Human Beings *or* Human Becomings?

SUNY series in Chinese Philosophy and Culture
———————
Roger T. Ames, editor

HUMAN BEINGS *or* HUMAN BECOMINGS?

A Conversation with Confucianism on the Concept of Person

Edited by
Peter D. Hershock and Roger T. Ames

Cover art: "The Three Vinegar Tasters" (The Three Teachings). Kanō Isen'in Naganobu (Japanese, 1775–1828). Honolulu Museum of Art.

Published by State University of New York Press, Albany

© 2021 State University of New York

All rights reserved

Printed in the United States of America

No part of this book may be used or reproduced in any manner whatsoever without written permission. No part of this book may be stored in a retrieval system or transmitted in any form or by any means including electronic, electrostatic, magnetic tape, mechanical, photocopying, recording, or otherwise without the prior permission in writing of the publisher.

For information, contact State University of New York Press, Albany, NY
www.sunypress.edu

Library of Congress Cataloging-in-Publication Data

Names: Hershock, Peter D., editor | Ames, Roger T., editor.
Title: Human beings or human becomings? : A conversation with Confucianism on the concept of person
Description: Albany : State University of New York Press, [2021] | Series: SUNY series in Chinese Philosophy and Culture | Includes bibliographical references and index.
Identifiers: ISBN 9781438481838 (hardcover : alk. paper) | ISBN 9781438481845 (pbk. : alk. paper) | ISBN 9781438481852 (ebook)
Further information is available at the Library of Congress.

10 9 8 7 6 5 4 3 2 1

Contents

Acknowledgments — vii

Introduction — 1
Peter D. Hershock and Roger T. Ames

Chapter 1
Compassionate Presence in an Era of Global Predicaments: Toward an Ethics of Human Becoming in the Face of Algorithmic Experience — 11
Peter D. Hershock

Chapter 2
Confucian Role Ethics and Personal Identity — 39
Roger T. Ames

Chapter 3
Deferential Yielding: The Construction of Shared Community in Confucian Ethics — 69
Gan Chunsong

Chapter 4
Confucian Self-Cultivation: A Developmental Perspective — 91
Jin Li

Chapter 5
Human Beings and Human Becomings: The Creative Transformation of Confucianism by Disengaged Reason — 121
Kwang-Kuo Hwang

CHAPTER 6
Understanding the Confucian Idea of Ethical Freedom through
Chen Yinke's Works for Mourning Wang Guowei   149
    Tang Wenming

CHAPTER 7
Life as Aesthetic Creativity and Appreciation: The Confucian Aim
of Learning   169
    Peimin Ni

CHAPTER 8
Confucianism on Human Relations: Progressive or Conservative? 187
    Stephen C. Angle

CHAPTER 9
From Women's Learning (*fuxue* 妇学) to Gender Education:
Feminist Challenges to Modern Confucianism   215
    Sor-hoon Tan

CHAPTER 10
Perspectives on Human Personhood and the Self from
the *Zhuangzi*   245
    David B. Wong

CONTRIBUTORS   265

INDEX   269

Acknowledgments

The conversation with Confucianism presented here began in conferences on the nature of personhood in an era of unprecedented technological transformations, hosted under the auspices of the Berggruen Institute at Stanford University in 2015 and in Qufu, China, the birthplace of Confucius, in 2017. Sustaining the conversation and bringing it to published fruition would not have been possible without the support of the Berggruen Institute and its China Center.

The Berggruen Institute is a response to the epochal, not incremental, transformations that are reshaping human life, social organization, and the world—transformations that are taking place now, in our own lives, and that will continue in those of our children and grandchildren. The Berggruen Institute seeks to deepen understanding of these great transformations, the ethical responses they demand, the social decisions they make possible, and how they are seen from different civilizational perspectives, with the objective of having enduring impact on the progress and direction of societies around the world. This book would not have come to be without the Berggruen Institute's support and its commitment to developing and promoting long-term answers to the greatest challenges of the twenty-first century.

Introduction

Peter D. Hershock and Roger T. Ames

Humans, at least since the first uses of fire, have been technological animals. The inventions of the wheel, the compass, the printing press, the internal combustion engine, and the telephone each have dramatically changed humanity's relationship to the world, as well as our relationships with one another. Yet, the transformations of human experience being precipitated by technology today are unprecedented.

We now know that human activity is capable of affecting planetary processes like climate. Humanity is experimenting with cloning, gene editing, and other forms of bio-engineering, mapping the neuro-topography of thought with functional magnetic resonance imaging, and realizing new kinds of human–machine interactions. Most profoundly, perhaps, artificial intelligence and related technical developments like machine learning and big data are blurring boundaries between both the commercial and the political, and the technical and the ethical.

These latest products of human ingenuity have the potential to radically augment human capacities or to entirely supplant them. They are already a catalyst for the emergence of new societal infrastructures and will fundamentally transform work and employment in the coming decades, challenging in the process all extant understandings of decision making and agency. In the face of such transformations—a decentering of the human that will be at least as consequential as that which occurred through the so-called Copernican revolution—serious and sustained reflection is required on what it means to be (or to become) human, and on the ethical and social safety implications of our new technologies.

The changes being driven by contemporary science and technology raise profound questions about fundamental values. We can now realistically contemplate the colonization of the moon and the development of brain–computer interfaces that could bring about truly digital consciousness. We have built computational machines that by themselves can learn how to design racecars and that can process tens of thousands of research papers in a single afternoon to predict new discoveries. We now also have the knowledge and technical expertise to realize a world in which no child needs to go to bed sick or hungry. And yet, hunger persists.

This disparity of human potentials and human realities is not merely factual—it is moral. The conjunction of remarkable technical expertise and continued failure to provide adequate nutrition to all stands as a powerful indication that we have yet to determine with sufficiently broad consensus what would count *as* a "solution" to world hunger. We have not yet persuaded ourselves that whatever changes we would need to make in our present ways of life to end hunger are worth the anticipated results. In short, the persistence of world hunger is not a technical problem. It is a moral predicament: evidence of unresolved conflicts among our own core values and interests. And hunger is just one of many such predicaments that we now face.

To address predicaments like the persistence of hunger in a world of excess food production or rising inequality in a world of historically unparalleled wealth production will require new kinds, scales, and scopes of ethical resolution. The global nature of these predicaments necessitates realizing new depths of ethical resolution, not only within communities and nations, but among them. Indeed, a guiding premise of this edited volume is that the interdependencies revealed by truly global predicaments compel questioning whether the resolve needed to address them can be realized within the horizons of any ethics committed to taking the individual—person, identity group, class, corporation, or nation—as the basic unit of moral analysis. The predicaments we now face make evident a new and profoundly unfamiliar and complex moral terrain.

Even at the personal level, the process of predicament resolution is always both contextual and reflexive. It involves us not only in changing *how* we live, but *why* we do so, and *as whom*. Global predicament resolution will require engaging in this reflexive process together, across both national and cultural boundaries. At the very least, it will require us to bracket imaginations of ourselves as singular agents acting in our own self-interest, and to deliberate together in full cognizance that either we win together or we lose together. At the heart of these deliberations will be questions about the meaning of personhood. What is it about who we take ourselves to be that allows global hunger to persist? Why are we falling so far short of doing what is needed to secure dignified lives for all? Who do we need to be *present as* to engage successfully in the boundary-crossing work of truly shared global predicament resolution?

Responding from an East-Asian Sinitic Perspective

The chapters in this book constitute an initial response to these questions from within Sinitic philosophical traditions. These traditions—Confucian, Daoist, and Buddhist—afford distinctive resources for conceiving of persons as relationally constituted and for developing a shared moral compass to guide our efforts to resolve global human predicaments in full recognition of our interdependence. In addition to their intrinsic merits as perspectives on the human experience, these traditions of thought and practice have the practical merit of being part of the cultural inheritance of roughly one-sixth of humanity. The sheer size of China's population and the fact that it will, in the coming decades, become home to the world's largest national economy mean, among other things, that Chinese perspectives must be integral to our shared efforts to resolve the global predicaments that humanity will be facing in this and coming generations.

In addition to this practical reason, there are both historical and philosophical rationales for turning to Sinitic traditions of thought. Although the roots of Confucianism and Daoism as elite traditions indigenous to what is now the Peoples Republic of China can be traced back to the Shang dynasty, they began to consolidate as canonical textual traditions during a time of great upheaval—the so-called Warring States period (475–221 BCE). Buddhist traditions began entering China during a comparable period of social, economic, and political transformation as the long-unified imperial China of the Han dynasty (206 BCE to 220 CE) broke apart into shifting arrays of violently competing kingdoms and warlord alliances. There is thus historical precedent for regarding the resolutely relational character of Sinitic articulations of the human experience as, at least in part, the result of their dynamic attunement to the demands of responding practically to social, cultural, economic, and political disruption and transformation.

Moreover, the philosophical resources afforded by these traditions are arguably the result of what amounted to sustained and substantially intercultural deliberations. By the Song dynasty (1127–1279), the mantra had become "the three teachings as one (*sanjiaoweiyi* 三教為一). Confucianism, Daoism, and Buddhism were being compared—by none other than the Song emperor Xiaozong (r. 1162–1189)—to the three legs of a *ding* ritual vessel symbolizing Chinese cultural and political authority. That is, they were understood to be distinct but complementary perspectives on the human experience. In fact, Buddhism had entered China from "the West"—Central and South Asia—as a manifestly "foreign" religion. And from the outset, Buddhist traditions both powerfully affected and evolved in sustained conversation with Confucian and Daoist interlocutors.

Thus, while Confucian, Daoist, and Buddhist thinkers have all broadly agreed that human nature is irreducibly relational and dynamic and that personhood is irreducibly interpersonal, they have differed markedly in their recommendations of how best to actualize an ethically informed understanding of who we should be present as to realize our full human potential. The continued vitality of China's philosophical traditions owes a great deal to the internal pluralism in each that has been a significant result of their critical engagements with one another and, more recently, with traditions originating outside of Asia, especially in Europe and North America.

The Chapters

The scholars who have contributed to this collection were invited to respond from within their chosen philosophical tradition to the question, "Who do we need to be—personally, culturally, socially, economically, and politically—to navigate the great transformations of the human experience that are now under way?" They were tasked, more particularly, with reflecting on the social and political implications of "rethinking personhood" in the context of these transformations in ways that might be deemed valuable by others drawing upon very different sets of resources.

Of the ten chapters included here, eight were written by Confucian thinkers whose work has often been expressly comparative, placing the Confucian tradition in conversation with other global philosophies. These contributions are framed by essays that come from outside the Confucian tradition. While Daoism and Buddhism have remained vibrant as both philosophical and religious traditions, the cultural fabric of China is undeniably woven with predominantly Confucian thread. Moreover, Confucian resources today, with the collaboration of both the academy and political forces, are being actively incorporated in Chinese efforts to address the predicament-laden transformations of the contemporary world. The Confucian perspectives offered here are thus justifiably granted centrality.

The two framing chapters—Buddhist and Daoist—serve a bordering function akin to that of the vocalists and dancers in a classical Greek *khoros* whose role was to create an expressive bridge between actors and audience members. That is, rather than being commentaries on the other contributions, these chapters are intended to establish a field of concerns about personhood that the remaining chapters bring into Confucian focus.

The volume opens with Peter Hershock's chapter, "Compassionate Presence in an Era of Global Predicaments: Toward an Ethics of Human Becoming in the Face of Algorithmic Experience," which sets out the predicament-laden nature of the intelligence revolution now taking place due to the confluence of big data, machine learning, and artificial intelligence. After briefly exploring human experience as being structurally informed and transformed by powerful and emergent value-deploying systems of *agentless* agency, Hershock offers a Buddhist response to who we need to be *present as* to engage successfully in truly shared and global predicament resolution.

Building on this vocabulary of human beings and human becoming, Roger Ames engages in chapter 2 in an extended philosophical meditation on culture and human nature. In "Confucian Role Ethics and Personal Identity," Ames ranges freely among classical sources, the contemporary Confucian thought of Tang Junyi, and the American pragmatism of William James, John Dewey, and George Herbert Mead to explore the embodied nature of what he terms "human becomings." What emerges is an understanding of personal presence based on the dynamic unfolding and consolidating of moral habits in the context of roles that stipulate the meaning of achieved excellence—a vision of relationally constituted persons in concert with others becoming not just human, but truly humane.

In chapter 3, "'Deference': On Sharing and Community in Confucian Ethics," Gan Chunsong begins with a detailed examination of the often underappreciated Confucian concept of deference or yielding (*rang* 讓). Following this, he embarks on a brief survey of the vicissitudes of Confucian thought and culture from the mid–nineteenth century through the final decades of the twentieth century, and its subsequent revitalization. He concludes with a visionary speculation on how the concept of deference might be pivotal in the articulation of a new approach to global governance that gradually decenters the nation-state in favor of modes of agency and community based on the priority of shared interests.

The following two chapters, by Jin Li and Kwang-Kuo Hwang, take social scientific approaches to enunciating Confucian personhood. In "Confucian Self-Cultivation: A Developmental Perspective," Li first outlines in broad strokes the core commitments embodied in Confucian self-cultivation as a lifelong endeavor to craft oneself as a person in community with others. She then fleshes out this conceptual scheme by working through case studies of Chinese parenting and the distinctive ways in which it merges socialization and self-cultivation through the practices of exemplar modeling, combining verbal instruction with embodiment, and following emotional engagement with reasoning.

Hwang is also concerned with developmental issues, but at an historical scale rather than at that of the human lifecycle. His chapter, "Human Beings and Human Becomings: The Creative Transformation of Confucianism by Disengaged Reason," maps Confucianism responsive adaptation to the demands of modernity. Beginning with discussions of personhood as explored by Martin Heidegger and Charles Taylor, Hwang lays out the necessity and root conditions of an "indigenous" psychology that mediates between the lifeworlds realized by cultural groups over the long-term history of their development, and microworlds constructed by individual scientists—a Confucian naturalism on the basis of which to reframe the work of social science.

Taking as his historical point of reference the turbulent Republican period China, Tang Wenming uses mourning as springboard for reflecting on the nature of freedom. His chapter, "Understanding the Confucian Idea of Ethical Freedom through Chen Yinke's Works for Mourning Wang Guowei," draws out the implications of seeing suicide as an ethical expression of "spiritual independence and freedom of thought." After setting the historical stage, Tang works through Axel Honneth's tripartite analysis of freedom realized in the objective system of social life, rather than in Kantian self-reflection or as a mere absence of constraints as in Hobbes. While stressing the immense influence of Hegel on modern Chinese philosophy, Tang argues on behalf of the need to qualify ethical freedom as a capacity for actualizing human relations in the context of an ongoing, normative reconstruction of the Confucian "five relations," grounded in the modern concept of personal freedom.

In chapter 7, "Life as Aesthetic Creativity and Appreciation: The Confucian Aim of Learning," Peimin Ni contests the received view that practices of self-cultivation in Confucianism have the aim of moral subjectivity, and that the Daoist ideal is to realize aesthetic subjectivity. Making use of classical textual materials, Ni links Confucian human-heartedness to tranquility, to virtue/virtuosity, but also ultimately to aesthetic enjoyment. That is, he argues that in Confucian self-cultivation through ritualized roles and relationships (*li* 禮), the ultimate point is not moral virtue (*de* 德), but rather an achieved, aesthetic virtuosity—a capacity for transforming daily life into a field of artistic activity.

Stephen Angle is similarly revisionist in his reading of Confucian tradition in his chapter "Confucianism on Human Relations: Progressive or Conservative?" Angle's argument is twofold. First, he takes exception to the view that Confucian conservatism and roles-defined patterns of relationality can be reduced to maintaining or restoring traditional relations. He then argues more positively that the Confucian ethos of relational conservation is consistent with an evolutionary Confucian tradition that is capable of critically incorporating modern values. This "Progressive Confucianism," as Angle understands it, sustains traditional emphases on developing virtue, but embraces an extension of these emphases to social relations, accepting that these relations and their parameters must change in significant ways. His chapter concludes with a consideration of how contemporary spousal relations might be given a progressive Confucian reading.

Concern for the evolution of social relations is central to Sor-hoon Tan's chapter, "From Women's Learning (*fuxue* 妇学) to Gender Education: Feminist Challenges to Modern Confucianism." Like Angle, Tan is critical of any naïve traditionalism that would seek the revival of Confucianism as it was understood and practiced historically. Her chapter begins with an in-depth survey of how gendered education within Confucian tradition discriminated against women and entrenched their inferior social position, followed by an account of gender relations in China today. She then explores what Confucian education and self-cultivation for women should mean in the contemporary world, emphasizing the importance of diversity and flexibility in roles and relationships as aspects of a critical and responsive Confucian feminism.

The final chapter in the collection, David Wong's "Perspectives on Human Personhood and the Self from the *Zhuangzi*," offers a constructive critique of Confucian preoccupations with human social relations. Elaborating on the perspectives on human being and becoming in the Daoist text the *Zhuangzi*, Wong argues for the importance of pluralism with respect to both values and identity. But he also argues for the merit of a Daoist understanding of pluralism, contrasting it with the position forwarded by Joseph Raz, according to which recognizing the worth of the commitments and values of others undermines an engaged expression of one's own commitments and values. He then turns to address the core ethical question of the meaning of "the good life," making use of Daoist insights to advocate learning practices that encompass all the different parts of ourselves as our potential teachers, even those nonconscious parts of ourselves most intimately related to other aspects of the natural world.

Direction without Destiny

One of the distinctive features of East-Asian Sinitic philosophies is their refusal to valorize destiny. Although imperial dynasties in premodern China were understood to enjoy a "celestial mandate," this mandate was understood to be revocable. The Sinitic disposition, if we can be forgiven the generalization, has for millennia been nonteleological. That is, it has expressed a resistance to the idea that human nature *is* one thing or another, or that reality is this way only or perhaps that way. In keeping with their intrinsic pluralism, Sinitic philosophies have tended to sort themselves out through what the contemporary interpreters of Japanese thought, Thomas Kasulis and James Heisig, have characterized as carefully articulated practices of argument by relegation, not argument by refutation. This is a deceptively simple difference. The Sinitic disposition is not to attempt discovering the one and only true destiny of humanity—to specify who we should all seek to be. Rather, the attempt has been to recognize the diversity of what is truly human and also to establish which ways of being truly human are to be given primacy.

To state this in perhaps more readily appreciated terms, the Sinitic disposition philosophically has not been to determine who *has* the truth or what the truth *is* once and for all, but rather to establish a hierarchy of approaches—in *this* particular historical period—for *truing* how we are humanly present. In our view, this disposition is one well worth fostering. The "Intelligence Revolution" that is now under way will force humanity to consider—with a practical immediacy that is without historical precedent—what to valorize as freedom, as justice, and as truly humane. Among the merits of Sinitic traditions of thought and practice is their readiness to endorse transformation in the (nondestined) direction of enhancing relational diversity—that is, to provide conceptual and practical support for realizing how our differences *from* each other might be crafted into progressively evolving differences *for* one another.

In a single generation, we have witnessed the dramatic ascendency of Asia, and of China in particular, occurring at the apparent expense of

Europe and America—a seismic shift that has transformed what was a familiar geopolitical order. Yet, more positively viewed, Asian development generally and China's growth more specifically have also brought into currency sets of cultural resources that have significant potential for reframing our engagements with the global predicaments that have beset us. The geopolitical order does not have to be structured in a way that is biased toward zero-sum, win-loss dynamics.

In seeking resources that will enhance human capabilities for resolving global predicaments like climate change, world hunger, or the algorithmic pairing of greater choice and control, primary among them are values and practices that will support replacing the familiar competitive pattern of single actors pursuing their own self-interest with collaborative patterns of players strengthening relations as a way of coordinating shared futures in which everyone is a winner. In our view, these are values and practices that will elicit appreciation of the possibility that freedom can be an expression of qualitatively deepening commitment and not just the enjoyment of numerically expanding experiential options.

As is now widely appreciated, the Sinitic traditions of Confucianism, Daosim, and Buddhism evince some persistent cultural assumptions and values: the holistic, ecological nature of the human experience; the high esteem accorded integration and inclusiveness; the *yinyang* interdependence of all things within their environing contexts; an aspiration toward deep diversity as the foundation of mutual contribution and achieved harmony; and the always provisional, emergent nature of natural, social, political, and cosmic orders. Collectively, these traditions celebrate the relational values of deference and interdependence and foster a modality of self-understanding rooted in and nurtured by unique transactional patterns of relations.

The shared argument of the authors included in this volume is not that the Sinitic cultures provide wholesale answers to the pressing problems of our times. That would be an argument aimed at refutation. Instead, the recommendations found in this collection are forwarded in a spirit of accepting accommodation tempered with practical considerations of what must, in any given instance, be granted priority. In an era of intensifying global predicaments, there is considerable urgency in taking full advantage of all of our world's cultural resources. Plurality is an undeniable fact of the contemporary world. Pluralism is among its necessary core values. What is to be avoided at all costs is advocacy of any single perspective, a one truth/one reality construction of human experience.

Who do we need to be present as to resolve the global predicaments of the twenty-first century? Our hope is that a chorus of offerings will be forwarded from within African, American, Asian, Australasian, European, Pacific Islander, and other indigenous perspectives. This volume is, we hope, but one of many contributing to the articulation of a diversity-enhancing vision of human and planetary flourishing in an era of unprecedented "creative destruction" that is at once technological, economic, social, cultural, political, and spiritual.

Chapter 1

Compassionate Presence in an Era of Global Predicaments

Toward an Ethics of Human Becoming in the Face of Algorithmic Experience

Peter D. Hershock

We are not usually inclined to think deeply about personhood. The socialization processes that begin in the home and that continue on playgrounds, in schools, and at work introduce us to our places in a world that precedes us, instructing us about who we are, and about who we both can and should be. Under normal circumstances, dwelling thoughtfully on what it means to be a person or to be human is a preoccupation only of agonized adolescents and professional philosophers—the pairing of which is, perhaps, telling.

My own conviction, however, is that our circumstances are no longer normal and that asking deep and probing questions about personhood ought now to be understood as a matter of both personal and public urgency. By this, I do not mean asking questions about how well we "fit" the places we have taken up or been assigned in the world by society or by chance, destiny, or divine plan—questions about our lots in life. It means asking much more complex questions about the "fitness" of our world and the systems of allotment prevailing within it—questions about structural constraints and affordances related to being or becoming, not just human, but truly humane. These are not ultimately metaphysical questions about who we *are*. They are ethical questions about who we need to be present *as*—questions about what we can and should *mean* to and for one another.

This conviction is rooted in recognition that we no longer live in a world of challenges that can be adequately and sustainably met as problems suited to purely technical solution. The most pressing challenges of the present and coming decades—among them, climate change; the degradation of both natural and urban environments; the persistence of global hunger; and rising inequalities of wealth, income, risk, and opportunity—are not technical problems. They are ethical predicaments that challenge us by offering increasingly dramatic (and often tragic) evidence of conflicts within and among our globally dominant systems of social, cultural, economic, and political values.

As I conceive the difference, problems occur when our accustomed practices no longer bring about desired results. Solving a problem entails identifying what would count as a solution in light of our abiding values, aims, and interests, and then discovering or developing new means to continue furthering them. Predicaments emerge with awareness of conflicts among our own values, aims, and interests. Predicaments cannot be solved precisely because our existing systems of values, aims, and interests prevent us from determining in advance what would count as a solution. Predicaments can be resolved only where resolution implies both *clarity* (about how things have come to be as conflicted as they have) and *commitment* (to alleviating that conflict). In short, predicament resolution entails changing our values, intentions, and actions to realize new and less conflicted patterns of outcome and opportunity.

Our collective failure to end world hunger, for example, is not due to a lack of natural or social scientific understanding of the proximate causal mechanisms involved. Neither is it due to a lack of the technological means or capacity for acting on our understanding. Hunger persists because we have yet to determine with sufficiently broad consensus what would count *as* a "solution," and because we collectively have failed to regard the changes we would need to make in our present ways of life as being *worth* the anticipated results. Addressing predicaments like global hunger or climate change requires new scales and scopes of resolution: that is, both greater clarity about how these predicaments have emerged and, more profoundly, shared commitment to realizing conditions in which these predicaments can no longer persist.

This characterization of our greatest global challenges notwithstanding, the fact remains of course that hunger, environmental degradation, and inequality are nothing new. And while anthropogenic climate change has only recently become accepted as a scientific reality, it has been an historical reality at least since the mid-nineteenth-century onset of the industrial revolution. So, even if it is granted that these are important ethical—and not merely technical—challenges, one might well ask why it is only now that they should be seen as urgently compelling us to ask deep and probing questions about who we need to be present as. What is it about our present historical moment that compels seeing inquiry into the meaning of personhood as intimately implicated in understanding and responding to these global-scale predicaments?

Predicament Resolution as Personal and Structural Transformation

Resolving predicaments is not just a matter of giving up one set of means for another to continue pursuing some constant set of ends or interests. In the case of addressing the conflict between environmental and economic values, aims, and interests that is at the heart of the climate change predicament, for example, it will not suffice to craft some "green" route to higher per capita GDP as a metric of economic health; it will entail, as well, crafting new metrics of economic vitality that will validate the structural embodiment of new configurations of economic aims and values that are consistent not merely with environmental sustainability, but with environmental flourishing. Predicament resolution entails reconfiguring constellations of importantly held values—an intentionality- and priority-transforming endeavor that can be undertaken only from within, by recursively evaluating those constellations in terms of our own core commitments. In other words, predicament resolution is inherently reflexive, involving us not only in changing *how* we live, but *why* and *as whom*. Predicament resolution is thus inseparable from personal transformation. In Buddhist terms that we will later explore in more detail, while problem solution is karma consolidating, predicament resolution is karma transforming.

Resolving predicaments that make evident conflicts *within* a given system of values, aims, and interests is always far from easy. Resolving predicaments that make manifest conflicts *among* such systems is immensely more difficult. Doing so requires, at the very least, a willingness to step out of the relative comfort of moral deliberations guided by appeal to some relatively stable constellation of values, aims, and interests, and to engage instead in the much more demanding ethical task of evaluating competing and often quite foreign constellations of values, aims, and interests.

As I have suggested elsewhere (Hershock 2012, 159ff), the shift from morality (what a community defines as what *we* should do) to law (what *no one* should do in a multicommunity polity) to ethics (what *anyone* should do in reasoned consideration of how best to act), may well have been spurred by needs to work through face-to-face conflicts among competing moral interests. The resolve needed to address predicaments that are not confined by national and cultural borders—predicaments like world hunger, climate change, and rising inequality—will necessarily be not just moral or legal, but ethical.

Yet, for reasons that will become more acutely apparent as our discussion proceeds, the kind of ethical resolve required to address global predicaments is at best only partially supported from within deliberations that grant foundational status to either virtue, duty, utility, or care. We are in need of an ethics that goes beyond considerations of how any individual morally and rationally motivated agent should act to evaluating how relational dynamics and human experience itself are being structurally informed and transformed by powerful and emergent value-deploying systems of *agentless* agency.

In his *Ethics of Information*, Luciano Floridi (2013) has argued persuasively that agent-oriented and action-oriented ethics do not afford us the critical resources needed in order to address the ethical entanglements peculiar to the social milieu that is emerging as a function of contemporary information and communications technologies. In such a milieu, he claims, what is required is a patient-oriented ethics capable of taking full account of temporally extended and spatially distributed forms of agency and the complexity that results in relation to both the origination and reception of morally charged actions. As Floridi makes clear (2013, 62), the kind of patient-oriented ethics that is needed must not only shift concern from the individual human being as the originator of moral action to the individual as recipient of the effects of value- and intention-driven conduct, in addition, it must warrant extending the horizons of ethical consideration to explicitly encompass other life forms, the environment, and eventually even what he terms the "infosphere" into which humanity is now enthusiastically migrating (2013, 16–18).

There is considerable merit in Floridi's insistence on expanding ethical consideration to include not just ethical agents but also ethical patients. But from a Buddhist perspective, this expansion is not quite sufficient to carry us beyond conventional ethics and their ontological presupposition that the individual is the basic unit of ethical deliberation. Buddhist thought and practice developed out of the meditative/phenomenological insights that dynamic relationality is ontologically basic, and that all "individuals" and "independent entities" are the result of intention- and value-inflected acts of abstraction. Although it may be conventionally true (*saṃvṛti*) to state that individual human beings and life forms and ecosystems are ethically distinct patients, the ultimate truth (*paramārtha*) is that there are no ethical patients, but only what we might call *ethical patience*—the value- and intention-inflected dynamics of our interdependence or relationality as such.

The shift of ethical primacy to qualitative considerations of relational dynamics and away from individual bearers of virtues and duties, individual calculators of consequence and utility, and even individual givers and receivers of care is, I think, justifiable on metaphysical or ontological grounds. This might be done in Buddhist terms, by invoking the interdependent origination, emptiness, and nonduality of all things that are hallmarks of Mahayana Buddhist philosophy. Alternatively, the justification might proceed along comparable Confucian lines (Ames 2011). In the present context, however, the most salient justification is practical.

The global predicaments with which we are now being confronted are not only evidence of conflicts among distinct systems of political, social, economic, cultural, and environmental values, held by competing individuals or groups (and thus, the result of what we might call individual karma). They are evidence also—and perhaps much more importantly—of conflicts among structurally embodied values, aims, and interests that are ever more powerfully and extensively shaping the relational dynamics constitutive of our increasingly complex interdependence (and thus evidence of what we might call collective karma). These conflicts are not the result of agent-originated actions, but rather of the recursively sustained conduct of various systems of agentless agency. Continued allegiance to the ethical primacy of the individual—whether as agent or as patient—is ultimately conducive to a conceptual blindness that exempts the structural ramifications of technology from effective ethical consideration and critique.

Distinguishing between Tools and Technologies

It is possible to make the need to move beyond conventional agent-, action-, and patient-oriented ethics more practically apparent by distinguishing clearly between tools and technologies. Tools are used and properly evaluated on the basis of their task-specific utility. Hammers are used to drive and pull nails. Computers are used to electronically process and transmit information. Tools quantitatively extend human abilities, and have greater utility the more precisely and powerfully they promote our interests. If tools don't work, we can put them away in the closet or the garage, we can recycle them to create other tools, or we can alter them to better suit our needs.

In sharp contrast, technologies cannot be used. They are not means to some specifiable set of ends. While tools are built or manufactured out of basic raw materials and occupy strictly limited and precisely located amounts of space, technologies are not made or manufactured and cannot be put away in a closet or garage. Technologies emerge as nonlocal relational phenomena through which transformative patterns are consolidated regarding how we conceive and promote our ends. Far from being task-specific, technologies continually generate new kinds of tasks, embodying broad strategies for realizing certain kinds of worlds or lived experience. In other words, technologies institutionalize patterns of *moral valence*. They cannot be value neutral, and can be evaluated only karmically—that is, in terms of how they affect the meaning and quality of our interdependence as such.

Consider telecommunications. As a technology, telecommunications consists of the full range of human conduct involved normalizing—that is, both making normal or usual and turning into a norm or value—the electronic processing, transmission, and storage of information. Prominent in this range of conduct is the use of such tools as computers and cell phones. But also included are the industrial processes and labor configurations by means of which these tools are produced, their transportation and marketing, the evolving culture of their uses, the invention of new vocabularies to capture these uses, and the lifestyle alterations they enable and encourage, including impacts on such morally laden patterns of conduct as those involved in maintaining friendships or committing to meetings. In short, telecommunications technology organizes a spectrum of human activities ranging from the mining of raw materials through the consumption and eventual disposal of information commodities.

Failing to recognize the difference between tools (as industrially produced entities) and technologies (as complexly emerging relationalities) has serious ethical consequences. First and foremost is a tendency to fall prey to the compositional fallacy that if something is good for each and every one of us, it must be good for all of us. Although it might be good for each and every one of us to drive a car to meet our local transportation needs, if all seven billion people on Earth were to do so, our city streets would be gridlocked, our air would be polluted to the point of being poisonous, and it would no longer make sense to try driving a car to school or work. What is good for each of us *as individuals* is not necessarily good for all of us *as communities*.

Less obviously, by restricting our "evaluation" of technologies to the utility of the tools they produce, we exempt those technologies from direct ethical critique. Doing so effectively blinds us to the fact that technologies are not task-accomplishing, but rather task-proliferating. That is, technologies expand by producing new ends to which the tools they produce can be applied. If they are successful, these tools become so widely used that the technologies from which they originate cross their own "threshold of utility" and begin creating problems of the kind that those immersed in these technologies will most readily see as soluble only by still further technological expansion. At this point, technology becomes indispensable. Stated generally, all technologies have thresholds of utility beyond which they ironically begin producing the conditions of their own necessity, thus rendering us increasingly dependent on them.[1]

Finally, identifying technologies with the tools they produce constitutes a failure to see that technology has become, in Jacques Ellul's (1983) terms, the complex and complete "milieu" in which we live and through which we define ourselves—the medium in which we craft our identities and frame our aspirations. Unlike tools that we can refrain from owning or using, and from which we thus have clear "exit rights," we no longer have any such rights with respect to technology. Even though I can elect not to own or use a smartphone, I cannot disengage myself from the ways in which relational dynamics have and continue to be shaped by smartphones, including the ways in which they foster regarding the optional as optimal and normalize deferring commitment in favor of maximizing choice.

Global Predicaments as Structural Products of Technological Irony

We will return later to consider the ethical implications of the erosion of exit rights in relation to now-emerging technologies of machine-learning and algorithm-generated experience. Prior to doing so, as a way of further clarifying why the need to resolve global predicaments raises ethical questions about who we need to be present as—and why these questions cannot be satisfactorily answered by conventional ethical means—it is useful to develop a better sense of the agentless origins of these predicaments as *structural tensions* in the historical manifestation of technological irony. Consider, for example, the emergence over the last half century of network society, reflexive modernization, and a global attention economy.

The Network Society. Advances in the sciences of computing and communications that were made in the context of Cold War research and development had the collateral effect of initiating a fundamental shift in the organizational dynamics of power—a shift from the 1950s dominance of the military-industrial complex to that of the military-industrial-communications complex. This transit has been critically framed by Manual Castells as the advent of *informational capitalism* and a global *network society* (Castells 1996, 1997, 1998).

Structurally, two facts about network dynamics are of particular significance. First, the value of membership in a network is a dual function of the quantity of nodes in the network and the quality of the informational exchanges among them. Second, network growth is a nonlinear function of negative (or stabilizing) feedback and positive feedback that *accelerates interactions* and *amplifies differentiation* among network nodes. What this means is that network-enabled (and, eventually, network-reliant) global informational capitalism accelerates flows of goods, services, and people in ways that *unpredictably* intensify and amplify both integration and fragmentation. In the context of global network society, increasing economic vitality necessitates increasing volatility.

Reflexive Modernization and World Risk Society. This structural pairing of vitality and volatility is central to what has been referred to as *reflexive modernization* and the rise of *world risk society* (Beck, Giddens, and Lash 1994): the emergence of conditions in which realizing continued economic growth and generally improved standards of living entails the production of unpredictable threats, risks, and hazards in the face of which responsible decisions nevertheless must be made. That is, reflexive modernization and world risk society occur when certain thresholds of scale, scope, and complexity are crossed, making it impossible to externalize the environmental, social, political, and cultural costs of sustained industrial/economic expansion or to inhibit the percolation of these costs into virtually every aspect of life.

Crucially, the threats, risks, and hazards produced under the structural regime of reflexive modernization do not mark *failures* of the technological and industrial systems by means of which economic growth and living standards have been realized. Rather, they are the ironic result of the extraordinary *successes* of these systems and the values embodied by them. That is, the primary causes for the inequalities, discontinuities, and risks associated with reflexive modernization and industrial globalization are not external, but internal (Beck 1999).

The Attention Economy. The combined advent of global informational capitalism and reflexive modernization has been conducive to the emergence of global realities characterized on one hand by intensifying structural tensions between integration and interdependence, and on the other by the accelerating multiplication and magnification of differences, including not only differences in wealth, income, risk, and opportunity, but also in lifestyle and lifeworld choices and identities. These structural dynamics, however, have also been inseparable from a dematerialization of the global economy and a capitalization of attention itself (Franck 1999)—the emergence of a new "colonial" regime based not on the extraction and exploitation of natural resources or even knowledge and information but rather on the systematic export and global dissemination of attention energy. With this "colonization of consciousness" (Hershock 1999), attention has become the primary currency of an economy in which power is extended not only over the distribution and consumption of material goods, over labor, over flows of information, and over the consolidation of conceptual capital, but also over the production of meaning as such (Hershock 2012, 134–147).

The primary structural tension inherent to the global attention economy is between an accelerating expansion of "emancipatory" (often market-mediated) *freedoms of choice*, including minority claims for rights-to-participation and rights-to-differ, and an intensification of "disciplinary" *compulsions to choose* under conditions of heightening ambiguity, uncertainty, and risk. This is resulting in an almost miraculous proliferation of experiential possibilities and options for identity construction and social affiliation, but also an ever more rapidly widening gap between developmental "winners" and "losers"—a gap that is now so immense that the richest eight individuals in the world have more wealth than that possessed by the 3.5 billion poorest people in the world (Oxfam 2017).

The structural changes associated with the emergence of a global network society, reflexive modernization, and the attention economy have been conducive to making the present moment one characterized by the greatest wealth generation in human history and also the greatest inequalities of wealth, income, risk, and opportunity the world has witnessed.[2] From a Buddhist perspective, this combination is not a matter of either historical accident or developmental necessity. It is a function of our collective human karma—a dynamic function of global convergence on a distinctive set of technologically embodied values, central among them control, choice, competition, and convenience. And our persistent failures to have more than cosmetic success in alleviating the conflicts and suffering caused by these inequalities and resultant feelings of injustice has much to do with the critical blindness induced and reinforced by ontological commitments to taking the individual, rather than relationality, to be the basic unit of political, economic, and ethical analysis.

It is in the context of these predicament-embodying, structural tensions that have come to define twenty-first-century globalization that questions about who we need to be present as assume critical urgency. The predicaments expressed by these structural tensions are not morally neutral events akin to thunderstorms or earthquakes—acts of nature in the occurrence of which we have no responsibility. We are caught up in a vibrant and yet volatile confluence of apparently agentless forces oriented toward deepening interdependence, accelerating differentiation, and expanding predicament generation—a confluence in which value systems are colliding with increasing frequency and intensity, and in ways that reveal both interpersonal and intercultural "fault lines" for which *no one can be held accountable*, and yet for which we have intimately *shared responsibility*.

Working across such personal and cultural "fault lines" is indispensable en route to building shared commitments of sufficient breadth and depth to engage in effective global predicament resolution. Yet doing so is no simple matter. Cultures do not exist in a simple and objectively observable fashion; they obtain as complexly dynamic "ecologies" of values and practices that have neither clear boundaries nor essential identities. And although cultural differences are often invoked in ways that reify them as external conditions preventing further movement in certain directions—something akin to fathomless crevices separating "us" from "others"—we are in actuality always intimately implicated in experiences of cultural differences. As Naoki Sakai and Meaghan Morris (2008) have insisted, cultural difference is not an observable fact, but rather a *felt relation*: an experience of uncanny feelings of unease, oddly opposed meanings, and crossed purposes.

Granted this, we can anticipate—in Jean-Luc Nancy's pregnant terms—that resolving global predicaments that enunciate cultural differences regarding, for example, the meaning of a "healthy" environment or "just" gender relations or "equitable" development, are ultimately going to depend less on constructing *common* institutions than on improvising *shared* structures of feeling that express sustainable new constellations of coordination-enriching values that have critical traction across national and cultural borders, as well as across what have been conventionally conceived of as the functionally independent domains of social, economic, political, and environmental relations.

The Case for Being Compassionately Present

It is in the context of this need to improvise shared structures of feeling that efforts have been mounting to build a global ethics of social justice around the "social emotion" of compassion. As Martha Nussbaum (2001) persuasively states in her book *Upheavals of Thought: The Intelligence of Emotions*, compassion is "embodied in the structure of just institutions" and generates "a breadth and depth of ethical vision without which public culture is in danger of being rootless and hollow" (403). Compassion, she argues, is not reducible to a fact of individual psychology. Rather, it involves making three judgments: (1) that some seriously bad things have happened to someone or some group; (2) that these bad things were not deserved by those affected; and (3) that the person or group that is undeservedly suffering is a significant element in one's own scheme of aims and interests.

Working from within a broadly liberal set of assumptions about personhood and the rational bases of action, Nussbaum avers that knowing we also might be affected by similar undeserved suffering is what motivates us to build institutions designed to mitigate conditions that stifle "human dignity and the capacity for action" or that create "social hierarchy and economic deprivation" (Nussbaum 2001, 413–414). The anticipated end of building these institutions is a just society that guarantees its citizens certain core capabilities that include both cultivatable "intrinsic capabilities" for freely choosing what to do and who to be, and "combined capabilities" for realizing a functional merger of personal abilities and a supportive socioeconomic and political environment (2011).

By advocating the cultivation of compassion as a means to social justice, Nussbaum challenges the widespread market-liberal assumption that the self-interest of individual agents is the natural and necessary cornerstone of civil society. Cultivating compassion is an affirmation of our mutual vulnerability and mutual relevance, and is the ultimate foundation for the construction of a morally—and not merely legally—just society.

It seems to me that Nussbaum is right to project compassion out of the psychological realm into that of public institution design. As Maureen Whitebrook (2014) has argued, as a political virtue, compassion must consist in something other than one-to-one acts of charity since it is possible to help someone who is manifestly in trouble without being motivated to identify and responsibly address the structural or institutional causes of his or her trouble and suffering. But the ways in which Nussbaum cashes out the three judgments undergirding compassion for others—entraining the alleviation of others' suffering with the pursuit of our own self-interest, and with guaranteeing equivalent capabilities for individual agency to all—makes it clear that her conception of compassion remains within the horizon of conventional ethical concerns about individual ethical agents, actions, and patients. And this, I think, seriously limits the social justice ramifications of compassion, especially in cases where the underlying causes of conflict and suffering are agentless and wherein the primary "patients" are not individual subjects, but rather patterns of relationality being subjected to structural distortion. Indeed, as we will later discuss, in the context of algorithmically personalized experience, eventualities that are deemed good by each and every one of us will not necessarily be good for all of us. It is entirely possible that each and every subject involved in the global attention economy will insist that all is good, even as they are being subjected to systematic and severe relational disadvantages.

If a primary driver for growing inequalities and suffering is, indeed, the reflexive pairing of risk- and hazard-production with amplifying compulsions to choose in conditions of structurally induced uncertainty and volatility, it would seem that securing greater individual freedoms of choice—even if "compassionately" motivated in Nussbaum's terms—will have the ironic effect of providing stabilizing feedback for the very systems responsible for and sustained by that pairing. Upon accepting the ontological primacy of relationality, it becomes evident that, particularly in the context of resolving boundary-crossing predicaments, compassion cannot consist in or depend upon some set of rationally derived judgments about others and what they are suffering. Rather, compassion and its political and social effectiveness must in significant degree be functions of the depth and quality of partnership realized among all of those who are attentively entrained with one another as stakeholders in a shared experiential domain.

Buddhist Compassion

Contrary to modern convictions about the ontological, ethical, and political primacy of the rationally self-interested individual agent, Buddhist traditions of thought and practice developed around the core insight that all things—including persons—arise interdependently and that what we conventionally take to be independently existing things and beings are conceptually constituted abstractions from ongoing relational dynamics. This insight was the result of a resolute, six-year search for the causes and conditions for conflict, trouble, and suffering (*duḥkha*), and the ethics that emerged as this insight and resolve were put to the therapeutic use of healing the "wound" of existence or "standing apart" from others. In light of this, Buddhist ethics might usefully be regarded as a kind of inverse utilitarianism. Rather than as calculus aimed at increasing the sum total of happiness and pleasure, Buddhist ethics is directed to qualitatively discerning how best to alleviate actually experienced conflict, trouble, and suffering.

As such, Buddhism offers an alternative to utilitarian calculations that has interesting parallels to Confucianism's "silver" alternative to the Western "golden rule."[3] In both cases, the alternative offered is an expression of normative humility—a readiness to refrain from establishing one's own preferences or interests as a universal standard. In the Buddhist case, this humility extends to the ostensibly final aim of realizing "nirvana," a term that simply means a "blowing out" or "cooling down" of the conditions for experiencing *duḥkha*. While happiness (*suḥkha*) is not dismissed as irrelevant, it is understood neither as the culmination of Buddhist practice nor as a cardinal point for orienting our efforts therein. Rather, happiness is an intermediary effect of calming and concentrative meditation techniques, the ultimate purpose of which is to realize *kuśala* conduct (Ch. *shan* 善)—to engage others and contribute to relational dynamics in ways that are not merely "skillful" or "wholesome," but superlative or virtuosic.

Importantly for Buddhist ethics, conducting ourselves in ways that are *akuśala* or "without virtuosity" encompasses everything that we would now conventionally define as "bad" and "mediocre," but also what is currently deemed "good." In much the same way that virtuosic musical performances establish new standards of musicianship, *kuśala* conduct and the relational dynamics eventuating from it effectively set new standards of ethical engagement. This, ultimately, is what is needed in order to alleviate and eliminate the root causes of conflict, trouble, and suffering (*duḥkha*).[4]

In keeping with the relational ontology that is experientially affirmed by insight into the interdependent origination of all things, *duḥkha* is not reducible to a subjective or psychological event, but must instead be understood and addressed as a function of relational distortions or interdependence gone awry. The central feature of this understanding is that these distortions are ultimately a result of actions carried out on the basis of habits (bodily, emotional, and cognitive), aversions and cravings originating in ignorance of the interdependence or relational nature of all things. In short, conflicts, trouble, and suffering are ultimately a function of our own karma.

Whereas "karma" was used in pre-Buddhist India to refer to actions subject to cosmic moral law, according to which individual agents engaging in "good" or "bad" actions will inexorably be rewarded with comparably "good" and "bad" experiential consequences, the Buddhist concept of karma directs attention to the experiential ramifications of values and intentionality (*cetanā*). Rather than reflecting a transcendent moral order, karma consists in a dynamic and recursive consonance among abiding patterns of values-intentions-actions and experienced opportunities and outcomes. In the language introduced earlier, to experience *duḥkha* is not to be confronted with a problem; it is to find ourselves intimately implicated in a predicament.

The key ethical entailments of this understanding of karma are, first, that all experienced realities imply responsibility; and, second, that since we can always change our intentions and the values informing, the relational dynamics constitutive of our life circumstances are also changeable. To be confronted with conflicts, trouble, and suffering is ultimately to become aware of the predicament-generating nature of our own constellations of values and commitments. Yet, by undertaking ongoing critiques both of our own constellations of values and intentions, and of the constellations of values embodied in our cultural, social, economic, and political institutions and practices, we can realize increasingly *kuśala* conduct. We can revise the meaning of our interdependence and resolutely extend its qualitative horizons.

This process of karmic revision and qualitative relational transformation was traditionally understood as based on the cultivation of wisdom (*prajñā*), attentive mastery (*samādhi*), and moral clarity (*śīla*), especially through the practices of generosity (*dāna*) and various forms of meditation, including insight (*vipaśyana*), concentration (*samādhi*), calming (*śamatha*), and mindfulness (*satipaṭṭhāna*) meditation. Importantly, however, those faring well on the path of Buddhist practice were often described as suffusing their entire situation with the relational qualities of compassion (*karuṇā*), equanimity (*upekṣā*), loving-kindness (*mettā*), and joy in the good fortune of others (*muditā*) (see, e.g., Tevijja Sutta, *Digha Nikāya* 1995, 13). That is, the effectiveness of Buddhist practice manifests in the degree to which each of us can be *present as* a radiant nexus of relational transformation.

This stress on being present in ways that are positively attentive to the well-being of others is encapsulated in the valorization of the historical Buddha's life as that of an itinerant teacher. Rather than becoming a "solitary buddha" (*pratyekabuddha*) who attained the wisdom needed to realize liberation from *duḥkha* without also resolving to help others do the same, the Buddha committed the remainder of his life to helping others author their own liberation from *duḥkha*. The early Buddhist personal ideal, exemplified in the person of the historical Buddha, was to be present as someone exemplifying the liberating marriage of wisdom and compassion.

In early Buddhist traditions, compassion was not understood as the syllogistic result of "apathetically" affirmed rational judgments regarding the serious and undeserved suffering of others whose interests and aims are deemed to be linked to one's own. Yet, it also was not understood to be a psychological event—the subjective experience of "feeling-with" or "feeling-for" others. Rather, compassion was understood to be a volitionally produced result of the practice of intentionally suffusing one's situation with awareness of conflict, trouble, and suffering; awareness of the patterns of the causes and conditions resulting in *duḥkha*; and awareness of the meaning-of and means-to dissolving those patterns.

As described by the early Theravada Buddhist commentator, Buddhaghosa (fifth century CE), in his *Visuddhimagga* or Path of Purification (chapter IX), compassion occurs when the suffering of others moves one's heart; when there is a firm intent to put an end to others' suffering; and when this intent is extended pervasively. Thus, compassion is not to be confused with the kind of sentimental sympathy that results in sorrow about the suffering of others—an experience that easily has the effect of reinforcing *duḥkha*-generating "cravings" and attachment to "self" (*atman*). Compassion, in a Buddhist sense, involves active and transformative engagement with others that is based on caring insight into the interdependence and interpenetration of all things—a form and quality of engagement predicated ultimately on being present without-self (*anatman*).

In later Mahayana Buddhist contexts, the personal ideal of embodying the pairing wisdom and compassion exemplified by the Buddha came to be identified with an explicitly intergenerational intention to support the liberation of all sentient beings (*bodhicitta*). This *mahakaruṇā* or "great compassion" was the defining characteristic of the personal ideal of the bodhisattva or "enlightening being" who vows to remain immersed in the world of recursively engendered conflict, trouble, and suffering in order to work for the liberation of all sentient beings. Crucially, given that sentient beings were understood to be numberless and their karmic situations infinitely varied, it was held that being able to keep this vow depended on a recursively generated capacity for unlimited "skillful means" or responsive virtuosity (*upāya*; Ch. *fangbian*, 孝便). Practicing compassion is thus not a matter of simply "caring about" and "caring for" others; it involves realizing capabilities-for and commitments-to making use of situationally available resources to bring about the predicament-resolving realization of increasingly liberating or enlightening relational dynamics.

In much the same way that musical virtuosity is an achievement of disciplined practice, the improvisational genius or responsive virtuosity exemplified by bodhisattva is an achievement of the disciplined practice of being compassionately present with and for others. The discipline involved, however, is not a matter of rule-following or behavioral regimentation. It is a process of what might be termed appreciative perfection—a process of progressively embodying truly humane and liberating modalities of presence.

In traditional Mahayana contexts this process has most commonly been identified with the practice of cultivating and ever more fully enacting six *pāramitās* or "utmost excellences": generosity (*dāna*), or noninstrumental offering; moral clarity (*śīla*), or the capacity to perceive the currents of value- and intention-generated meaning and action presently shaping the karmic landscape and to participate in the liberating redirection of those currents through an ongoing situational purification of intent; patient willingness (*kṣānti*), or the steadfast readiness to act as needed to reorient relational dynamics in conditions of persistent uncertainty; valiant effort (*vīrya*), or a heroic enthusiasm and energy for the practice of virtuosic engagement; attentive poise (*dhyāna*), or the meditatively enabled realization of interest freed from both attraction and aversion; and wisdom (*prajñā*) as the situationally apt enactment of *kuśala*, or virtuosic relational dynamics, based on liberating insight into the interdependent, essence-less, and karmically configured nature of all things.

The personal ideal of the bodhisattva committed to compassionately embodying the six *pāramitās* offers a vision of who we need to be present as in order to engage in global predicament resolution. And, I think it offers a vision of human becoming that is capacious enough to be granted widespread assent and that is also conducive to realizing the mutual nonobstruction of personal and social good. But it is also an ideal, the viability of which is under threat by technological transformations of the human milieu that have the potential to dissolve capabilities-for and commitments-to addressing structural and institutional causes of conflict, trouble, and suffering as we increasingly frame our values, aims, and interests from behind experiential "veils of ignorance" that have been tailored to fit our individual needs and interests by an agentless regime of algorithmic agency.

The Threat of Algorithmic Experience

We are on the verge of an era-defining transformation of human experience. This transformation is not inevitable. But it will prove inexorable in the absence of concerted, ethically robust efforts to challenge prevailing suppositions about the moral status of global information and communications networks and the agentless forms of agency that are becoming pervasive within them. If that happens, we may well come to live as "gods," but we will be like the blissfully unenlightened gods occupying the heavenly realms in the Buddhist cosmos: beings dwelling in conditions so desirous that they are unsuitable for embodying the bodhisattva ideal.

In keeping with karmic insight that we can only respond effectively and sustainably to the relational distortions and predicaments we face by first understanding how they have come to be as they have, it is perhaps helpful to briefly describe the technological origins and practical manifestations of this transformation.

It will soon be technically feasible to map in real time the movements and activities of every person on earth and to tailor each person's mediated experience to reinforce and eventually shape the character of his or her interests and preferences. This possibility reflects an unplanned convergence among several initially unrelated currents of information and communication technology research and development. Central among these, I think, is a current of dramatic advances miniaturization and processing speeds that enabled data production to be made mobile, convenient, and nearly ubiquitous. To give a sense of the scale shift in data production, while 100 gigabytes of data were produced per *hour* in 1997, five years later, 100 gigabytes were being produced every *second*. By the end of this year, it is estimated that 50,000 gigabytes of data will be generated every second, including roughly 204 million emails, 216,000 Instagram posts, 277,000 Twitter posts, and seventy-two hours of YouTube videos.[5] At present, 2.5 quintillion bytes of new data are being produced every day.[6] Indeed, of the total amount of data in the world, 90 percent was produced in just the last two years.[7] We have entered the era of so-called *big data*—an era of astonishingly high-volume, high-velocity, and high-variety data generation.

The iconic tools of the miniaturization and mobility revolutions—the smartphone and tablet computer most prominent among them—proved to be remarkably well-suited to supporting and accelerating the construction and scaling up of social media platforms like Facebook, Weibo, and YouTube, and to normalizing twenty-four-hour access to internet search engines like Google and Baidu. The immense popularity of these wireless-connected devices is in large part a function of the user-friendly options for sharing images, music, video, and text that are afforded by having a presence on new social media platforms, as well as the ever-proliferating array of information services offered by internet service providers that have come to be available anytime and anywhere. In combination, the mobility of these devices and the attractiveness of the platforms and services to which they provided uninterrupted access facilitated a massive shift of social energy from offline to online environments, making connectivity practically habitual. The result has been a radical "democratization" of data production and sharing, including highly personal data regarding entertainment preferences, subjects of interests, shopping behavior, commuting habits, and travel plans.

As dramatic as this shift has been, an entirely new and potentially much more extensive dimension of data production has been opened with the incorporation of miniature, networked sensors into such everyday objects as medicine bottles, pens, running shoes, refrigerators, and automobiles. This fusion of everyday objects and online connectivity ushers in a kind of "augmented reality" that has been christened the "internet of things"—a world of "enchanted objects" (Rose 2015) and truly pervasive data production. While using, for example, a web-linked pen to take notes at a meeting, a virtual copy is being created and converted into printed text, the time and location of the meeting are being recorded, and all of this data is being continuously uploaded to a cloud server, enabling access to these notes (in real time) by anyone, from anywhere with a connection to the internet. Web-linked running shoes produce data about one's pace, the routes one runs, how often, and with how many calories burned. The cap of an "enchanted" medicine bottle changes color to remind you to take your medication, records if and when you did so, and can be made to pass this data on to your health care provider. It is now estimated that by 2026 there will be some 150 billion such networked sensors embedded in objects of daily use, resulting in a doubling of the total amount of data in the world every twelve hours. With the internet of things, data production becomes ambient.

This unrelenting escalation in the volume, velocity, and variety of data generation and storage over the last two decades might have produced nothing more than global "data smog." But the rise of big data also happened to come at a crucial juncture in machine-learning research and development. Traditional artificial intelligence research aimed to create software that would enable electronic entities like computers to replicate human-reasoning processes. Machine-learning research, by contrast, took the approach of developing learning algorithms: software that is capable of converting data to information with sufficient facility to carry out real-world actions like recognizing faces, signatures, or speech by learning from its own mistakes and authoring new and increasingly effective algorithms. Machine learning is based on algorithms that write new algorithms. In other words, machine learning marks a shift of coding responsibility from humans to computers.

The problem with machine learning is that it is completely dependent on trial-and-error and incremental adaptation. Without a huge amount of readily accessible and relevant data, machine learning is simply too slow and inept to be practically viable. With big data, machine-learning algorithms suddenly had the raw data needed to begin realizing their full potential. It became possible to convert "data smog" into almost unlimited kinds of useful information. In short, machine learning has made it possible to extract value from big data.[8]

Unsurprisingly, one of the most striking achievements made possible by algorithmically mined big data is the broad and multiple-layered commercialization of the internet that has occurred over just the last fifteen years.[9] Based on data gathered from credit/debit card purchases, web searches, and text, image, and video postings to social media, it is now possible for internet search engines and recommendation platforms to engage in increasingly accurate predictive analytics and to deliver ever more effectively personalized product and service advertising and pricing to individual consumers. Algorithms are being used to develop consumer credit ratings, to organize airline flight schedules, and, with considerable controversy, as part of the judicial process to undertake "risk assessments" and make "evidenced-based" recommendations regarding bail, sentence, and parole provisions.

Data profiling has also made possible carefully tailored and invisibly conducted "persuasive computing," "trend reinforcement," and political "nudging." With access to big data, digital assistants such as Siri, Cortana, Alexa, and Now communicate well enough today in natural language to be able to serve as private secretaries providing meeting reminders, offering advice on commuting options and where to get coffee or have lunch, and generating comprehensive grocery lists and recipes for upcoming dinner parties. And, because they do so with full access to all of one's past data-producing behavior, they are able to do so in ways that are uncannily effective. Indeed, we are on the verge of what Sherry Turkle (2011) has called the "robotic moment" when "affective computing" becomes effective enough for digital assistants and digital therapists to seem "alive enough" to engage as socially intelligent beings.

As might be expected, these technical advances have also been put to use in government-run surveillance programs to identify and build profiles of individual users of web browsers, instant messenger services, email, Skype video calls, landline and mobile phone calls and text messages, and social media interactions. For example, in 2012, the "Karma Police" program operated by the British Government Communications Headquarters (GCHQ) was acquiring some 50 billion metadata records every day about online communications and web-browsing activity, with plans to double that by the end of the year (Gallagher 2015). While information about this GCHQ data-mining operation and a similar program run by the American National Security Agency have been leaked to the public,[10] it can be safely assumed that many other nations have similar surveillance programs capable of monitoring all communications across entire countries, including capabilities for accessing the *content* of communications, not just metadata about their origin, destination, and routing.

All of these developments raise important legal and ethical questions. The case of government surveillance is particularly interesting since the raw data being gathered depends on access to privately owned and operated information and communications infrastructure, placing network and social media platform providers in positions of considerable structural power. At the same time, however, the legal right to gather and monetize personal data is crucial to the commercial success of network and social media platform providers. It is in the interest of these providers and industry more broadly to gain government recognition of this right to use personal data with often only default permission by individual citizens. In most countries, bargains on privacy issues have been cut between government and industry in ways that allow both surveillance and commercialization to proceed, if not hand in hand, then at least without conflict.[11] And, no less legally complicated and ethically troubling connections obtain among government censorship of internet traffic, consumer desires for unrestricted traffic (so-called net neutrality), and the industrial practices of throttling or blocking internet traffic and prioritizing certain forms of internet content—practices that are crucial to making network provision commercial viable.

If, as noted earlier, political validity depends on economic vitality, and if economic vitality depends increasingly on maximizing the production and both predictive and persuasive use of personal data, then it follows that politics is becoming increasingly predicated on gathering and manipulating personal data. In addition to electronic espionage, the political uses of big data and machine learning now include the global dissemination of fake news, the hacking of foreign elections, and the use of human trolls, web robots, and populist citizenry to "crowdsource" censorship and engage in both overt and covert annexations of social media.

In the face of these complex relations among government, industry, and the public, it might be expected (at least in liberal democratic countries) that network and social media platform consumers/users would lobby for stricter regulation of personal data use, whether by government or industry. But, in fact, consumers/users globally have proven to be content to tolerate default invasions of their privacy in exchange for the ease and effectiveness of online experiences that have become not just habitual but crucial to the formation and maintenance of their own social identities. And, while the causes for this complacency are undoubtedly quite complex, it is instructive to consider the historical case of pre-reunification East Germany, where empirical studies conducted by the government showed that access to foreign media led to a net increase of support for the regime, rather than calls for its reform or removal (Kern and Hainmueller 2009). Indeed, it can be convincingly argued that the shift from mass media such as network television and radio, to cable television, to streaming services and other forms of web-delivered entertainment has had the practical effect of allowing consumers/users to "opt out" of politics (Prior 2007).

These claims run directly counter to the widely embraced belief—most passionately expressed during the early days of the so-called Arab Spring—that social media have played important roles in galvanizing dissent and opening spaces of citizen group empowerment. In fact, the emancipatory political role attributed to social media appears to have been more a matter of modern mythmaking than a reflection of on-the-ground political realities (Morozov 2012). The weight of evidence globally is that political claims lodged on the internet by citizen groups have been modest (if not trivial) in scope and have done little to pressure political and corporate leaders into enacting real social reforms. Indeed, they appear instead to have had the ironic effect of increasing "the hegemonic authority of bureaucratic actors who recognize that the Internet creates a diversion that minimizes the likelihood of street-level response" (Maratea 2014, 124). As Evgeny Morozov pointedly notes, "The most effective system of Internet control is not the one that has the most sophisticated and draconian system of censorship, but the one that has no need for censorship whatsoever" (2012, 58)—an insight not lost on contemporary authoritarian regimes.

Contemporary regimes of surveillance, censorship, and privacy invasion are causes for profound legal and ethical concern. But, to the extent that they are framed in terms of individual consumer, corporate, or national actors and interests, it seems to me that focusing on these specific concerns is liable to obscure the paradigm shift needed to appreciate the full threat of algorithmically tailored experience. In doing so, it encourages continued reliance on familiar agent-, action-, and patient-oriented approaches to ethics, distracting us from the much more challenging task of crafting an ethics suited to critical engagement with the relational distortions and exploitations of attention that are now being brought about by agentless forms of agency.

The Predicament of Algorithmic "Karma"

Facilitated by networked mobile devices, there has occurred over the last decade a gradual and yet profound decoupling of physical and social presence and a dramatic migration of social life from offline to online environments. This has been celebrated by some as opening up almost utopian spaces for identity construction and expressions of social, cultural, and political difference. But, unlike offline social environments and public spaces, the online environments made possible by network connectivity are not spaces of chance encounters; they are environments designed to satisfy individual human interests. Online experience is algorithmically crafted to induce the most commercially valuable behavior possible by steering us toward web content that accords as closely as possible with our own manifest likes and interests, attracting and holding our attention for as long as possible. Simply put, the values expressed in our online conduct are used recursively to reconfigure our online reality.

Granted that attention is the single most important fuel of the new global informational economy, and granted that attention is the most basic resource for intentional, relational transformation, and thus indispensable to making any positive changes in our lives, the algorithmic tailoring of experience is very likely to amplify current trends toward widening gaps of wealth, income, risk, and opportunity. Just as important, though, it also poses new and very real structural threats both to our development of the kinds and depths of resolve needed to engage in predicament resolution, and to our pursuit of relational equity as an index of capacities-for and commitments-to acting in our own self-interest in ways deemed valuable by others.[12] Understanding and responding to these threats ultimately requires confronting the karmic implications of algorithmically tailored experience.

In theory, all web content is accessible to us. But in actuality, as learning algorithms process ever-increasing amounts of our personal data, our online experience is becoming ever more suitably and uniquely our own. We may have the impression that we have access to everything available on the web—the entire content of an infinitely rich informational reality. But that is not the case. To play with a phrasing gleaned from the Mahayana Buddhist text, the Diamond Sutra: what we take to be "everything" is not everything, even though we have no reason not to refer to it as "everything." It *is* all that we know, even though it does not include everything that could be referred to *as* everything. To dwell within algorithmically tailored online environments is to take up residence in individually tailored "filter bubbles" (Pariser 2011), And, with the internet of things and new technologies (like Google Glass) that aim to blend online and offline experiences to produce personalized "augmented realities," these bubbles eventually will make shared reality entirely optional.

Some might think this is nothing to be concerned about. If the data-profiling, predictive analytics, and persuasive computing capabilities that have resulted from the merger of big data and machine learning are making it possible to so effectively customize the human experience that we are each afforded virtually frictionless freedoms of choice, so what? If everything we experience is something that we want to experience, if our individual online and augmented realities adaptively anticipate and provide each of us what we desire, is this not our technological dream come true—the dream of limitless experiential control?

Seen through the lens of the Buddhist teaching of karma, however, this dream takes on nightmarish qualities. The core value of our now dominant technological lineage—control—allows us to exert *independence from* and *power over* our circumstances. That may often be good. But it is not *kuśala*. As control-biased technologies cross the threshold of utility, control becomes practically essential, resulting in experiences of our circumstances as increasingly in need of alteration or control. And this ultimately means living in increasingly controlled environments and, thus, being increasingly *subject to control*. And so the karmic cycle tightens: the better we get at getting what we want, the better we get at wanting; but the better we get at wanting and getting what we want, the less we will finally want what we get.

Big data and machine learning are dramatically amplifying the independence and power afforded by control-biased technology, but they are also raising the experiential and karmic stakes of doing so. A point will come when we will have no exit rights from the filter bubbles being crafted for us by agentless forms of structural agency—a loss of rights for which no one will be accountable and yet for which we will each be responsible. The cost of unlimited freedoms of experiential choice will be the normalization of digital solipsism—the valorization of living increasingly comfortably behind experiential "veils of ignorance" that have been tailored algorithmically to fit our individual needs, aims, and interests. In Buddhist terms, we each will take up personal residence in a karmic *cul-de-sac*—a karmic dead-end. We will be enabled to live godly lives, but they will be lives without any prospect of freedom from the compulsion to choose or freedom to engage compassionately in global predicament resolution.

Relational Ethics and the Prospect of Truly Liberating Structures of Feeling

Herbert Marcuse presciently noted in his 1964 book, *One-Dimensional Man*, that powerful social, political, and economic elites seem best able to use technologies to control people's lives when the people being controlled believe that these same technologies are crucial to their own prospects for living more comfortable, secure, and liberating lives. But in an era of algorithmic experience, Marcuse's astute ethical concern is rendered impotent by its agent orientation. Yet, the recursive complexity of the link between structurally delivered control and personal beliefs and desires in the present era renders patient-oriented concerns no less impotent.

Buddhism can plausibly be seen as offering an action-oriented alternative. In the Araṇavibhanga Sūtta (*Majjhima Nikāya* 1995, 139:6ff), for example, the Buddha explicitly corrects the agent bias of a group of students, encouraging them to refrain from blaming or praising people's behavior and to concentrate instead on simply explaining the causal and correlational links between actions and experiential consequences. And, as the narratives of the Buddha's own enlightenment make clear, insight into karma—that is, insight into the experience-shaping of dynamics of intentional action—is the necessary prelude to realizing liberation from conflict, trouble, and suffering.

But, if Buddhist ethics are in some degree action-oriented, this does not seem to be in a Kantian manner of determining which actions are intrinsically good and thus categorically binding on us as rationally moral beings. The improvisational genius or skillful means (*upāya*) that characterize the actions of bodhisattvas point toward an ethos of situational responsiveness rather than dutiful adherence to some rationally derived norms. Indeed, in Chinese Buddhism, it was understood that, to have liberating interactions with others, bodhisattvas would often have to engage in "unconstrained conduct" (*wu'ai xing* 無礙行), acting in ways that are "without precedent" (*wuwei* 無為) and contrary to customary moral and societal norms.

At the same time, while the emphasis on karma in Buddhist ethics is undeniable, it is not the immediate consequences of action that are of primary ethical concern, but rather the values and intentions informing action. Indeed, since actions undertaken on the basis of craving forms of desire are karmically binding, providing every member of a given population with the means to satisfy every experiential desire would arguably be deemed unethical. A society structured to afford the greatest number of people and the greatest total control over the content of their experience might be considered a good society by most people, but this would not necessarily make it a liberating one.

Finally, it's hard to reconcile the quantitative foundations of classical utilitarianism and the disregard for personal and situational uniqueness that are implicit in an aggregative hedonic calculus with the Buddhist ethos of realizing qualitatively superlative (*kuśala*) conduct and the compassionate responsiveness crucial to the bodhisattva ideal. There is an important sense in which capacities-for and commitments-to superlative responsiveness cannot be measured, but only evaluated in explicitly evolving qualitative terms.

That the Buddha's liberation came with insight into the interdependence or relationality of all things, and that he devoted the remainder of his life to improvising means by which others could author their own liberation, suggests that the Buddhist alternative to agent- and patient-oriented ethics is not focused on actions and their consequences, but rather on relational dynamics as the primordial and irreducibly values-infused presence from within which agents, patients, and actions relating them can be differentiated and abstracted as putatively independent. Both the personal example of the Buddha and the personal ideal of the bodhisattva point toward an ethics of compassionate engagement dedicated to alleviating *duḥkha*, whenever and wherever possible, by engaging with others in virtuosically responsive and karma-transforming shared predicament resolution. In keeping with these examples, I think our best hope of resisting the experiential allure of agentlessly crafted algorithmic experience is by fostering a robust, contemporary ethos of compassionate human becoming—an ethos best articulated in the conduct of truly diversity-enhancing intercultural philosophy.

Notes

1. On these ironic or "revenge effects" of technology, see Tenner (1997) and Hershock (1999).
2. For a more in-depth discussion, see Hershock (2015).
3. The "golden rule" is to "treat and act toward others as you would have them treat and act toward you," while the "silver rule" is to "*not* treat or act toward others as you would *not* have them treat or act toward you."
4. For a textual source supporting this reading of Buddhist ethics, see the Sakkapañha Sūtta, *Digha Nikāya* (1995, 21).
5. One gigabyte of storage is enough for sixteen hours of high-quality music or 65,000 pages of a Word document.
6. That is 2,500, 000,000,000,000,000 bytes, or the equivalent of 10 million high-definition video discs.
7. www.vcloudnews.com/every-day-big-data-statistics-2-5-quintillion-bytes-of-data-created-daily
8. For a comprehensive, if very hopeful, introduction to algorithm-based machine learning, see Domingos (2015).
9. By way of illustration, consider that in the United Kingdom in 2001 roughly 154 million pounds were spent on online advertising; by 2014, that figure had risen to 7.1 billion pounds, or 40 percent of total advertising expenditures. In the European Union as a whole, total online advertising in 2014 was 24.6 billion euros (Horten 2016, 25).
10. Through the famous Edward Snowden affair and Wikileaks.
11. For a clear and insightful examination of these government-industry interactions, see Horten (2016).
12. On relational equity in contrast with comparative equity as equality of opportunity, see Hershock (2015).

References

Ames, Roger T. 2011. *Confucian Role Ethics: A Vocabulary*. Honolulu: University of Hawai'i Press.
Beck, Ulrich. 1999. *World Risk Society*, London: Polity Press.
Beck, Ulrich, with Anthony Giddens and Scott Lash. 1994. *Reflexive Modernization: Politics, Tradition and Aesthetics in the Modern Social Order*. Stanford, CA: Stanford University Press.
Buddhaghosa. 2011. *Visuddhimagga*, translated by Bhikkhu Ñāṇamoli as *The Path of Purification*. Kandy: Buddhist Publication Society.
Castells, Manuel. 1996. *The Rise of the Network Society*. Vol. 1 of *The Information Age: Economy, Society and Culture*. Cambridge, MA: Blackwell.

———. 1997. *The Power of Identity.* Vol. 2 of *The Information Age: Economy, Society and Culture.* Cambridge, MA: Blackwell.

———. 1998. *End of Millennium.* Vol. 3 of *The Information Age: Economy, Society and Culture.* Cambridge, MA: Blackwell.

Dīgha Nikāya. 1995. Translated by Maurice Walshe as *The Long Discourses of the Buddha.* Boston: Wisdom Publications.

Domingos, Pedro. 2015. *The Master Algorithm: How the Quest for the Ultimate Learning Machine Will Remake Our World.* New York: Basic Books.

Ellul, Jacques. 1983. "The Search for Ethics in a Technicist Society." mc7290.bgsu. wikispaces.net/file/view/4_Ellul_1983.pdf

Floridi, Luciano. 2013. *Ethics of Information.* Oxford: Oxford University Press.

Franck, Georg. 1999. "The Economy of Attention." *Telepolis*, July 12, 1999. www.heise.de/tp.artikel/55567/1.htmal

Gallagher, Ryan. 2015. "From Radio to Porn: British Spies Track Web-Users Online Identities," *The Intercept*, September 24, 2015. theintercept.com/2015/09/25/gchq-radio-porn-spies-track-web-users-online-identities

Hershock, Peter D. 1999. *Reinventing the Wheel: A Buddhist Response to the Information Age.* Albany, NY: SUNY Press.

———. (2012). *Valuing Diversity: Buddhist Reflection on Realizing a More Equitable Global Future.* Albany, NY: SUNY Press.

———. 2015. "The Value of Diversity: Buddhist Reflections on More Equitably Orienting Global Interdependence," in Roger T. Ames and Peter D. Hershock (eds.), *Value and Values: Economics and Justice in an Age of Global Interdependence.* Honolulu: University of Hawai'i Press.

Horten, Monica. 2016. *The Closing of the Net.* London: Polity Press.

Kern, Holger Lutz, and Jens Hainmueller. 2009. "Opium for the Masses: How Foreign Media Can Stabilize Authoritarian Regimes," *Political Analysis* 17(4): 377–399.

Majjhima Nikāya. 1995. Translated as *The Middle Length Discourses of the Buddha* by Bhikkhu Nanamoli and Bhikkhu Bodhi. Boston: Wisdom Publications.

Maratea, R.J. 2014. *The Politics of the Internet: Political Claims-making in Cyberspace and Its Effect on Modern Political Activism.* Lanham, MD, Lexington Books.

Morozov, Evgeny. 2012. *The Net Delusion: The Dark Side of Internet Freedom.* Washington DC: Public Affairs.

Nancy, Jean-Luc. 2000. *Being Singular Plural.* Translated by Robert Richardson and Anne O'Byrne. Stanford, CA: Stanford University Press.

Nussbaum, Martha. 2001. *Upheavals of Thought: The Intelligence of Emotions.* Cambridge: Cambridge University Press.

———. 2011. *Creating Capabilities: The Human Development Approach.* Cambridge, MA: Belknap Press.

Oxfam International Report. 2017. "An Economy for the 99%." www.oxfam.org/en/research/economy-99

Prior, Markus. 2009. *Post-Broadcast Democracy.* Cambridge: Cambridge University Press.

Rose, David. 2015. *Enchanted Objects: Innovation, Design, and the Future of Technology.* New York: Scribner's.
Sakai, Naoki, and Meaghan Morris. 2008. *Translation and Subjectivity: On Japan and Cultural Nationalism.* Minneapolis: University of Minnesota Press.
Tenner, Edward. 1997. *Why Things Bite Back: Technology and the Revenge of Unintended Consequences.* New York: Vintage Books.
Turkle, Sherry. 2011. *Alone Together: Why We Expect More from Technology and Less from Each Other.* New York: Basic Books.
Whitebrook, Maureen. 2014. "Love and Anger as Political Virtues," in Michael Ure and Mervyn Frost (eds.), *The Politics of Compassion.* London: Routledge.

Chapter 2

Confucian Role Ethics and Personal Identity

ROGER T. AMES

Introduction: "Human *Beings* or "Human *Becomings*?"

What is a human "being"? This was a perennial Greek question asked in Plato's *Phaedo* and in his *Republic*, and in Aristotle's *Categories* as well. And there were many different answers, two of which are pointed at metonymically in the "up" and "down" gestures of Plato and his student Aristotle in Raphael's famous "School of Athens" fresco. And one persistent answer to this question was an ontological one, predating Plato's psyche with the Egyptian transfiguration of the *ka* and *ba* life-forces animating the spiritual entity *akh* in the afterlife, and with the Pythagorean doctrine of the reincarnation of an immortal soul that anticipates and informs Plato's *Phaedo*. From these deep historical roots, the "being" of a human being has come to be understood popularly in Christian doctrine as some variation on a permanent, ready-made, and self-sufficient soul. Early on in the narrative, "know thyself"—the signature exhortation of Socrates' doctrine of "recollection" (*amnanesis*)—is to remember and thus know this soul fully. Each of us *is* a person, and from conception, has the integrity of *being* an individual person.

How, or *in what way* (*dao* 道), do persons in their roles and relations *become* consummately human (*ren* 仁)? This then was the perennial Confucian question asked explicitly in all of the *Four Books*: in the *Expansive Learning* (*Daxue* 大學), in the *Analects of Confucius*, in the *Mencius*, and again in *Focusing the Familiar* (*Zhongyong*). And the answer even before the time of

Confucius was a moral, aesthetic, and ultimately religious one. Persons (always and necessarily plural) *become* humans by cultivating those thick relations that constitute our native conditions and that guide the trajectory of our life narratives—that is, the whence and whither of our life's journey within family, community, and cosmos.[1] And "cultivate your persons"—*xiushen* 修身—the signature exhortation of the Confucian canons—is the ground of the Confucian project of becoming consummate as the unique persons we aspire to become (*ren*). We are to cultivate our conduct assiduously as it is expressed through those specific family, community, and cosmic roles and relations that we live together. In this Confucian tradition, because we depend upon our associated lives lived in the roles of family and community to become persons, our assertive "I" is always a "we," and our socialized "me" is always an "us."

What is at stake here is the deliberate Mencian answer to perhaps our most basic and important philosophical question: what does it mean to become fully human? How do we explain birth, life, and growth of the human "being"?—by reduplicative causal accounts (the infant is a ready-made adult), by teleological accounts (the infant is simply preliminary to the existing ideal), or as a human "becoming" that appeals to a contextual, narrative account available to us through a phenomenology of reflective and purposeful personal action? How do we define what it means to be a human "being"?—by speculative assumptions about innate, isolatable causes that locate persons outside of the roles and relations in which they live their lives, or alternatively, as having "become" human by taking full account of the initial, native conditions and context within which persons are inextricably embedded, and then by assaying the full aggregation of consequent action as their life stories unfold?

In our own world in which individualism has become an ideology with a seeming monopoly on intellectual consciousness, we are going to have to ask whether our own default common-sense assumptions about *individual* human "beings" are consistent with the Confucian project as it was situated and developed within the natural *qi* cosmology that serves this tradition as the context for such personal growth, or whether a narrative understanding of person is not a better reading of ancient Confucian philosophers.

The Confucian Project: Achieved Relational Virtuosity

In appealing to an understanding of Chinese natural cosmology as the relevant interpretive context for this Confucian project, I want to provide a language that will distinguish this worldview from the reductive, single-ordered, "One-behind-the-many" ontological model that grounds classical Greek metaphysical thinking about persons and cosmos wherein one comes to "understand" the many by knowing retrospectively the foundational and causal ideal that lies behind them. Instead, we find that in Chinese cosmology there is a symbiotic and holistic focus-field model of order that is illustrated rather concisely in the organic, ecological sensibilities of the *Expansive Learning* 大學. The meaning of the family is implicated in and dependent upon the productive cultivation of each of its members, and by extension, the meaning of the entire cosmos is implicated in and dependent upon the productive cultivation of each person within family and community. Personal worth is the source of human culture, and human culture in turn is the aggregating resource that provides a context for each person's cultivation.

While certainly having important theoretical implications, the enduring power of this Confucian project is that it proceeds from a relatively straightforward account of the actual human experience. It is a pragmatic naturalism in the sense that, rather than relying upon metaphysical presuppositions or supernatural speculations, it focuses instead on the possibilities for enhancing personal worth available to us here and now through enchanting the ordinary affairs of the day. A grandmother's love for her grandchild is at once the most ordinary of things, and the most extraordinary of things.

Confucius by developing his insights around the most basic and enduring aspects of the ordinary human experience—family reverence, deference to others, friendship, a cultivated sense of shame, education, community, and so on—has guaranteed their continuing relevance. One characteristic of Confucianism that is certainly there in the words of Confucius himself and that has made his teachings so resilient in the Chinese tradition, is its porousness and adaptability. His contribution was simply to take ownership of the cultural legacy of his time, to adapt the wisdom of the past to his own present historical moment, and then to recommend to future generations that they do the same.[2]

The personal model of Confucius that is remembered in the *Analects* does not purport to lay out some generic formula by which everyone should live their lives. Rather, the text recalls the narrative of one special person: how he in his relations with others cultivated his humanity, and how he lived a fulfilling life, much to the admiration of those around him. We might take liberties and play with the title of the *Analects*, reading "discoursing" (*lunyu* 論語) more specifically as "role-based discoursing" (*lunyu* 倫語). Indeed, in reading the *Analects*, we encounter the relationally constituted Confucius making his way through life by living his many roles as best he can: as a caring family member, as a strict teacher and mentor, as a scrupulous and incorruptible scholar-official, as a concerned neighbor and member of the community, as an always critical political consultant, as the grateful progeny of his progenitors, as an enthusiastic heir to a specific cultural legacy, indeed, as a member of a chorus of joyful boys and men singing their way home after a happy day on the river Yi. He offers us historical models rather than principles, and exhortations rather than imperatives. The power and lasting value of his insights lie in the fact that, as I will endeavor to show, these ideas are intuitively persuasive, and readily adaptable to the conditions of ensuing generations, including our own.

Indeed, invoking the Chinese natural cosmology as context, what makes Confucianism more empirical than empiricism—that is, what makes Confucianism a *radical* empiricism—is that it respects the uniqueness of the particular, and the need for a generative wisdom that takes this uniqueness into account in anticipating a productive future. Rather than advancing universal principles and assuming a taxonomy of natural kinds grounded in some notion of strict identity, Confucianism proceeds from always provisional generalizations made from those *particular* historical instances of successful living, the specific events recounted in the narrative of Confucius himself being a case in point.

"Culture," "Human Flourishing," and "Human Nature"

We might look to the term "culture" and the metaphors in which it is embedded within our own narrative to register the assumptions we bring with us in making horticulture and husbanding an apposite metaphor for the production of culture. Indeed, it is because we default to these same assumptions that the essentialist interpretation of Confucianism on "human nature" (*xing* 性) persists as the prevalent understanding.

In his *Keywords: A Vocabulary of Culture and Society* (1976) Raymond Williams famously describes "culture" as one of the two or three most complicated terms in English.[3] He attributes this in part to the relative recency with which the meaning of "culture" has been metaphorically extended from its original sense of the physical processes of nurturing and cultivation—that is, the practices of horticulture and husbandry—to point toward a characteristic mode of material, intellectual, spiritual, and aesthetic development. Just as our common sense dictates, we see these practices as teleologically driven in bringing to fruition characteristic forms inherent in the object of cultivation where human intervention serves as both a source of discipline and control, and as an external facilitation. The assumption is that the plant or animal flourishes if it is unimpeded and properly nourished.

It was only in the eighteenth century that "culture" was first used consistently to denote the entire "way of life" of a people, and only in the late nineteenth and early twentieth centuries that it was identified with specific civilization-distinguishing patterns of practices and values. In this latter case, it was used in the context of theories of progressive "social evolution" as something that sets apart and divides societies, making one more advanced than another. One contemporary legacy of this emerging sense of contest is the contemporary media's frequent characterization of multicultural tensions in education as "culture wars."

As in premodern Europe, there was no single term in premodern Chinese and Japanese that had a conceptual reach comparable to that of contemporary uses of the word "culture." But the term that came to be used throughout the geographical region to appropriate and translate this emerging modern concept differs markedly in its metaphorical implications from those assumed with the English word "culture." While Chinese and Japanese abound with words that, like "culture," are rooted in instrumental physical processes of cultivation and nourishing (for example, *xiu* 修, *yang* 養, *xu/chu* 畜), these terms are bypassed as points of metaphorical departure in favor of 文化 (*wenhua*)—a compound word that combines the characters for "the inscribing and embellishing of the literary/civil/artistic traditions" (*wen*) and "transforming" (*hua*). Whereas metaphorically rooting "culture" in practices of plant and animal domestication invites seeing cultural norms as having a transcendent disciplinary force with respect to that which is being "cultured," *wen* was understood (with significant political implications) as *collaborating* with nature and *elaborating* upon it rather than as regulating its spontaneous growth.

As is demonstrated by its use in texts dating to the Han dynasty (202 BCE–220 CE), the term *wenhua* is an ancient one. *Wenhua* is a *kanji* term derived from classical Chinese that first appears in the court bibliographer Liu Xiang's 劉向 (77–76 BCE) *Shuoyuan* 說苑: "It is only when civilizing efforts do not bring them up to standard that punishments are to be imposed."[4] And, by at least the fifth century, Chinese literary theorists such as Liu Xie 劉勰 (465?–522?) identified *wen* explicitly with the self-arising (*ziran* 自然) and ceaselessly creative (*shengsheng buxi* 生生不息) dynamics of the natural world (*dao* 道), affirming that nature and nurture were not opposed, but rather a co-evolving, contrapuntal process understood to be at the heart of realizing a symbiotic, natural and societal, harmony. Moreover, in sharp contrast with the contemporary use of "wars" as a metaphor for cultural tensions, from ancient times *wen* was contrasted explicitly with the destructive and dehumanizing use of military force (*wu* 武). *Wen* instead denotes the expansively civil dimension of the human experience that emerges when the life of a community is guided by an aesthetically and critically enriching counterpoint between persistent canonical texts and those continuing commentaries that have been crafted in each generation as a response to current conditions. In sum, the conceptual genealogy of *wenhua* implies that culture emerges through an *intrinsic* relationship between persistence and change (*biantong* 變通)—a relationship between tradition and transformation in which cultural conservation and prospective change, far from being opposed, are complementary and mutually enhancing. Indeed, it is this complementary, contrapuntal dynamic that has immediate relevance for the Confucian notion of "human nature" (*xing*) as conduct.

Tang Junyi 唐君毅 on "Human Nature" (*renxing* 人性) *as* Conduct

Tang Junyi grounds his work in his understanding of Chinese natural cosmology, and has offered a series of generalizations that he takes as defining of a persistent yet always changing Chinese cosmology. These propositions proffered by Tang Junyi provide yet another vocabulary for reiterating and reinforcing the characterization of Chinese cosmology we might abstract from the "Great Tradition" 大傳 commentary on the *Book of Changes* 易經. Tang in his final proposition invokes a feature of Chinese cosmology that provides insight into the vectoral yet always contingent nature of the human experience. For Tang Junyi as a Confucian, "human nature" (*xing* 性) is a provisional, generalized disposition at once persistent and yet always under revision in its interactions with other things. In Tang's own words, Chinese cosmology entails the holographic notion that "'human nature' is nothing but the unfolding of the natural and cultural processes themselves" (*xing ji tiandao guan* 性即天道觀).[5]

For Tang Junyi, any teleological or genetic assumptions we might have about being human must be qualified by the spontaneous emergence of novelty within any specific context, and by the creative advance in the continuing present of any situation. "Human nature," then, is a generalization regarding the aggregating yet open-ended disposition of human beings over time, and is nothing more or less than an expression of the ongoing attainment of relational virtuosity (*ren* 仁) within our inherited natural and cultural legacy (*tiandao* 天道). That is, the nature of each person must be recovered from and understood in terms of the continuous unfolding of the entire cosmos. In fact, rather than referencing some fixed endowment, it is for Tang precisely the indeterminate possibility for creative change that is the most salient feature of the human *xing*. What is given in the *xing* of persons—that is, in their initial conditions—is most importantly the propensity for growth, cultivation, and refinement.

In Tang Junyi's general discussion of the Confucian understanding of the "nature" (*xing* 性) of things, he quite appropriately begins from the etymology of the term by allowing for its immediate association with "life" (*sheng* 生) itself. Expanding upon this connection, he acknowledges the irreducibly relational and contextual character of the content of the human experience, and notes that for this reason the *xing* of anything, including human beings, necessarily has two referents: it denotes the continuing life and function of a particular thing itself, and also refers to that which in a thing continues the life of other things.[6] The nature of the earth, for example, lies not only in its own conditions—something porous in which different kinds of plants can be productively grown or something solid on which suitable human habitation can be built. The nature of earth also lies in its propensity to grow and give life to other things—the way in which it is life-giving for other plants and animals.[7] Analogously, Confucian persons are defined relationally and collaterally—not only what they "are," but more importantly, what they "do" with and for other persons and things in the world.

Tang Junyi further clarifies what he means by the cosmological proposition that "human nature is nothing but the unfolding of the natural and cultural processes themselves" (*xing ji tiandao guan* 性即天道觀):

> Within Chinese natural cosmology what is held in general is not some first principle. The root pattern or coherence (*genben zhi li* 根本之理) of anything is its "life force" (*shengli* 生理), and this life force is its "natural tendencies" (*xing* 性). Anything's natural tendencies are expressed in the quality of its interactions with other things and events. "Natural tendencies" or "life force" then entailing spontaneity and transformation have nothing to do with necessity. . . . The emergence of any particular phenomenon is a function of the interaction between its prior conditions and other things and events as external influences. So how something interacts with other things and events and the form of this interaction is not determined by the thing in itself. . . . Thus

the basic "nature" of anything includes this transformability in response to whatever it encounters.⁸

To illustrate this notion of contingent emergence, Tang provides a gloss on the opening passage of the *Zhongyong* 中庸. In his commentary on this text, Tang seeks to preclude any essentialistic interpretation of human nature. In explanation of "what *tian* (conventionally translated 'Heaven') commands is called natural tendencies" (*tianming zhi wei xing* 天命之謂性), he states explicitly:

> What is meant by this claim is not that *tian* according to some fixed fate determines the conduct and progress of human beings. On the contrary, *tian* endows humans with a natural disposition that, being more or less free of the mechanical control of their established habits and of external intervening forces, undergoes a creative advance within their context that is expressive of this spontaneity.⁹

Tang then goes on to distinguish humans from other things by their degree of complexity and their self-conscious freedom and creativity:

> It is only in having more interactions with other things that something increases its creative impulse. . . . The quality of something is a function of what novelty emerges and is manifested in its interactions with other things and events. It is also a function of the ongoing tendency to expansiveness that comes with being self-consciously able to constantly seek out more and better interactions, and being able to abandon the mechanical control of one's own past habits and those mechanical habits from external intervening forces. But this is not something that the ordinary run of things can do—it is only we humans that can do it.¹⁰

It is in this sense that the *Book of Rites* 禮記 can claim that "humans are the heart-and-mind of the world" (*renzhe tiandi zhi xin ye* 人者天地之心也).¹¹ It is through an irreducible intersubjectivity that persons become reflexive and self-conscious in their conduct, and thus have the freedom and creativity to strive after optimal relations. To speak of "human nature" for Tang, then, is to generalize the aggregating yet open-ended narratives of particular humans over time.

In Tang Junyi's extensive work on "human nature" (*renxing* 人性) he demonstrates a great sensitivity to the existential coloring of the classical Confucian conception of what it means to become human. For Tang, "Since any particular existent has life, in saying that it has a *xing*, what is important is not in saying what the nature and character of this entity is, but in saying what the direction of its life's existence is."[12] It is only in that it has life and growth that it has *xing*. And among things, as we have seen, humans are a special case. The *xing* of humans cannot be approached in the same way as our understanding of the *xing* of other phenomena because humans have an internal perspective on their own evolving constitution that is not available to them in the investigation of other things. In reflecting on the relationships between experience and conceptualization, Tang asserts that:

> It is not certain that human realization can exhaust human possibilities; if one wants to understand human possibilities it is not like seeking to know the possibilities of other things that can, on the basis of inference and hypothesis, be known objectively. Rather it comes from the way in which persons realize their internal aspirations and how they come to know them. Once we have an understanding of this human *xing*, we will of our own accord surely have the linguistic concepts through which to express it. Such linguistic conceptualization follows upon what is known, and is formed continuously as the opportunity presents itself.[13]

Tang thus emphasizes the primacy of the realization of the human aspirations over the conceptualization and articulation of them, giving full notice to the personal locus of that realization. He disassociates the conversation among classical Chinese philosophers over the meaning of *xing* from the contemporary science of psychology to the extent that in the latter case there is a desire to treat the human "being" as an objective phenomenon. For Tang, it is the reflexive and self-conscious existential project that is the fundamental distinguishing characteristic of the classical Confucian conception of *xing*. In fact, it is precisely the indeterminate possibility for creative change that Tang identifies as the most salient feature of the human *xing*:

> Usually what is meant by "nature" as quality or character, as when Westerners refer to it in the language of "property, characteristics, propensity, and essence" is a fixed quality, disposition, or directionality. But when we reflect upon what nature is from

the perspective of the experience of the inner aspirations that we as humans have in relation to our world, there is a real question as to whether or not we can say that humans have any fixed nature. This is because the world that humans encounter and the aspirations they bring to it both entail limitless change. . . . For the most part, the discussion of human nature in Chinese thought has had as its one common feature a reference to this capacity for boundless change as wherein the special nature of the human lies. This then is the human's spiritual nature (*lingxing* 靈性) that differs from the fixity and lack of spirituality in the nature of other things.¹⁴

What is an initial condition in the nature of human beings is most importantly the propensity for growth, cultivation, and refinement—a human capacity for radical changeability. It is thus that throughout Tang's analysis, and especially in reference to the human phenomenon, he underscores the fundamental relationality and collaterality of *xing*:

It is my opinion that in looking at the beginnings of a theory of human nature in China's early philosophers, the basic idea was not to take humans or their *xing* as some objective thing that can be looked at and discussed in terms of its universal nature or its special nature or its possibilities. As humans encountered the myriad things and heaven and earth, and as they encountered their inner experience of their own aspirations, what was important for them was to reflect on what the *xing* of this human is, and what the *xing* of heaven and earth and the myriad things is. The way the human was perceived within the mainstream of Chinese thought was as a kind of thing amidst and among the myriad things, and not just as one kind of the myriad things.¹⁵

If we were to summarize the notion of person that follows from Tang Junyi's description of "human nature" (*renxing* 人性), taking the notion of "growing and living" (*sheng* 生) within its contextualizing relations as its defining feature, we would have to allow that such an irreducibly complex agency is vital and inherently active, and is not only responsive to its environments but is further characterized by the freedom and creativity to be self-defining and self-aware. This reflexive "self-" has to be understood as irreducibly transactional: shaping and being shaped in its contextualizing relations. This agency is first and foremost a striving and a "doing" that is an expression of life and growth, and that in the production of enhanced meaning brings with it aspiration, frustration, and sometimes even satisfaction. Such an understanding of agency is wholly naturalistic in that it makes no appeal to a metaphysics of self or to any unifying substratum such as soul or mind, and thus is more of a centered, concentrated vitality than a unity. This agency is hylozoistic—at once psychic and physical—that is always embodied and embodying as a porous membrane that strives to achieve meaning and coherence in the changing configuration of its relations. It offers a revisionist and emergent understanding of agency that is animated and projective, and that having developed its own inflected and reflexive sense of itself out of its intersubjective relations with others, becomes increasing enculturated through the semiotic processes and symbolic competencies that come to shape it in these associations. It is radically embedded, and can be understood only by moving from field to focus, from the totality to the particular, taking into account the full compass of its contextualizing relations. Indeed, this agency is an expression of the ongoing attainment of relational virtuosity (*ren* 仁) within our inherited cultural legacy (*tiandao* 天道), allowing Tang to insist that "human nature is nothing but the unfolding of the natural and cultural processes themselves" (*xing ji tiandao guan* 性即天道觀). It is this sense of growth in its achieved personal uniqueness and its intimate continuity with the totality through family and community relations that provides a direct line from the self-conscious deference, veneration, and gratitude of the moral life to the spirituality we associate with an increasingly religious sensitivity. This notion of agency breathes life into the Confucian vocabulary, transforming terms such as "excellence" (*de* 德) into striving after and "getting" (*de* 得) and "appropriateness" (*yi* 義) into a self-conscious sense of responsibility and accountability for the quality of meaning in one's relations with others.

I want to argue that, with respect to this notion of human nature, Tang Junyi's "New Confucianism" is not so new. This collateral and multilateral understanding of person is in fact consistent with the Confucianism espoused in the *Expansive Learning* that sets the Confucian project. And this Confucian project can be described as a radical empiricism directed at achieving the highest integrated cultural, moral, and spiritual growth for the person-in-community. For Confucius, communal harmony begins here in indefatigable personal cultivation. And through growth in familial, communal, and natural relations, the aspirant seeks to ascend to cosmic consequence in spiraling radial circles. The Confucian sages are no more than ordinary persons who, through their resolute commitment and assiduous discipline in their family and communal relations, learn to do the most ordinary of things in extraordinary ways. Indeed, the familiar Confucian claim that "everyone can become a sage" is an assertion that the spontaneous emergence of real significance in the ordinary business of the day is itself the meaning and content of sagely virtuosity. As is stated in the *Zhongyong*:

> The vision of the moral life (*dao*) is not at all remote from people. If someone were to take it as being remote, it would not be the true vision.[16]

This idea that the inspired life is nothing more than the transformation of immediate human relations is a familiar theme in the Confucian canons:

> The Master said: "How could consummate conduct (*ren*) be at all remote? No sooner do I seek it that it has arrived."[17]

Achieving Personal Identity through Embodying (*ti* 體) Propriety (*li* 禮)

In attempting to consolidate an understanding of the Confucian notion of personal identity, we might begin from the challenge that William James directs at the familiar "substance" understanding of the "essence" and "attribute" unity of the foundational individual. James uses the analogy of "climate" to illustrate the redundancy that a superordinate substance like "soul" or "self" or "mind" introduces into an analysis of personal identity:

> The low thermometer to-day, for instance, is supposed to come from something called the "climate." Climate is really only the name for a certain group of days, but it is treated as if it lay *behind* the day, and in general we place the name, as if it were a being, behind the facts it is the name of. But the phenomenal properties of things . . . do not inhere in anything. They adhere, or cohere, rather, with each other, and the notion of a substance inaccessible to us, which we think accounts for such cohesion by supporting it, as cement might support pieces of a mosaic, must be abandoned. The fact of the bare cohesion itself is all the notion of the substance signifies. Behind that fact is nothing.[18]

The Confucian alternative to locating personal identity in some superordinate soul or self or mind is to find this same coherence *in media res* in the achieved coordination and integration of one's embodied roles and relations. In the *Zhongyong*, we are told explicitly that family feeling is the ultimate source of the civility and propriety fostered within our ritualized roles and institutions:

> Consummate conduct (*ren* 仁) means comporting oneself as a human being (*ren* 人), wherein devotion to one's kin is most important. Appropriateness (*yi* 義) means doing what is fitting (*yi* 宜), wherein esteeming those of superior character and conduct is most important.[19] The degree of devotion due different kin and the degree of esteem accorded those who vary in excellence of character and conduct is what gives rise to the achievement of propriety in our roles and relations (*li* 禮).[20]

In considering personal identity from a Confucian point of view, we must appreciate fully the way in which both our somaticity and our relations with others enables us to achieve and sustain coherence as a person. At the same time, we must resist the familiar, uncritical assumption that being embodied and being "en-roled" necessarily commits us to the notion of superordinate and discrete, individual "selves." The character for "body" (*ti* 體) that has "bones" (*gu* 骨) as its classifier emerges relatively late in antiquity. Although by the time of the silk manuscripts recovered at Mawangdui in 168 BCE *ti* does occur in this present form, it appears earlier on the bronzes with a "lived body" (*shen* 身) signific (figure 2.1), and then on the bamboo strip manuscripts with a "flesh" (*rou* 肉) signific (figure 2.2).

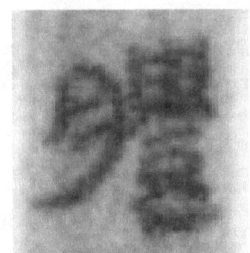

Figure 2.1　　　　　　　　　　Figure 2.2

We can use these three alternative classifiers that constitute the different forms of this character as a heuristic for parsing *ti*'s range of meaning. We must allow that *ti* with the "bones" (*gu*) classifier references the "verbal body" as a process of "configuring, embodying, and knowing" the world. *Ti* with the "lived body" (*shen*) classifier references the vital, existentially aware, lived-body in its dynamic social relations with others. And *ti* with the "flesh" (*rou*) classifier references the carnal body—body as flesh and bones. At the most primordial level, the body via these three mutually entailing modalities serves as the bond that conjoins our subjectivity with our environments and that mediates the processes of thinking and feeling with our patterns of conduct.

In the Confucian tradition, the body is an inheritance we receive from our families, and as a current in a genealogical stream that reaches back to our most remote ancestors, brings with it a sense of continuity and belonging, as well as the religious significance such feelings entail. Respect for one's own body is to show reverence for one's ancestors; disregard for one's own body is to bring shame to one's lineage. As is stated in the first chapter of the *Classic of Family Reverence* (*Xiaojing* 孝經):

> Your physical person with its hair and skin is received from your parents. Vigilance in not allowing anything to do injury to your person is where family reverence begins . . . .[21]

This responsibility to preserve one's body intact is a major theme throughout the Confucian canons. A passage in the *Record of Rituals* reads:

> The Master said: "Among those things born of the heavens and nurtured by the earth, nothing is grander than the human being. For the parents to give birth to your whole person, and for one to return oneself to them whole is what can be called family reverence. To avoid desecrating your body or bringing disgrace to your person is what can be called keeping your person whole."[22]

Confucius' protégé, Master Zeng, is a name often associated with family reverence (*xiao* 孝) in the canonical literature, and it is recorded in the *Analects* that on his deathbed he said the following:

> Master Zeng was ill, and summoned his students to him, saying, "Look at my feet! Look at my hands! The *Book of Songs* says:

> Fearful! Trembling!
> As if peering over a deep abyss,
> As if walking across thin ice.[23]
>
> It is only from this moment hence that I can be sure I have avoided desecration of my body, my young friends."[24]

This relationship between the responsibility one has for keeping one's body intact and the appropriate attention to family reverence (*xiao*) works in the other direction as well. Traditionally, in the application of penal law (*xing* 刑), amputory and branding punishments were often meted out for serious crimes as a deliberate strategy for not only alerting the community to the presence of a ne'er-do-well in its midst, but also as a way of assuring that such felons wear their shame before their ancestors in the world beyond.

But "body" is only a metonym for much more than the carnal person. Nathan Sivin has explored the correlations between body, cosmos, and state in the pre-Qin and early Han dynasties, claiming that "the ideas of Nature, state, and the body were so interdependent that they are best considered a single complex."[25] Perhaps the writings ascribed to Dong Zhongshu 董仲舒 are the locus classicus for describing the many correspondences between the human person and the cosmos—between the microcosm and the macrocosm.[26] Therein Dong describes not only associations between the changing seasons of the year and the rise and fall of the human passions, but he also explores the many ostensive correlations between the anatomy and physiology of the human body and the structure of the material cosmos.[27] Further, early in the tradition an elaborate vocabulary evolved that associates specific family relations with different parts of the body: the "living person" (*shengshen* 生身) is a metaphor for one's parents, "bones and flesh" (*gurou* 骨肉) for one's children, "hands and feet" (*shouzu* 手足) for one's brothers, "stomach and heart-mind" (*fuxin* 腹心) for one's friends, and "of the same womb" (*tongbao* 同胞) for one's countrymen.

In the *Book of Rites* and several other canonical texts, a further correlation is pursued in associating the proper structure of the cosmos (*li* 理) as a whole with propriety in human roles and relations (*li* 禮), suggesting that human morality has its counterpart in the harmonious workings of the cosmos.[28] What is significant in this reflection on our embodied persons is that physically, socially, and religiously our bodies are a specific matrix of nested relations and functions, and are invariably a collaboration between our persons and our many environments. No "body"—not the vital, the social, or the carnal—does anything by itself.

Achieving Personal Identity through Realizing Propriety (*li* 禮) in Embodied Living (*ti* 體)

In this Confucian tradition, we might say that "body" (*ti* 體) and its cognate character "realized propriety in one's roles and relations" (*li* 禮) express two ways of looking at the same phenomenon: that is, they reference a living body and embodied living respectively. As is stated in the *Book of Rites*:

> Now the great body of ritual proprieties (*li zhi dati* 禮之大體) embodies (*ti* 體) the heavens and the earth, emulates the four seasons, takes *yin* and *yang* as its standard, comports with human feeling, and is thus called "ritual proprieties (*li* 禮)." As for those who would denigrate it, they have no idea where these ritual proprieties come from.[29]

Peter Boodberg in searching for the common ground shared by these cognates *ti* and *li* allows that "Form, that is, organic form . . . appears to be the link between the two words, as evidenced by the ancient Chinese scholiasts who repeatedly used *t'i* [*ti*] to define *li* in their glosses."[30] Deborah Sommer goes back to the usages of *ti* in the *Book of Odes* to expand on this organic meaning of *ti*:

> . . . as a polysemous corpus of indeterminate extent that can be partitioned into subtler units, each of which is often analogous to the whole and shares a fundamental consubstantiality and common identity with that whole. . . . When a *ti* body is fragmented into parts (literally or conceptually), each part retains, in certain aspects, a kind of wholeness or becomes a simulacra of the larger entity of which it is a constituent.[31]

This abstract understanding of *ti* is derived from its association in the early literature with vegetable propagation that is "accomplished not with seeds but by dividing the roots, stems, tubers or other fleshy parts of plants into segments that are then replanted to develop into 'new plants.' "[32] Sommer observes that "for people of an agriculturally based society, the notion that plants can be multiplied through vegetative division would have been a commonplace."[33] There is both continuity and origination in the process of sprouting potatoes being dissected and grown again, of the inedible crowns of pineapples producing their next generation of fruit, and of the unusable roots of defoliated coriander and scallions generating a new harvest of leaves and stems.

In her survey of this early literature, Sommer concludes that "*ti* bodies often act more like plants than like humans."[34] But I would not find the same contrast between humans and plants here. Indeed, I would want to take her analysis a step further as a real insight into the early Chinese way of thinking about human genealogical continuity itself, giving us an opportunity to extrapolate from horticulture to human culture. Another of Tang Junyi's propositions that he uses to describe Chinese natural cosmology is "the inseparability of the one and the many, of uniqueness and multivalence, of continuity and multiplicity, of integrity and integration" (*yiduo bufenguan* 一多不分觀).[35] If we take human procreativity as an illustration of this proposition, such a characterization is another way of affirming *paisheng* 派生, the genealogical derivation of a distinctive and uniquely "one" person. At the same time, within the ongoing, ceaseless process of shaping and being shaped called *huasheng* 化生, the "many" progenitors persist and live on in this process of transformation into someone else. That is, while persons emerge to become specifically who they are as individuals, the parents and grandparents of such individuals continue to live on in them, just as these new individuals too will live on in their progeny. The focus-field language that we have proposed as a way of thinking about the relationship between particulars and the totality seems immediately relevant to the kind of holography Sommer alludes to when she says that "each new plant in some sense is still the parent plant, and there exists a material continuity of identity from one life form to the next. . . . Mother and daughter plants are at once autonomous and yet consubstantial."[36]

We might take a clarification of this *ti* embodiment genealogy yet another step. This process of division, diffusion, and derivation can be further illuminated if we reflect on the complex transmission of always embodied knowledge from generation to succeeding generation. The body is the site of a conveyance of the cultural corpus of knowledge—linguistic facility and proficiency, religious rituals and mythologies, the aesthetics of cooking, song, and dance, the modeling of mores and values, instruction and apprenticeship in cognitive technologies, and so on—as a continuing, intergenerational process through which a living civilization itself is perpetuated.

Turning to *li* 禮, the communal *shen* 身 body is diffused in the dynamic, ritualized roles and relations that constitutes it, and just as the *ti* body does not carry with it a superordinate notion of "self" or "soul"—some ghost in the machine—likewise, realizing propriety in living one's roles and relations that complements this body in constituting one's person is also primordial. That is, the quality of one's conduct is not mediated by or reduplicated in some notion of a discrete "agent" or "character" that would isolate and locate persons outside of their social and natural relations. Instead, the identity of persons lies in the achieved amalgamation, the integration, and the sustained coherence of their continuing habits of conduct within the embodied roles that constitute them.

Any real harmony must be mediated through a robust sense of propriety in the roles and relations that situate us within family and community:

> Achieving harmony (*he* 和) is the most valuable function of realizing ritual propriety in our roles and relations (*li* 禮). In the ways of the Former Kings, this achievement of harmony through realizing propriety made them elegant, and was a guiding standard in all things large and small. But when things are not going well, to achieve harmony just for its own sake without regulating the situation through realizing propriety will not work.[37]

The Focus-Field, Holographic Conception of Persons

The focus-field notion of persons assumed in this cosmology stands in stark contrast to a metaphysical realist conception of an inner, private domain and a shared outer world. It begins from this doctrine of internal, constitutive relations and requires a fundamentally different understanding of persons in which their particular identities and the unsummed totality—their foregrounded focus and its field—are two holographic and thus mutually entailing ways of perceiving the same phenomenon. Just as each played note in a symphony has implicated within it the entire performance, so each focal event has implicated within it its entire, unbounded field. Indeed, to grasp this holographic understanding of "bodyheartminding" (*xin*) the following, oft-cited passage from the *Mencius* that calls into question the distinction between an inner self and an outer world might require a more literal reading than it usually receives:

> 7A4: 孟子曰: 萬物皆備於我矣。
>
> Mengzi said, "The myriad happenings of the world are all implicated here in me."

Corollary to the reconceiving of this inner-outer dynamic as a vital, nonanalytic continuity of "bodyheartminding" is an alternative reading of the full range of such dualistic distinctions—subjective and objective, self and other, agent and action, the cognitive and the affective, nature and nurture, and so on.

In order to make sense of this Mencian claim—"the myriad happenings of the world are all implicated here in me"—we will need an alternative to our common-sense understanding of the inner and outer as two separate domains. We must clarify the background cosmological assumptions about the processive nature and the radical contextuality of the human experience, and about the perceived relationship between particular persons and their experienced world. In this effort, we might want to attempt to recover the way in which the Mencian notion of *xin* 心 is understood within this early cosmology.

Most obviously, as noted above, it is a commonplace that *xin* does the work of both cognizing and feeling in a life experience that includes both felt thoughts and cognitively informed feelings. Similarly, there is no strict dichotomy between intellection and sensation, between body and mind, between structure and function, between thinking and doing, between center and context, between nature and culture. These aspectual distinctions are nonanalytic and mutually entailing; they do not serve to separate and isolate different components within bodyheartminding nor fragment the activities that are defining of it.

Taking our cue from Chinese medicine as a practical application of this cosmology, we have to avoid the formalism that comes with a doctrine of external relations by acknowledging the inseparability of physiology and anatomy, of function and structure. Indeed, it is because traditional Chinese medicine has a dynamic, symbiotic understanding of the coterminous relationship between structure and function often captured in the expression "forming and functioning" (*tiyong* 體用)—or more simply, "trans-*form*-ing"—that it can provide us with a significantly different way of understanding the myriad "things" that Mencius finds to be "all implicated here in me." As medical anthropologist Judith Farquhar observes in her attempt to make sense of what we might call this Chinese *qi* 氣 cosmology: "*Qi* is both structural and functional, a unification of material and temporal forms that loses all coherence when reduced to one or the other 'aspect.' "[38]

Systemic physiological functions have parity if not privilege over the more persistent, localized anatomical structures in traditional Chinese medical sensibilities, requiring that explanations be holistic and inclusive rather than being overly specific and thus exclusive. These functions also have an existential as well as a more objective character. The term *zhenmai* 診脈, for example, is certainly localized as "taking this pulse," but more importantly it is using one's tactile sensitivity to feel and interpret the visceral dynamics of the living body holistically, and as such has synoptic reference not only to the organism itself as experienced from within, but also to the organic, lived relationship this organism has with its external landscape. In "taking this pulse," the medical practitioner is ultimately feeling the pulse of the living cosmos.

If we use the language of focus and field to give an account of "bodyheartminding," it is first and foremost the dynamic focus of a specific systemic center of thinking and feeling that extends out radially as a physiological, psychological, and sociological experience to the furthest reaches of the unbounded cosmos as its contextualizing field. Indeed, *xin* is only derivatively and abstractly taken to be the physical organ that then becomes metonymic for a full complex of interactions and events, where this one focal aspect is isolated as a symbol for the holistic and eventful functions—both physical and psychic—that constitute a continuing human life.

We might cite a second related passage in the *Mencius* that describes and advocates for the symbiotic and mutually entailing phases of making the most of our "bodyheartminding," an effort that in turn enables us to grow our initial conditions in family and community fully and to make our own distinctive contribution to the realization of our cosmic context:

> 7A1: 盡其心者知其性也。知其性則知天矣。存其心養其性所以事天也。

> Those who make the most of their "bodyheartminding" (*xin*) realize their natural tendencies (*xing*). And in realizing their natural tendencies they are realizing their natural and cultural context (*tian*). Keeping up their bodyheartminding and nourishing their natural tendencies is the way to do service to nature and culture (*tian*).[39]

The familiar dualistic separation of inner and outer domains appeals to a doctrine of external relations and brings with it a familiar exercise called "introspection," where introspection is usually understood as turning from our normal outward orientation to a reflective examination of our own internal mental states and feelings. Inspired by this Mencian understanding of "bodyheartminding," however, we might want to challenge this definition of what takes place when we look "inward" by inventing an alternative term—"*intra*-spection." Such a neologism would signal the fact that the process of "*looking into* our own bodyheartminding" is at the same time a *looking outward* into the quality of the coalescence this "bodyheartminding" has achieved with its contextualizing world. Indeed, such "intraspection" as a looking "into" the productive connectivity of our bodyheartminding with the "outer" world is both inner and outer at the same time. The point is that bodyheartminding is holographic, and indeed, since "everything is here in me," in "making the most of our bodyheartminding" we are literally bringing the entire cosmos into more meaningful focus and resolution from our own unique perspectives. And in so doing, we thus come to function most productively and influentially in our relations with what is happening in the world around us.

We might recall the first *Mencius* passage cited above, but now consider the fuller passage rather than just the first phrase. It again expresses this "inner-outer" focus-field dynamic:

7A4: 孟子曰: 萬物皆備於我矣。反身而誠，樂莫大焉。強恕而行，求仁莫近焉。

Mengzi said, "Is there any enjoyment greater than, with the myriad happenings of the world all implicated here in me, to turn personally inward and to thus find resolution with these happenings. Is there any way of seeking to become consummate in my person more immediate than making every effort to act empathetically by extending myself into the places of others?"

Again in this passage we see that becoming consummate as a human being is a holographic process, where the inner resolution of our connectivity with all of the happenings in the world, and the outer reach and influence we are to have on other things are in fact coterminous and mutually entailing. There is a symbiosis between consolidating our relations within the focus and thereby bringing these relations into meaningful and clear resolution (*cheng* 誠) on the one hand, and extending the field of relevance of this focal identity outward by deferring to and producing meaning in our expanding circle of personal relations (*shu* 恕). Sincerity and resolve as achieved in our relations "within" are manifested as consummate conduct in our relations "without." In this way, not only are the myriad happenings of the world implicated here in me, but more importantly, they are made increasingly meaningful by virtue of my capacity to give full resolution to my connectivity with them in my own person.

Resonances between the Confucian Focus-Field Person and Classical Pragmatism

We might appeal to the pragmatic holographic conception of relational person as both an associative and contrastive analogy that can serve us in bringing this Confucian version of relationally constituted person into clearer resolution. John Dewey in his phenomenology of human conduct combines the process psychology of William James and the social psychology of George Herbert Mead to locate persons within their natural and social relations. As Mead insists, "self" is coterminous with the world:

> The self cannot arise in experience except as there are others there. The child experiences sounds, etc., before it has experience of its own body; there is nothing in the child that arises as his own experience and then is referred to the outside things. . . . Only a superficial philosophy demands the old view that we start with ourselves. . . . There is no self before there is a world, and no world before the self. The process of the formation of the self is social.[40]

These pragmatists are revolutionary in dispensing with the "old psychology" that begins from assumptions about a superordinate and discrete *psyche*. As Dewey observes:

> The doctrine of a single, simple and indissoluble soul was the cause and the effect of failure to recognize that concrete habits are the means of knowledge and thought. Many who think themselves scientifically emancipated and who freely advertise the soul for a superstition, perpetuate a false notion of what knows, that is, of a separate knower.[41]

Dewey instead, in a different language but still analogous in many ways to the Confucian notion of relationally constituted persons, arrives at an understanding of person as a dynamic combination of habit and impulse:

Now it is dogmatically stated that no such conceptions of the seat, agent or vehicle will go psychologically at the present time. Concrete habits do all the perceiving, recognizing, imagining, recalling, judging, conceiving and reasoning that is done. "Consciousness," whether as a stream or as special sensations and images, expresses the functions of habits, phenomena of their formation, operation, their interruption and reorganization. . . . A certain delicate combination of habit and impulse is requisite for observation, memory and judgment.[42]

Another way of getting at this more holistic understanding of how our specific acts of conduct occur within an unbounded "field" of action might be to invoke the language of these classical pragmatists and borrow some powerful images provided by Dewey and James themselves. The first point Dewey would make is that we need to abandon our common-sense assumption that we live our lives inside our skins and recognize the extent to which life is "out there" in a way that is organic, interactive, and fully collaborative with the changing world:

The thing essential to bear in mind is that living as an empirical affair is not something which goes on below the skin-surface of an organism: it is always an inclusive affair involving connection, interaction of what is within the organic body and what lies outside in space and time, and with higher organisms, far outside.[43]

On this basis, Dewey offers us a societal, dynamic, and interactive conception of how mind itself comes into being, where it is "located" in "the qualities of organic action," and how it functions as "a characteristic way of inter-activity." This Deweyan conception of "mind" as a dynamic, extended habitude resonates interestingly with the Mencian notion of a diffused yet centered process of "bodyheartminding" as we have described it above. Dewey continues:

Domination by spatial considerations leads some thinkers to ask *where* mind is. . . . [A]ccepting for the moment the standpoint of the questioner (which ignores the locus of discourse, institutions, and social arts), limiting the question to the organic individual, we may say that the "seat" or locus of mind—its static phase— is the qualities of organic action, as far as these qualities have been conditioned by language and its consequences. It is usual

> for those who are posed by the question of "where" and who are reluctant to answer that mind is "where" there is a spaceless separate realm of existence, to fall back in general on the nervous system, and specifically upon the brain or its cortex as the "seat" of the mind. But the organism is not just a structure; it is a characteristic way of inter-activity which is not simultaneous, all at once, but serial. It is a way impossible without structure for its mechanism, but it differs from structure as walking differs from legs or breathing from lungs.[44]

Dewey's point is that "mind" is both focused as a locus of persistent habits and diffused as a field of psychophysical activities being carried out in the unbounded world of experience. This participatory, eventful understanding of mind can for Dewey be further clarified in the idiomatic, nondoctrinal, and organismic way that we use the word "soul:"

> To say emphatically of a particular person that he has soul or a great soul . . . expresses the conviction that the man or woman in question has in marked degree qualities of sensitive, rich and coordinated participation in all situations of life. . . . To see the organism *in* nature . . . will be seen to be *in*, not as marbles are in a box but as events are in history, in a moving, growing never finished process.[45]

And Dewey provides an image that illustrates how the holographic focus of our habitual behaviors in having both "everything" and "all the time" as their penumbra is thus a construal of the synchronic and diachronic totality from one particular perspective:

> We find also in all these higher organisms that what is done is conditioned by consequences of prior activities; we find the fact of learning or habit-formation. . . . Thus an environment both extensive and enduring is immediately implicated in present behavior. Operatively speaking, the remote and the past are "in" behavior making it what it is. The action called "organic" is not just that of internal structures; it is an integration of organic-environmental connections. It may be a mystery that there should be thinking but it is no mystery that if there is

thinking it should contain in a "present" phase, affairs remote in space and in time, even to geologic ages, future eclipses and far away stellar systems. It is only a question of how far what is "in" its actual experience is extricated and becomes focal.[46]

In the *Pluralistic Universe*, James uses a phenomenology of consciousness to reflect on and to give vivid expression to what he calls "the pulse of inner life," a pulsation that, in being both holistic and specific at the same time, requires that we abandon any notion of "inner" and "outer" as exclusive domains. As we did with the Mencian notion of *xin*, we must reconceive the relationship between inner and outer in focus-field, holographic terms where they are simply two ways of foregrounding and emphasizing different aspects of the same phenomenon:

> In the pulse of inner life immediately present now in each of us is a little past, a little future, a little awareness of our own body, of each other's persons, of these sublimities we are trying to talk about, of the earth's geography and the direction of history, of truth and error, of good and bad, and of who knows how much more? Feeling, however dimly and subconsciously, all these things, your pulse of inner life is continuous with them, belongs to them and they to it. . . . The real units of our immediately felt life are unlike the units that intellectualist logic holds to and makes its calculations with. They are not separate from their own others, and you have to take them at widely separated dates to find any two of them that seem unblent . . . my present field of consciousness is a centre surrounded by a fringe that shades insensibly into a subconscious more. . . . Which part of it properly is in my consciousness, which out? If I name what is out, it already has come in. The centre works in one way while the margins work in another, and presently overpower the centre and are central themselves. What we conceptually identify ourselves with and say we are thinking of at any time is the centre; but our full self is the whole field, with all those indefinitely radiating subconscious possibilities of increase.[47]

We might want to clarify the notion of "potential" to underscore the inseparability of person and context in this Confucian conception of relationally constituted, focus-field persons. The "potential" for becoming human is not simply the first inklings, something inborn "within" the person exclusive of family relations. In the first place, there is no such person. Since persons are constituted by their relations, the "potential" of a person in fact emerges *pari passu* from out of the specific, contingent transactions that, in the fullness of time, eventuate in this particular person in this particular family. Thus, the best sense we can make of "potential" here is that rather than being ready-made, it evolves with the ever-changing circumstances; rather than being generic or universal, it is always unique to the career of the relational person; and rather than existing as an inherent and defining endowment, it can only be known post hoc after the unfolding of the particular narrative.[48] The argument, then, is that the preponderance of the content of "human nature" (*renxing* 人性) is acquired rather than given as it is expressed in the habitude of "consummatory conduct" (*ren* 仁), "acting optimally appropriate in meaningful relations" (*yi* 義), "realizing propriety in these roles and relations" (*li* 禮), and "acting with intelligence and wisdom" (*zhi* 智). "Natural tendencies" (*xing* 性) are no more an essential and inborn given than is "consummatory conduct" (*ren* 仁). Both are a source and a product: that is, the articulation of tentative native conditions in the robust consequences of habituation. "Acting with wisdom" is not applying wisdom to a situation, but a condition of acting that arises with the efficacy of one's actions.

Turning to causality, then: given the constitutive nature of relations, causality is not some agency outside and prior to the perceived configuration of things happening, but rather a function of the creative and thus causal nature of the relations themselves. There is a fallacy in taking human nature as causal in the sense that it reduplicates itself in action—the idea that our conduct is *ren* because we are potentially *ren*. Rather habits of moral conduct and native conditions should be understood as symbiotic and mutually determining. When we ask, which comes first, the chicken or the egg? we have to allow that they come together or not at all. From the perspective of classical Western metaphysics, we might say that Chinese cosmology shaves with Ockham's razor not once, but twice. Chinese cosmology does not appeal to the notion of a transcendent and independent God as the source of the world, but begins from what is happening in the autogenerative world itself (*ziran* 自然). And Chinese cosmology does not appeal to an independent nature or soul as the source of human conduct, but begins from a phenomenology of what unfolds and aggregates as moral habits within human conduct itself.

Notes

This chapter is excerpted from a manuscript I am currently writing tentatively titled "'Human Becomings': Theorizing Persons for Confucian Role Ethics."

1. See *Analects* 12.1: "Through self-discipline and achieving propriety in one's roles and relations one becomes consummate in one's conduct." 克己復 禮為仁。

2. *Analects* 7.1.

3. Raymond Williams, *Keywords: A Vocabulary of Culture and Society*. New York: Oxford University Press, 1976.

4. 文化不改, 然後加誅。

5. Tang Junyi (1991) Vol. 11, 22–24.

6. Tang Junyi (1991) Vol. 13, 28–29.

7. *Zuozhuan* Duke Zhao, 25. He also cites the example of medicine that is most often defined in terms of its effects on the human subject.

8. Tang Junyi (1991) Vol. 4, 98–100. 中國自然宇宙論中, 共相非第一義之理。物之存在的根本之理為生理, 此生理即物之性。物之性表現於與他物感通之德量。性或生理, 乃自由原則, 生化原則, 而非必然原則。。。。 蓋任一事象之生起, 必由以前之物與其他之交感, 以爲其外緣。而一物與他物之如何交感或交感之形式, 則非由任一物之本身所決定。。。。因而一物之性之本身, 即包含一隨所感而變化之性。

9. Tang Junyi (1991) Vol. 4, 100. 所謂天命之為性, 非天以一指定命運規定人物之行動運化, 而正是賦人物以多多少少不受自己過去之習慣所機械支配, 亦不受外界之來感之力之機械支配, 而隨境有一創造的生起而表現自由之性。

10. Tang Junyi (1991) Vol. 4, 100. 且物必愈與他物感通, 而後愈有更大之創造的生起。。。。個體的德量, 由其與他物感通, 新有所創造的生起而顯; 亦由時時能自覺的求多所感通, 求善於感通, 並脫離其過去之習慣之機械支配, 及外界之物之力之機械支配, 而日趨宏大。但此非一般物之所能, 唯人乃能之耳。

11. Tang Junyi (1991) Vol. 4, 22.

12. Tang Junyi (1991) Vol. 13, 28. 然就一具體存在之有生, 而即言其有性, 則重要者不在說此存在之性質性相之爲何, 而是其生命存在之所向之爲何。

13. Tang Junyi (1991) Vol. 13, 21–22. 人之現實性不必能窮盡人之可能性, 而欲知人之可能性, 亦不能如人之求知其他事物之可能性, 而本推論與假設以客觀知之; 而當由人之內在的理想之如何實踐, 與如何實現以知之。即對人性有知, 自亦必有名言概念, 加以表達。然此名言概念, 乃順此所知, 而隨機以相繼的形成。

14. Tang Junyi (1991) Vol. 13, 24. 如西方人之 Property, Characteristics, Propensity 及 Essence 諸名之所指, 皆是一定之性相性質或性向。然吾人若由人之面對天地萬物與其所體驗之內在理想, 而自反省其性之何所是時, 是否可言人有定性, 則大成問題。因人之所面對之天地萬物與理想, 皆為變化無方者。。。。中國思想之論人性, 幾於大體上共許之一義, 即為直就此人性之能變化無方處, 而指為人之特性之所在, 此即人之靈性, 而異於萬物之為一定而不靈者。

15. Tang Junyi (1991) Vol. 13, 21. 依吾人之意, 以觀中國先哲之人性論之原始, 其基本觀點, 首非將人或人性, 視爲一所對之客觀事物, 來論述其普遍性, 特殊性, 或可能性, 而主要是就人之面對天地萬物, 並面對其內部所體驗之人生理想, 而自反省此人性之所是，以及天地萬物之性之何所是。緣是而依中國思想之諸大流，以觀人之性，則人雖為萬物中之一類，而不只為萬物之一類。

16. *Zhongyong*, 13. See Ames and Hall (2001), 93–94.

17. *Analects* 7.30.

18. James (2000), 42.

19. Note the paronomastic definitions for *ren* 仁 and *yi* 義 as *ren* 人 and *yi* 宜 respectively: that is, definition by semantic and phonetic association.

20. *Zhongyong*, 20. See Ames and Hall (2001), 101. In deference to the Confucian commitment to family as the putative ground of moral sensibilities, we have challenged the conventional translation of the title of this text as "Doctrine of the Mean" with "Focusing the Familiar," and in so doing have sought to underscore the cognate relationship between "family" and "familiar."

21. See Rosemont and Ames (2009).

22. Lau (1992); *Liji* 25.36/128/6.

23. *Songs*, 195.

24. *Analects* 8.3.

25. See Sivin (1995), 5.

26. For example, *Chunqiufanlu* 春秋繁露, 23 and 46.

27. Ibid., 56.

28. See Zhang Zailin (2008), 20–22.

29. Lau (1992); *Liji* 50.1/174/18. 凡禮之大體，體天地，法四時，則陰陽，順人情，故謂之禮。訾之者是不知禮之所由生也。

30. Boodberg (1953), 326. This might explain the abbreviated graph for *ti* 體 that is constituted by "person" (*ren* 人) and "root or trunk" (*ben* 本) as *ti* 体. See Ames (1993), 169.

31. Sommer (2008), 294.

32. Ibid., 295.

33. Ibid., 296.

34. Ibid.

35. Tang Junyi (1991) Vol. 11, 16–17.

36. Sommer (2008), 296.

37. *Analects* 1.12.

38. Judith Farquhar, *Knowing Practice: The Clinical Encounter of Chinese Medicine*. Boulder: Westview (1994), 34.

39. It is because it is important to appreciate the performative implications of *zhi* 知—conventionally translated as "knowing"—that we have rendered it here as "realizing" something in the sense of "making it real" rather than limiting it as simply "knowing" something cognitively.

40. Mead (1982), 156.

41. Dewey (1922), 176.

42. Dewey (1922), 176–177.

43. John Dewey, *The Essential Dewey* Vol. 1. Edited by Larry A. Hickman and Thomas M. Alexander. Bloomington: Indiana University Press (1998), 147.

44. Dewey (1998), 151.
45. Dewey (1998), 152.
46. Dewey (1998), 146–147.
47. William James, *A Pluralistic Universe*. New York: Longmans, Green and Co., (1912), 286–288.
48. For Dewey too (1998): "Potentialities cannot be known till after the interactions have occurred. There are at a given time unactualized potentialities in an individual because and in as far as there are in existence other things with which it has not as yet interacted." Lincoln is not Lincoln independent of the circumstances of history, nor are the circumstances of history the making of Lincoln. Indeed, Lincoln is a collaboration between person and circumstances expressed as thick habits of conduct. "The idea that potentialities are inherent and fixed by relation to a predetermined end was a product of a highly restricted state of technology" (223–224).

References

Ames, Roger T. 1993. "The Meaning of Body in Classical Chinese Philosophy." Self as Body in Asian Theory and Practice. Edited by R.T. Ames, W. Dissanayake, and T. Kasulis. Albany, NY: SUNY Press.

Ames, Roger T., and David L. Hall. 2001. *Focusing the Familiar: A Translation and Philosophical Interpretation of the* Zhongyong. Honolulu: University of Hawai'i Press.

Ames, Roger T., and Henry Rosemont, Jr. 1998. *The Analects of Confucius: A Philosophical Translation*. New York: Ballantine.

Boodberg, Peter A. 1953. "The Semasiology of Some Primary Confucian Concepts." *Philosophy East and West* 2(4).

Dewey, John. 1998. *The Essential Dewey*. Volume 1. Edited by Larry Hickman and Thomas Alexander. Bloomington: Indiana University Press.

———. 1922. *Human Nature and Conduct*. New York: Henry Holt and Company.

Farquhar, Judith. 1994. *Knowing Practice: The Clinical Encounter of Chinese Medicine*. Boulder: Westview.

Fingarette, Herbert. 1983. "The Music of Humanity in the Conversations of Confucius." *Journal of Chinese Philosophy* 10.

James, William. 2000. *Pragmatism and Other Writings*. New York: Penguin.

———. 1912. *A Pluralistic Universe*. New York: Longmans, Green and Co.

Kwan, Tze-wan. (n.d.). "Multi-function Character Database" at humanum.arts.cuhk.edu.hk/Lexis/lexi-mf

Mead, George Herbert. 1982. *The Individual and the Social Self: Unpublished Work of George Herbert Mead*. Edited by David L. Miller. Chicago: University of Chicago Press.

Rosemont, Henry Jr., and Roger T. Ames. 2009. *The Chinese Classic of Family Reverence: A Philosophical Translation of the Xiaojing* 孝經. Honolulu: University of Hawai'i Press.

Sivin, Nathan. 1995. "State, Cosmos, and Body in the Last Three Centuries B.C." *Harvard Journal of Asiatic Studies* 55(1).
Sommer, Deborah. 2008. "Boundaries of the *Ti* Body." *Asia Major* Third Series, Vol. XXI, Part I.
Tang Junyi 唐君毅. 1991. *Complete Works* 唐君毅全集. Taipei: Xuesheng shuju.
Zhang Zailin 張再林. 2008. 作爲身體哲學的中國古代哲學 (Traditional Chinese Philosophy as the Philosophy of Body). Beijing: China Social Science Press.

Chapter 3

Deferential Yielding

The Construction of Shared Community in Confucian Ethics

GAN CHUNSONG

Translated by Daniel Sarafinas

"Deferential yielding"[1] has garnered only minimal scholarly attention as a concept within Confucian ethical thought, yet we can find the values of being "cordial, proper, deferential, frugal, and yielding"[2] in the *xue er* (学而) chapter of the *lunyu* (论语, the Analects of Confucius) when Zi Gong 子贡 investigates if it is these values that makes Confucius (*kong zi*, 孔子) stand out from common people. As the successor to Confucius' thought, Mencius (*mengzi*, 孟子) describes the principle of propriety (*li* 礼) as "the feeling of modesty and deferential yielding" in his discussion concerning the root of morality. From these examples we can see that, regardless of whether we consider it a psychological foundation or mode of behavior, deference serves as a fundamental aspect of Confucian values. While work on the Confucian concept of deferential yielding is limited, in this chapter I will attempt to analyze the concept through its connected virtues and its use within social systems in order to enrich our understanding of Confucian ethics.

Deferential Yielding as a Principle of Confucian Morality and its Relationship with Other Moral Concepts

When Confucian ethics is considered, the concepts of "benevolence" (*ren* 仁), "righteousness," (*yi* 义), or "propriety" are generally among the first brought to mind. If we survey the evolution of pre-Qin moral concepts, we find that the notion of "deferential yielding" has been continually marginalized within the Confucian moral system, and by the end of the Warring States period the notion of "propriety" had become central to the increasingly systematized Confucian moral principles.

One possible explanation for this is that when the idea of private property had not yet fully developed, the characteristic of "deferential yielding" was very important. During the prehistorical period of legend, the sovereignty of the earliest Chinese kings was not decided by inheritance, but was rather based on "yielding the throne" (*shan rang* 禅让) to someone more worthy or capable. For example, Emperor Yao 尧 did not pass on his royal title to his own son, but "yielded" it to Shun 舜, who had more power of moral persuasion. Similarly, Shun passed the royal title to Yu 禹 for his ability to control the floods and win the hearts of the people. These events were recorded in detail in the earliest classic texts. Deferential yielding became a kind of system as well as a great virtue of a nobleman. *The Book of Documents* (*shangshu* 尚书) praises Yao as being "capable of all respect and *deferential yielding*."

> Examining into antiquity (we find that) the Di Yao was styled Fang-Xun. He was reverential, intelligent, accomplished, and thoughtful—naturally and without effort. He was sincerely courteous, and capable of (all) yielding. The bright (influence of these qualities) was felt through the four quarters (of the land), and reached to (heaven) above and (earth) beneath. He made the able and virtuous distinguished, and thence proceeded to the love of (all in) the nine classes of his kindred, who (thus) became harmonious. He (also) regulated and polished the people (of his domain), who all became brightly intelligent. (Finally), he united and harmonized the myriad states.[3]

This early description of the system in which the king transfers authority to a morally upright individual has been called into question, however. Some works, such as the *hanfeizi* (韩非子), believed that the explanation for the early kings "yielding the throne" (*rangwang* 让王) was because they were exhausted from their service, not because of their great virtue. From another perspective, this sort of suspicion and explanation indicates that these early kings worked extraordinarily hard in their government affairs.

The reason early Confucians admired "yielding the throne" as an ideal system of transferring power was that it embodied the notion of "all under heaven is common to all" (*tianxia wei gong* 天下为公). According to Confucian thought, the authority of that which is "under heaven" (*tianxia* 天下) cannot be usurped by a small number of privileged people. Because that which is under heaven is shared by all under heaven, it is contrary to "ruling the country like one's own family" (*jia tianxia* 家天下). In Zheng Xuan's 郑玄 commentaries on this subject, he writes "it is appropriate to concede power and position to one who is virtuous and talented for the sake of serving the common people, rather than holding power and position for oneself." The thought of Kong Yingda 孔颖达 also revolves around developing this idea. He writes "the position of the monarch belongs to all people under heaven. It is necessary to yield the position and power to someone virtuous for the benefit and interest of the people rather than pass it on to one's own offspring. For example, in ancient times power and position was passed on to Yao and Shun rather than Zhu Jun 朱均." "All under heaven" is posited here as the combination of "common to all" (*gong* 公) and the system of yielding the throne. It importantly points out that, from the fundamental principle that all under heaven cannot be privately possessed, the participatory sharing manifested through the essence of "yielding" is fair and appropriate.

Yao, Shun, and Yu were those sagacious rulers who did not see all under heaven as their own privately owned property, which gave the later generations a standard for the position and behavior of the monarch. Regardless of whether it is "under heaven" or a country, its leader must have an impartial heart for under heaven to be on the side of the ruler.

Other schools of thought in early China also affirmed the importance of the concept of deferential yielding. The Mohists (*mojia* 墨家) promoted the ideas "yielding the throne in favor of the esteemed" (*shanrang shangxian* 禅让尚贤) and "yielding the throne in favor of the virtuous" (*shanrang shangde* 禅让尚德). These ideas produced a real influence in the actual practice of governance, although the practice of "yielding the state" (*rangguo* 让国) did not accomplish the political results in the states of Wei 魏 and Yan 燕

as well as Yao and Shun's "yielding the throne." For example, when King Wei Hui (魏惠王) wanted to transfer authority over the state to Hui Shi (惠施),[4] Gongsun Yan 公孙衍, the general of the state of Wei, incited Shi Ju 史举 to campaign for King Wei Xiang 魏襄王 to abdicate his throne,[5] and King Kuai of Yan 燕王哙 prudently listened to Lu Maoshou's 鹿毛寿 advice and abdicated the kingdom to his son.[6] Regardless of whether it is someone agitating for the abdication of the throne or a king actually carrying it out, the underlying reason for one to do so is that the legitimacy of the virtuous person occupying that position lies in the will of the people, and has its grounds in "virtue and talent" (*xianyi* 贤义), "reputation" (*shengming* 声名), and other moral standards. The unearthed text from the Warring States period, *tangyu zhi dao* 唐虞之道, also gives a systematic explanation of "yielding the throne" as that which is virtuous:

> Those today who [would] emulate/employ virtue [may] not employ it before their age [has come], [and must] not turn arrogant when they [come to] rule the people, or become pleased with themselves if they finally [come to] serve as king to the world. When they occupy a low position, they [must] not think lightly of being a commoner, and when they come to possess the world, they [must] not attach importance [to themselves] because of it. Possession of the world may not augment them, and loss of the world may not diminish them. The ultimate in humanity is to bring profit to the world rather than to profit one's self. "Yielding" refers to the upholding of virtue and the investing in worthies. When virtue is upheld, the world has its ruler and the age is enlightened. When worthies are invested, the people are moved [through] instruction and transformed by the way. Ever since there have been living people, there has never been a case where they could be transformed without [the model of] yielding.[7]

Yielding allows the sage with an impartial heart to govern all under heaven and establish order. This kind of spirit can be described using relatively modern terminology as "participatory sharing." This was gradually condensed into a core value of Confucianism by Confucius and Mencius. Mencius, for example, in his discussion with King Xuan of Qi 齐宣王, says that nothing is wrong with pursuing joy, but it is only by "making joy a thing common between oneself and the people" (*yumin tongle* 与民同乐)⁸ that one is able to truly receive the support of the people.

The *Mencius* internalizes the spirit of "deferential yielding" such that it becomes a kind of innate ability or innate knowledge of right and wrong that one need not go through a process of training to achieve. Moreover, Mencius promotes the idea of innate knowledge, believing it to be a kind of moral consciousness that distinguishes humans from other animals. He posits the "four principles," or the four moral tendencies of humans, as the foundation for this innate knowledge. He says "the feeling of commiseration is the principle of benevolence. The feeling of shame and dislike is the principle of righteousness. The feeling of modesty and deferential yielding is the principle of propriety. The feeling of approving and disapproving is the principle of knowledge. Men have these four principles just as they have their four limbs."⁹ In this chapter, deferential yielding is portrayed as the moral root that produces etiquette and ritual. It appears that humans are born with these four kinds of moral consciousness as a matter of nature, just as one is born with a body.

If one wants to utilize this kind of morality of deferential yielding to administer society, one must also insist on participatory sharing. In the Liang Hui Wang I chapter of the Mencius, Mencius and King Hui of Liang (梁惠王) discuss a story of how a sagely ruler should share his own gardens and include the participation of the common people such that it results in their support of him with the hope that the ruler would imitate this method, thus obtaining the true support of the people. The chapter says:

> Mencius, another day, saw King Hui of Liang. The king went and stood with him by a pond, and, looking around at the large geese and deer, said, "Do wise and good princes also find pleasure in these things?" Mencius replied, "Being wise and good, they have pleasure in these things. If they are not wise and good, though they have these things, they do not find pleasure. It is said in the Book of Poetry, 'he measured out and commenced his marvelous tower; he measured it out and planned it. The people addressed themselves to it, and in less than a day completed it. When he measured and began it, he said to them—Be not so earnest: But the multitudes came as if they had been his children. The king was in his marvelous park; the deer reposed about, the deer so sleek and fat: And the white birds came glistening.

> The king was by his marvelous pond; how full was it of fishes leaping about!' King Wen used the strength of the people to make his tower and his pond, and yet the people rejoiced to do the work, calling the tower 'the marvelous tower,' calling the pond 'the marvelous pond,' and rejoicing that he had his large deer, fishes, and turtles. The ancients caused the people to have pleasure as well as themselves, and therefore they could enjoy it. In the Declaration of Tang it is said, 'O sun, when wilt thou expire? We will die together with thee.' The people wished for Jie's death, though they should die with him. Although he had towers, ponds, birds, and animals, how could he have pleasure alone?"[10]

The spirit of participatory sharing embodied by deferential yielding is particularly aimed at the powerful and wealthy. This is to say that a very important dimension of deferential yielding is the requirements it demands of those who occupy society's upper classes. In a hierarchical social order, deferential yielding is manifested as those members in positions of power or from respected families making concessions or yielding to communities that occupy other social positions. A virtuous leader should not bully or push around those more vulnerable and weaker members of society, but should embody that state in which all things of heaven and earth are seen as one body, thus allowing one to cherish all people under heaven. In the *lunyu*, Confucius requires rulers to use the rites and deferential yielding as a method to govern the state, such as in the *liren* 里仁 chapter in which Confucius says, "If rulers are able to effect order in the state through the combination of observing ritual propriety and deferring to others (*rang* 让), what more is needed? But if they are unable to accomplish this, what have they to do with observing ritual propriety?"[11] This passage means that the monarch not using the rites and deferential yielding is equivalent to deviating from the principle of "rule by ritual propriety" (*lizhi* 礼治).

Deferential yielding is the essence and expression of propriety. The interpretation of propriety's meaning and rules in *The Book of Rites* (*liji* 礼记) has many explanations of the relationship between propriety and deferential yielding. In the *Quli* 曲礼 chapter, for example, it says:

> The course (of duty), virtue, benevolence, and righteousness cannot be fully carried out without the rules of propriety; nor are training and lessons for the rectification of manners complete;

> nor can the clearing up of quarrels and discriminating in disputes be accomplished; nor can (the duties between) ruler and minister, high and low, father and son, elder brother and younger, be determined; nor can students for office and (other) learners, in serving their masters, have an attachment for them; nor can majesty and dignity be shown in assigning the different places at court, in the government of the armies, and in discharging the duties of office so as to secure the operation of the laws; nor can there be the (proper) sincerity and gravity in presenting the offerings to spiritual Beings on occasions of supplication, thanksgiving, and the various sacrifices. Therefore, the superior man is respectful and reverent, assiduous in his duties and not going beyond them, retiring and deferential yielding—thus illustrating (the principle of) propriety.[12]

While there is an aspect of propriety that is expressed as strict and solemn, beneath these ceremonial elements must emerge a spirit of deferential yielding. The Confucians maintain a critical attitude toward a confrontational approach because competition and fighting is the most important reason for the destruction of the order of propriety, and thus they use the principle of yielding to avoid this sort of conflict.

> Music comes from within, and ceremonies from without. Music, coming from within, produces the stillness (of the mind); ceremonies, coming from without, produce the elegancies (of manner). The highest style of music is sure to be distinguished by its ease; the highest style of elegance, by its undemonstrativeness. Let music attain its full results, and there would be no dissatisfactions (in the mind); let ceremony do so, and there would be no quarrels. When bowings and deferential yielding marked the government of the kingdom, there would be what might be described as music and ceremony indeed.[13]

Deferential yielding and harmony represent the core spirit of a civilization characterized by the rites and music (*yue* 乐) and are the fundamental principles for the Confucian's construction of an orderly society. Through the rites and deferential yielding one can achieve the absence of contention and disputes, and with the assistance of music one can ultimately achieve order through rites and music. In addition to political order, people also require a yielding attitude in their daily life. Yielding can be seen as a virtue as well as one kind of method to establish good social customs.

The Confucian classic *The Great Learning* (*daxue* 大学) says "from the example of one family being benevolent, the whole state becomes benevolent; from the example of one family being yielding, the whole state becomes yielding; from the ambition and perverseness of one man, the whole state may be led to rebellious disorder; such is the nature of influence."[14] The meaning of this passage is that if every family reveres benevolence and love (*renai* 仁爱), the whole state will love one another. If the people are able to share and participate in this, then the rites and deferential yielding will be promoted throughout the state. Conversely, if one person is utterly greedy, then it may lead to all people becoming selfish. The difference between what is expressed in *The Great Learning* and the previously discussed virtuous ruler's exemplary behavior being that which inculcates a general culture of the rites and deferential yielding into society is that *The Great Learning* indicates that it is the cultivation of the individual and the family that serves as the root on which social order of the state is founded.

It is not only the Confucians that regarded deferential yielding as an important kind of quality, as it appears that it was a common value among the pre-Qin Hundred Schools of Thought (*zhuzi baijia* 诸子百家). Even the Confucian's principle intellectual competitors, the Mohists (*mojia* 墨家) and Daoists (*daojia* 道家), regarded the quality of deferential yielding as very important.

In the *luwen* (鲁问) chapter of the *mozi* (墨子), Mozi warns people that the spirits desire that when in a high rank one should give up one's position in favor of those more virtuous, and that when wealthy one should share one's wealth with the poor; this is the way one can make one's household safe and sound. The chapter says:

> Mozi had recommended Cao Gongzi to Song. He returned in three years and saw Mozi, saying: "When I first came to your school I had to wear short jackets and eat vegetable soup. Even this I could not have in the evening if I had had it in the morning. And I had nothing to offer and sacrifice to the ghosts and spirits. Now, on your account my family has become better off. And I could respectfully offer sacrifice and worship ghosts and spirits at home. Yet several members of my household died off, the six animals do not breed, and I have myself been troubled with ailments. I doubt if your way is after all to be adopted."

Mozi said: This is not fair. For what the ghosts and spirits desire of man is that when in high rank and receiving much emolument, he give up his position in favor of the virtuous; that when possessing much wealth, he share it with the poor. How can the ghosts and spirits merely desire to snatch food and drink? Now, when in high rank and receiving much emolument you did not give up your position in favor of the virtuous. This is your first step to bad fortune. Possessing much wealth, you did not share it with the poor. This is your second step towards misfortune. Now you serve the ghosts and spirits by merely offering them sacrifice; and you wonder whence come all the ailments. This is like shutting one out of a hundred gates and wondering whence the thieves entered. How can you invoke ghosts and spirits for blessing like this?[15]

Mozi is speaking from the position of the lowest social strata of the people and believes that those who hold a position in society but do not yield that position in favor of someone more suitable, or those who hold wealth but do not share it with the poor are the causes of social crisis. At about the same time as Mozi wrote this, the Daoist school of thought began raising issues with the ideas of the Confucian *junzi* (君子, nobleman, gentleman). As such, the Daoists and Confucians can be seen as having a constructive dialogue, and although the method each school employs may be different, the goals of each are consistent with one another insofar as they agree that a sage is one who takes the heart-mind of the common people as the starting point when handling one's own affairs. The classic Daoist text the *Laozi* (老子) says:

The sage has no invariable heart-mind of his own; he makes the heart-mind of the people his heart-mind.
To those who are good (to me), I am good; and to those who are not good (to me), I am also good;—and thus (all) get to be good. To those who are sincere (with me), I am sincere; and to those who are not sincere (with me), I am also sincere;—and thus (all) get to be sincere.
The sage has in the world an appearance of indecision, and keeps his heart-mind in a state of indifference to all. The people all keep their eyes and ears directed to him, and he deals with them all as his children.[16]

Although this does not explicitly utilize the concept of deferential yielding, the idea of making the heart-mind (*xin* 心) of the people as one's heart-mind is a reminder to the ruler to start off from the perspective of the common people, and this has an intrinsic consistency with the spirit of the rites and deferential yielding.

Deferential Yielding and Contending, Assuming One's Duty

As mentioned previously, as a Confucian moral principle, deferential yielding forms a compatible and supplementary relationship with other more fundamental virtues such as "ritual propriety." But what is the relationship between deferential yielding and the other Confucian moral principles? The Qing Dynasty scholar Cheng Yaotian (程瑶田) also explored this question.

Cheng Yaotian, who later changed his name to Rang Tang (让堂), discusses the relationship between the concept deferential yielding and those of "contending" (zheng 争) and "assuming one's duty" (*ren* 任) in his writings:

> To yield one's power in order to give it away to someone of virtue seems to be contrary to contending for power. The sage believed there were proper ways to compete in archery, although contending is inevitably involved. Bowing, for example, is a sign of declining out of courtesy. Yielding seems to be the opposite of assuming one's duty. The sage says "it is necessary to assume one's duty." Zilu, for example, was reluctant to yield his position, which was actually just him sighing out of emotion rather than literally meaning it. It is important for a man to remain benevolent even when he has to confront his teacher, which is a true representation of "yielding out of deference." Archery, therefore, goes hand in hand with the spirit of "yielding out of deference." The sage believed that this spirit should be the most important aspect in contending for power in a prudent manner.[17]

This is a very important point. As opposed to the Daoist philosophy of retiring from society, the Confucians put particular emphasis on taking on one's social responsibility. Thus, in the *lunyu* we see the attitude of "in striving to assume duty in your conduct, do not yield even to your teacher,"[18] which is to say, if one happens upon a mission to fulfill some social need, deferring or declining is simply not adequate. Hence it must be pointed out that the Confucian's emphasis on "setting to task" and "not yielding," especially when it refers to a duty or a mission, is particularly in regard to wealth and position.

Yielding as a mode of behavior is oriented toward social harmony. "Harmony is the key to judging in daily life. When getting along with others, one easily puts aside his own emotions, and those surrounding him can see this. All that they see and hear is harmony."[19] Connected to this is accumulating virtue, which goes together with the outstanding characteristics of the gentleman. A gentleman is a true representation of the virtues and morals of heaven, which is in a harmonious relationship with the laws of the universe. Thus, harmony is cultivated in a natural manner. "Only the accumulation of virtue can guarantee harmony."[20] Cheng Yaotian believes that contention is not always the result of a conflict of interests, but might be some small issue that makes one feel resentful, and this will lead to the destruction of a harmonious situation. When this happens, one must know how to forgive. If one simultaneously possesses these four seeds of virtue, then "the elimination of mean attitudes and behaviors would help the common people return to a state of purity and honesty, which helps create a harmonious society."[21]

Deferential yielding as a virtue is highly esteemed, even to the extent that the character *rang* 让 has been used to create many new words, such as the word for showing courtesy or consideration for someone (*lirang* 礼让), or the word for being respectfully modest (*jingran* 敬让). Yielding includes the sense of modestly declining or complaisance for the sake of others, and its essence is the will for status and wealth to be shared amongst members of society. On the other hand, contention, which is antithetical to deferential yielding, and isolating oneself, which is antithetical to participatory sharing, are both examples of moral deficiencies. Within traditional Chinese ethical thought, "contending" implies an unwillingness to allow others to partake because one intends to dominate them, and not contending implies a willingness to sacrifice one's own interests in order to gain the trust of others. The Han dynasty Confucian classic *Virtuous Discussions of White Tiger Hall* (*baihutong delun* 白虎通德论) contains the sentence "where is the propriety in bowing in deference? It is in the honorable person taking a loss to oneself, not contending." That is to say, it is through taking a loss to oneself that harmony of the community is achieved.

Thus, theories that take their shape from the concept of deferential yielding form the values underlying Chinese national community and familial community. Because deferential yielding promotes harmony between family members and members of society in traditional Chinese society, it is recognized in many different ways, especially in stories told within the family and used in moral education. The ancient story about Kong Rong 孔融 eating only the smallest pears and leaving the bigger for his brothers is a classic story that promotes sharing amongst family members, and is told in elementary school classes even today.

This story appears in a *Biography of Kong Rong* chapter in the *Book of the Later Han* (*houhan shu* 后汉书) commented on by Li Xian 李贤, in which it says "at the age of four, when eating pears with his older brothers, Rong picked out the smallest pears. When the elders asked him why he did so, he responded 'I am the smallest, so I should pick the smallest.' What a wonderful family member!" The meaning behind him always picking the smallest pears because he is the youngest is clear. This story was later included in an ancient Chinese early education primer, the "Three Character Classic" (*sanzi jing* 三字经).

The Manifestation of Deferential Yielding and Participatory Sharing in Economic Activity

As a Confucian principle of "commonality" and "participatory sharing," deferential yielding is constantly emphasized by Confucians and serves as a kind of expectation for a design of the system. Confucius continually admonished rulers for whom fairly distributing wealth is a factor in receiving support from the people; he says: "I have heard that the ruler of a state or the head of a household does not worry that his people are poor, but that wealth is inequitably distributed; does not worry that his people are too few in number, but that they are disharmonious."[22] The meaning here is that having little wealth is not important for those ruling a country or a family; the crucial aspect is sharing that wealth in fair proportion. According to the principles of Confucianism, "equal" (*jun* 均) does not necessarily mean distributing in equal proportions, but rather comes close to the principle of distributive justice, that is, to reasonably distribute social wealth according to one's social position.

This kind of principle of distribution is repeatedly emphasized by Confucian scholars. For example, in his discussion with King Hui of Liang, Mencius, a very important figure in the development of Confucian thought, mentions the point of view of "having pleasure common with the people" (*yumin tongle* 与民同乐). From Mencius's perspective, if the ruler is able to contemplate the interest of the common people, allowing people to live in peace and work happily, while simultaneously enjoying the pleasure of wealth and hunting out in the fields, the common people will not harbor any resentment, even to the point that they would judge the status of his health from the activities in which he engages, wishing him more happiness. Therefore, it is not the case that the ruler should not enjoy pleasure, but rather that he should share his pleasure with the common people.

Another important successor of Confucian thought, Xunzi 荀子, put particular emphasis on the idea of "distinctions" (*fen* 分). He believed that every person will pursue wealth and pleasure, and if this pursuit cannot be controlled or moderated, society will be led into a state of chaos. His discussions on the origin of ritual practices in particular contain the principle of distributive justice. He writes:

> What is the origin of ritual? I reply: man is born with desires. If his desires are not satisfied for him, he cannot but seek some means to satisfy them himself. If there are no limits and distinctions in his seeking, then he will inevitably fall to wrangling with other men. From wrangling comes disorder and from disorder comes exhaustion. The ancient kings hated such disorder, and therefore they established ritual principles in order to curb it, to train men's desires and to provide for their satisfaction. They saw to it that desires did not overextend the means for their satisfaction, and material goods did not fall short of what was desired. Thus both desires and goods were looked after and satisfied. This is the origin of rites.[23]

From Xunzi's perspective the most important function of ritual practice is to determine "limits and distinctions" (*duliang fenjie* 度量分界). Although "distinctions" has the connotation of social position for Xunzi here, the more important meaning lies in determining definite principles of distribution to allow the receiving and sharing of social wealth, and this is the foundation for the stability and sustainability of a society based on the system of rites.

Under this spirit of sharing, the Confucian and Legalist opinions regarding economic policy diverged. The divergence was centered on whether or not the states should amass their wealth to establish a large and powerful government, which would then create a powerful military and carry out the construction of large-scale public works. The Confucians tended toward a kind of laissez-faire economic policy, that is, they advocated that the government not excessively intervene in the economic activity of the people. When asked by his student about what kind of economic policies should be carried out, Confucius responded clearly and simply, "be generous and yet not extravagant" (*hui er bufei* 惠而不费).²⁴ His explanation of this was "give the common people those benefits that will really be beneficial to them,"²⁵ which means that what the common people think is the most beneficial method should be protected and supported. This is the way to let the common people obtain the most benefit and keep the government from managing too many affairs. In *The Great Learning* it is said:

> Virtue is the root; wealth is the result. If he make[s] the root his secondary object, and the result his primary, he will only wrangle with his people, and teach them rapine. Hence, the accumulation of wealth is the way to scatter the people; and the letting it be scattered among them is the way to collect the people.²⁶

This illustrates the belief that the core of governance lies in virtue, and if the government is overly attached to accumulating wealth, the people will abandon the ruler. On the other hand, if the ruler is willing to share wealth with the people, they will rally around him.

Around the year 300 BCE, states such as the Qin and the Qi reformed their taxation systems, which increased their strength, causing rulers to welcome Legalist thinkers who advocated government policies of intervention. The Confucians, however, did not reform their fundamental position, opposing the government's monopolization of wealth and advocating decreased taxes and forced labor of the common people. Confucianism's consistent position was fighting for the benefit of the people. Although during the Warring States period the Qin were successful because of their interventionistic financial policies, they ruled for only seventeen years, which reinforced the Confucian's belief that gaining political power through plundering from the people is unsustainable. This is why they criticized the Legalists as those who support "gathering wealth by heavy taxation," which is the opposite of "participatory sharing." Although the Confucian theory of "participatory sharing" is similar to Aristotle's "proportional equality" in the sense that it is not absolute egalitarianism, it was already regarded as "the order of heaven" (*tianli* 天理) by Han dynasty Confucians, or to use today's language, it was regarded as "natural law." The famous Han dynasty philosopher Dong Zhongshu 董仲舒 (179–104 BCE), said "those who have gained a major part of benefits and interests shall not obtain all of the benefits and interests. Based on the law of the universe, it is necessary to leave some leeway instead of taking it all. Such a law of the universe holds true to managing affairs in the human society. Therefore, the sage follows such laws; those governmental officials who are granted with fabulous salary should bear in mind that they should not scramble for the personal benefits and interests against the common people."[27] The meaning of this passage is that if one has already obtained much, but still wishes to possess even more, it is natural that the ruler will not be able to satisfy these needs. This is why the government should not contend with the people over profits, but rather should allow the people to share amongst themselves the products of the natural world.

China's history has seen several important debates concerning the economic system, such as the debate between Sang Hongyang 桑弘羊 and the *Xianliang Wenxue* (贤良文学, Book of Virtuous Literature),[28] or the debates between Wang Anshi 王安石 and Sima Guang 司马光. Strictly speaking, these debates cannot be simply described as debates between Confucians and Legalists, but what is interesting is that in the 1970s Chinese historians started to describe Chinese history as a battle between Confucians and Legalists, and Sang Hongyang and Wang Anshi were both referred to as Legalists.

For example, when reforming the laws, the Northern Song statesman Wang Anshi regarded increasing the financial capabilities of the country as an important strategy for governing the country. He reinterpreted classic Confucian texts such as the *Rites of Zhou* (*zhouli* 周礼), orienting it around "the ability to keep the national financial balance based on earnings and spending" and "the state sets the rules and regulations for the common people to observe and follow in their daily life." He implemented prompt regulation of commodity prices through control of the price of goods, information, and distribution quantities. This kind of increase in the state's control over finances has been regarded as disturbing free economic activity since the pre-Qin. Wang Anshi, thus, was met with intense opposition from people like Sima Guang. These critics cited Mencius, "distinction between righteousness and benefit," and the *Great Learning*'s "it would be better to have a minister who robs (a wealthy family) of its revenues than one who accumulates and hoards more,"[29] and believed that only discussing finances was the Legalist's "method of commerce administration," not a proper strategy for political administration.

Competition and Deferential Yielding

In 1840, after Western countries forced their way into China, Confucian values slowly began to be called into question. Facing continuous economic and military defeats, people at first believed it to be a problem of insufficient military equipment, later that it was a case of institutional and administrative disparities, and finally that there were deficiencies in terms of culture and values. During this self-analysis, it was thought that Confucianism overemphasized "yielding," leading to a lack of competitive spirit, and it was believed that this is what led to the Chinese people's inability to resist Western economic and military invasions within their process of modernization. Starting with Liang Qichao 梁启超 writing *On the New People* (*xinmin shuo* 新民说), the idea of creating a new kind of character and identity for the people of China was promoted, a new identity with the important characteristic of a competitive spirit, thereby criticizing the attitude of "courteous yielding" (*lirang* 礼让). Some even went so far as to praise the spirit of Yang Zhu 杨朱, who would not pluck a single hair from his body even if it meant benefitting all under heaven, believing this to be respecting one's own rights. From their perspective, benefitting oneself is part of one's natural instincts. However, people also exhibit social characteristics and cannot exist isolated from a group, but must establish a community in which the individual's interest is protected first and foremost. Liang Qichao derived "benefitting the other" and "benefitting the group" from "benefitting oneself," and derived "the significance of loving the other" from "the heart of loving oneself." This kind of ethical value perspective that takes "benefitting oneself" as its core is quite disparate from the traditional values that advocate deferential yielding, and we can see this as a result of the influence of Western Enlightenment thinkers as well as the national crisis that led to a new value perspective.

This kind of discourse regarding the relationship between public and private interests has been continuously repeated in contemporary China's discussion regarding "national character." Fei Xiaotong 费孝通 believed that the principle of ethics for Chinese people is defined by closeness to one's own bloodline, and that the scope of those with whom one shares is limited to those with whom you are related by blood. When engaged in social activity or distributing resources, accordingly, one would be inclined to show more consideration to those with whom one has close relations, and ignore those with whom one's relations are distant, leading to a lack in spirit of communal sharing.

However, not all of these new intellectuals had a thoroughly negative attitude toward traditional Chinese ethics, including Liang Shuming 梁漱溟 (1893–1988), who had the opposite perspective of Fei Xiaotong. He thought that Chinese should uphold "relationship centered ethics" (*lunli benwei* 伦

理本位), which is to say, when engaging in social affairs the relationship to their counterpart provides them with an understanding of their responsibilities and duties toward those people. In his book *The Substance of Chinese Culture* Liang Shuming writes, "a harmonious compromise can be reached when a problem is encountered. That is, each yielding to the other creates a harmonious compromise which solves the problem, and this has become the proper way for Chinese people, as the world knows. As the popular saying goes 'when one contends, both people become ugly, when one yields, both people achieve.' Non-westerners surely understand this mentality of seeing contending as ugliness."[30] Liang Shuming provides four justifications within his explanation of the philosophy of deferential yielding. The first is that animals with the capability of reason are able to overcome their natural, biological instincts. The second is that Chinese relationship-centered ethics extends relation-based ethics of the family to all social relationships, and is therefore able to uphold the principle of each person attaching importance to the other. The third is that there is not much antagonism between groups within Chinese society, and as a result harmony is promoted over confrontation. The fourth is that one cannot understand Chinese people's mode of behavior from an egoistic standpoint.[31]

Relationship-centered ethics does not compel Chinese people to act based on what they need for themselves, but rather they are compelled by the duty to the relationship, attaching more importance to the other and using what society acknowledges as "propriety/social etiquette" (*li* 礼) as a guide to one's behavior. This kind of behavior, corresponding to "overcoming oneself and observing proprieties" (*keji fuli* 克己复礼), is considered "justice" within Chinese culture. It is through this perspective that Liang Shuming carries out a comparison between Chinese and Western ethics. Using a Western standard, the lack of public virtue in Chinese ethics appears to be a kind of selfishness, but looking at it from a Chinese perspective, Westerners emphasize rights over this or that between each other, do not understand honoring one's parents and respecting one's elders, and do not understand "treating each other with propriety" (相与之礼) and regarding attaching more importance to the other in interactions, and this is certainly one kind of selfishness.

After the founding of the People's Republic of China in 1949, a socialist system that exhibited equality as its primary characteristic was established. In the name of collectivization and nationalization what was at one time the most fundamental economic function of the family within the Chinese value perspective was rejected. State-owned businesses made companies that administered over their worker's birth, old age, sickness, death, and education take over many social responsibilities. This kind of practice of "sharing" made the contradiction between Chinese people's value concepts and the economic development of Chinese society increasingly more acute, which brought the Chinese economy to the brink of collapse. Following the period of reforms and opening up to the world after 1978, the economic functions of the family were restored. On a psychological level, the catch phrase "let some people get rich first" implies this kind of orientation, namely, people believe that the egalitarianism of the period of socialism impaired efficiency, and under the dual role of power and wealth, social wealth became increasingly concentrated, creating a larger gap between the wealthy and poor. The Chinese academic world began to criticize the relationship between this kind of phenomenon and the "ideals" of socialism, and the government also saw that these elements could lead the country to unrest. Therefore, after 2,000 years, constructing a "harmonious society" (*hexie shehui* 和谐社会) became the Chinese government's new objective. It was under these circumstances that the traditional Chinese value *deferential yielding* became a way to formulate a rational system of distribution and encourage the charitable hearts of entrepreneurs and wealthy people. Regardless of whether it is the government or the people, everyone recognizes that participatory sharing is an important foundational value to promote the healthy development of society.

Since 2010, Chinese society has become reacquainted with Confucian ethics, and the concepts of deferential yielding and participatory sharing promoted by Confucianism have gradually been recognized, not only within social life, but also within the integration of Confucian ethics and the core values of socialism. Even more emphasis is being given to equality and fairness in the distribution of wealth. In terms of international relations, as a fundamental concept for the development of peace in foreign relations, "the notion of the community of common destiny" promotes the sharing of benefits. Xi Jinping 习近平 said: "to create a community of common destiny for mankind we must establish a partnership in which all are treated as equals with mutual commerce and mutual understanding, build a security pattern featuring fairness and justice contributed to and shared jointly by nations, strive for open, innovative, and inclusive development prospects that benefit all, advance inter-civilization exchanges featuring harmony in diversity and inclusiveness, and build an ecosystem that puts Mother Nature and green development first."[32] The construction of this community must have the attitude of mutual commerce and mutual understanding, particularly regarding international relations. In the present world structure of national interests, constructing a new kind of civilizational order using the notions of courteous yielding and participatory sharing within Chinese culture will not only cause the Chinese people to obtain the support of a new set of values, but will also contribute to the world.

For a long time now, China has had to confront an unequal international order, and therefore a critical attitude has been preserved toward the principle of "distinction between in-group and foreigners" implied within the notion of the nation-state. Most people, however, express skepticism concerning the ability for people to abandon working toward their own country's interests in favor of the common interests of humanity. Confucian thought created a logic that spreads from the individual to the family, to the country, and ultimately to the entire human community. This kind of logic is much more suitable when considering the problem of shared interests within the multinational community. Regarding the community of common destiny, we can consider the following eight points

First: China, as a country inheriting the tradition of Confucian culture within the current international system, should carry on the value system characterized by deferential yielding and participatory sharing. Within the system of nation-states, China should first emphasize the compatibility between nationalism and cosmopolitanism, and ultimately should become a country with the ability to attract others through its moral force and social order.

Second: Taking a cosmopolitan worldview, reconfigure the relationship between national interests and global interests and reconsider and critique personal and national interests as paramount notions, moving towards a global worldview.

Third: Reconsider the pattern of human development since the enlightenment and search out the circumstances and principles for energy sustainability and the possibility of continued human development. Reconsider the understanding of human beings since the enlightenment and sufficiently recognize the relationship between the independence of the individual and duty to society. Recognize that the family is the first step for the individual to enter society and that using familial affection as a starting point to understanding the world is not mutually exclusive with understanding the world through social contracts.

Fourth: Institutionally implemented under the condition of protecting national sovereignty, establish a new system of conditions for the sovereignty of the nation-state, determine various areas of development for people using a division of power, and set up a political and legal system that takes the interests of the individual, family, and global community as its standard.

Fifth: Gradually reduce every country's armed forces and transfer each country's military spending to the people. Establish a committee according to the votes of each sovereign nation and authorize this committee to create a military force tasked with protecting world order and dealing with individuals or groups who wish to damage this world order.

Sixth: Establish a diverse, self-managed society and administration made up of independent citizens to partially replace the function of the system of nation-states.

Seventh: Reform the current system of representation within the United Nations, primarily by changing the operating method of the power system such that the United Nations has a more effective governing force. Then, during the process of nation-states transitioning into autonomous organizations, gradually dissolve the United Nations and establish an administrative organization of independent people that has the duty of maintaining order and ensuring safety.

Eighth: Establish an agreed upon political organization in order to determine the fundamental principles of human life, which would be tasked with amending and improving the current institutional systems by responding to the constantly changing forms of society and the economy.

In today's search for China's unique mode of development, sketching out the world's future may seem abstruse, however, as a major contributor of value to world civilization, China ought to contribute ideas and methods to achieve a sustainable human existence, joining all others seeking global justice and order. The spirit of assuming responsibility (not yielding) and the participatory sharing of interests can serve as value principles for when we reflect on the construction of community.

Notes

1. Translator's note: I will be translating the term *rang* 让 as "yielding" or "deferential yielding" throughout this chapter for the sake of clarity and simplicity, but it should be noted that the term carries the connotations of complaisance, allowance, and concession as well.

2. *Analects*, 1.10. All translations of the *Analects* here will be using Roger T. Ames and Henry Rosemont, Jr, *The Analects of Confucius: A Philosophical Translation* (New York: Ballantine Books, 1999), with minor emendations.

3. *The Book of Documents—The Canon of Yao* 尚书尧典, 1. When referring to passages from classic Chinese texts, I will cite the chapter and section number as they appear in the online version of the text on the Chinese Text Project website (www.ctext.org). This website is commonly used by scholars in the field and provides easy and instant access to the original texts, English translations by James Legge, as well as lexical information.

4. See *lushi chunqiu-buqu* 吕氏春秋-不屈.

5. See *zhanguo ce- wei di er* 战国策-魏第二.

6. See *zhangguo ce-Yan diyi* 战国策-燕第一 and *shiji-yanshijia* 史记-燕世家.

7. Translation (with minor emendations) from Scott Cook, *The Bamboo Texts of Guodian: A Study and Complete Translation* (Ithaca, NY: Cornell University Press, 2012).

8. Mencius 梁惠王下, 11. Trans. Legge

9. Mencius, Gongsun Chou I. 孟子·公孙丑上. Trans. Legge.

10. Mencius, Liang Hui Wang Shang. 孟子-梁惠王上. Trans. Legge.

11. *Analects* 4.13.

12. *Book of Rites*, Quli I 礼记-曲礼上, 8. Trans. Legge.

13. *Book of Rites*, Yueji 礼记-乐记, 11. Trans. Legge.

14. *The Great Learning* 大学, 11. Trans. Legge (translation modified).

15. Mozi, *luwen* 墨子-鲁问, 15. Trans. W.P. Mei, ctext.org. Translation modified.

16. *Laozi*, ch. 49. 老子-第四十九章. Trans. Legge, ctext.org.

17. Cheng Yaotian 程瑶田, *Zhurang pian* 主让篇, From the *Complete Works of Cheng Yaotian* (*cheng yaotian quanji* 程瑶田全集), 19–20.

18. *Analects* 15.36.

19. *Cheng Yaotian*, 95.

20. *Cheng Yaotian*, 95.

21. *Cheng Yaotian*, 96.

22. *Analects* 16.1.

23. From Burton Watson, with emendations. 2009. Watson, *The Analects of Confucius* (Translations from the Asian Classics). New York: Columbia University Press, 2009.

24. *Analects* 20.2.

25. *Analects* 20.2.

26. *The Great Learning*, 13. Trans. Legge.

27. The *Fanlu Commentaries on the Spring and Autumn Annals* (*Chunqiu Fanlu* 春秋繁露), *Duzhi* 度制.

28. This book was one of the texts used for the imperial examination system that determined who was able to enter civil service.

29. *The Great Learning*, 16.

30. Liang Shuming 梁漱溟, "The Essentials of Chinese Culture" (*zhongguo wenhua yaoyi* 中国文化要义), from *The Complete Works of Liang Shuming* (*Liang Shuming quanji* 梁漱溟全集), 201–202. edited by the Committee of the Academy of Chinese Culture (Jinan: Shandong Remin Press, 2005).

31. *Shuming*, 202.

32. Xi Jinping 习近平, 2016, "Promoting the Construction of a New Kind of International Relations with Mutually Profitable Cooperation as its Core" (*tuidong goujian yi hezuo gongying we hexin de xinxing guoji guanxi* 推动构建以合作共赢为核心的新型国际关系), from the *Instructional Book on Important Lectures Given by General Secretary Xi Jinping* (*Xi Jinping zong shuji xilie zhongyao jianghua duben* 习近平总书记系列重要讲话读本), 265. Beijing: People's Publishing House.

Chapter 4

Confucian Self-Cultivation
A Developmental Perspective

JIN LI

The Master says "Through overcoming self (克己) and observing ritual propriety (复禮) one becomes authoritative in one's conduct (仁)." If for the space of a day one were able to accomplish this, the whole empire would defer to this authoritative model.

—*Analects* 22.1

If we were able to see, side by side, a raw block of stone and a finished artwork sculpted from it, we would marvel at the magical transformation of a lifeless and meaningless stone into an aesthetic embodiment of artistic meaning (Searle 2014). Although we would still marvel at the artist's craft in creating such a transformation, we may not find it magical if we were able to observe the actual process of this transformation. What seems to change our view is our apparent apprehension of two things: (1) the artist's vision of the finished artwork, and (2) the day-to-day, incremental process of sculpting undertaken by the artist to realize that vision in stone. Of course, before seeing the fruit of their labor, artists must also persist through the repetitive monotony of chipping and grinding the tone in a series of seemingly insignificant steps, in addition to overcoming distractions in life. Nevertheless, if they follow through persistently, they will be able to bring the envisioned work into being.

Confucian learning through self-cultivation is similar to the sculpting process. Like the incremental work involved in sculpting, Confucian self-cultivation aims at crafting the self in accord with an all-around vision of what it means to be a virtuous person (Tu 1985; Li 2012). In the *Analects* we find frequent references of this process of refining raw stone to polished jade ware that has come to stand as a symbol for the ideally cultivated human self in Chinese culture. Furthermore, the purpose of life as envisioned by Confucius himself and by later Confucians is to work on the self as a project (Tu 1979), analogous to the making of an artwork by the sculptor. But there is a nontrivial difference: the raw stone is the artist herself. The process of self-cultivation is one of overcoming or chipping away the parts of the self that might impede the process of becoming a better self. Given that the goal is to embody human virtue, the process is not only a morally motivating and spiritually uplifting; it is also an aesthetically fulfilling journey (Rosemont 2003; Tu 1985).

In this chapter I first outline the need for self-cultivation via learning as conceptualized by Confucians. Next, I discuss how Confucian self-cultivation is practiced, particularly in the socialization of children. I offer some examples of illustrative data collected from Chinese immigrant mother-child conversations about how mothers talk about learning in socializing their children toward self-cultivation. Whenever appropriate, I discuss Western thought and European American socialization practice as a comparative reference in order to highlight the process of Confucian self-cultivation.

Need for Self-Cultivation in Human Development

Humans are born with the potential to develop. However, humans are not fully developed persons at birth. Each infant has a long, obstacle-filled journey ahead. To develop into a functional member of society, or better yet, to realize one's full potential, one needs to develop intellectually, emotionally, socially, morally, as well as aesthetically, and, perhaps, spiritually. Much of this development requires a dual process. One the one hand, one's development depends wholly on the intimate nurturance of one's social world, starting at home. Without this initial care, the infant cannot survive (Bowlby 1969). With reduced—that is, insufficient care—while a child may "survive," it is likely to suffer from a host of adverse developmental consequences (Stamoulis, Vanderwert, Zeanah, Fox, and Nelson 2015). However, while essential, family nurturance alone does not suffice. As one grows older, one also needs additional support from one's community (e.g., neighborhood, school, and peers), and from within the larger spheres of one's social contexts. This process of social support begins in the family and continues throughout one's life (Lightfoot, Cole, and Cole 2018).

On the other hand, humans are self-conscious and self-directed creatures, able to reflect on and monitor their own well-being, action, and adjustment (Damasio and Carvalho 2013). Thus, in addition to their ability to receive nurture and to internalize the values, norms, and behaviors of their culture, children are also capable of molding their own lives. This capacity is especially evident when children have acquired requisite cognitive, emotional, social, and moral competences that they can use in their own development (Lightfoot et al. 2018). This part of the dual process is termed *purposeful learning*. Not only are humans capable of such learning, they are normatively regarded as responsible for it across cultures (Harkness and Super 1996).

The Confucian learning tradition, broadly construed, consists in this latter process of self-cultivation. However, Confucian self-cultivation does not just rest on human capacities that modern biological and psychological sciences have verified. There is a set of hard-to-dismiss values that are more widely practiced in the so-called Confucian-heritage cultures (CHCs, including China, Taiwan, Hong Kong, Singapore, Korea, Japan, and Vietnam) than in the West (and other cultures). These values have stood the test of time, and are therefore in need of careful consideration. A growing body of philosophical and empirical research exists on Confucian self-cultivation both in the non-CHCs and within CHCs (Ames 2011; Ames and Hall 2001; Fung 1999; Han 2016; Kato 2016; Kwak 2016; Ivanhoe 2000; C. Li 2014; J. Li 2012; Sun 2008; Wong 2004). Despite an unprecedented and wholesale assault against it, as well as concomitant concerted Westernization in recent history (Yue 2009), this learning tradition has persisted in East Asia and across the East Asian diaspora (Li 2016). Confucian self-cultivation is even witnessing a revival in China where the tradition has been under severe attack for the last 150 years (Bell 2008; Sun 2015).

This long and vital tradition holds two interrelated sets of beliefs that guide the actual practice of self-cultivation, one regarding a distinctive view of the self and the other regarding the purpose of self-cultivation.

View of the Self

A comparison with the dominant Western perspective on the self will shed useful light on Confucian self-cultivation. The Western self, according to philosophical writing and modern psychological research, is defined as essential, bounded, innate, linear, or atomistic (Ames and Hall 2001; Giordano 2014, Markus and Kitayama 1991). Although the Western self also needs the social world's nurturance to develop and social relationships to flourish, Western cultures place a higher value on the notion of the individual and his or her unique qualities. This view has its roots in Greek antiquity and was developed further, first through Christian scholarship on personal identity and the soul, and subsequently by modern science (Martin and Barresi 2006; Taylor 1989). Empirical research in psychology comparing Western with East Asian selves shows consistently that the former is much more strongly identified with independence than the latter (Heine, Kitayama, and Lehman 2001; Markus and Kitayama 1991; Wang 2001).

In contrast, Confucianism defines the human self as fundamentally relational (Ames 2011; Ames and Rosemont 1998). This philosophical perspective is rooted in the fact that humans do not survive, grow, and flourish as individuals, but in webs of relationships. All human children are born into such a preexisting web. While the most important relationship has traditionally been that between a mother and her child, in the present-day world this relationship is no longer strictly biological and can occur between a child and anyone who assumes the role of a primary caregiver. This primordial relationship is not a stand-alone dyad, however. Rather, it is situated in a family with other adults (e.g., grandparents, aunts, and uncles), other children (i.e., siblings), and kinship peers (e.g., cousins). The moment children are born, they start to receive love and care from the caregiver and other family members. This is, and has been, the only way human infants in any culture survives. At the same time, the family provides ongoing interactions with the infant that provide intellectual stimulation and model speech patterns, social regulations, emotional responses, moral thinking/feelings, and behavioral norms (Li 2012; Wu 1996).

Thus, conceptually, Confucian thought regards the self as more particular, porous, malleable, and interrelational (Ames and Hall 2001; Ames and Rosemont 1998). As such, the social condition of human existence renders impossible any view of the self as an ontologically singular "being" (or *Sein* in German) wrapped inside the person's skin, as Western philosophy so pervasively and tenaciously insists (Martin and Barresi 2006). The self is an ontological reality inescapably intertwined in the relationships the person has had since infancy. Because each person's relationships are with *particular* caregivers and *particular* others in the family, the self is also bound to be *particularly* shaped by those relationships. The people one engages in crucial social contexts, especially those with whom one has intimate relationships, are constitutive, not external and accidental, to the self (Giordano 2014, 2015). One's development continues to unfold as a result of these specific relationships.

Confucianism further presumes that, rather than having fixed, innate, and unchanging qualities, the self is malleable by ongoing experience, self-reflection, and behavioral adjustments. At no point is the self taken to be an ontological existence fixed in time and space—a kind of "being" (*Sein*) (Kaufman 1956). The relational nature of the self is both an effect of the social context and at the same time a cause of changes of the context (Li 2012). This dialectic process engenders needs for continual and mutual adaptation between the self and others. Thus, it is unthinkable for the Confucian self to be anything but evolving. For this reason, Ames and Hall (2001) use the term *human becoming* to denote the Confucian self, eschewing references to the *human being* that are familiar and natural to us in both Western philosophical as well as common parlance.

Parenthetically, the social and developing nature of the human self, as anthropologists have long recognized, is allied with processes of enculturation through which children are guided into membership in their natal culture (Levine 1990; Rogoff 2003). Becoming a member of one's culture involves learning how to relate to others in social webs shaped by the given culture's social norms, preferences, and moral precepts. Unequivocally, a large body of modern developmental research over the last century has documented the indispensably social nature of child development and relationality (Lightfoot, Cole, and Cole 2013).

Purpose of Self-Cultivation

The Confucian philosophical outlook resting on the relationality and malleability of the self naturally accords a tremendous degree of agency to humans. This agency, as Confucius himself envisaged, is rooted in the resolve one can generate to shape one's own life, socially as well as morally. Although physical well-being (survival and death) and some practical success (wealth and status) are easily understood by most people, they are not under easy human control. As Confucius' *Analects* 12.5 states, "Life and death are a matter of one's lot; wealth and honor lie with Heaven" (生死有命, 富貴在

天; Ames and Rosemont 1998). The real power of human agency lies in unlocking one's potential to become a better person socially and morally. Self-cultivation is the pathway to accomplish that goal.

Confucian self-cultivation is oriented according to a set of cardinal human virtues: benevolence (仁), rightness (義), ritual propriety (禮), wisdom (智), trustworthiness (信), integrity (廉), and sense of shame (恥). They have been so deeply rooted in the CHCs, particularly in the family, that these virtues continue to be cultivated in children and sought for one's own self-cultivation (Li, Fung, Bakeman, Rae, and Wei 2014). In school curriculum throughout CHC history, Confucian texts were required reading because they were the core of the civil service examination from the seventh century until the abolition of the exam system in 1905. When cultivated, these virtues become deeply a part of oneself and last for a lifetime (Zagzebski 1996), guiding one's thinking, feelings, and behavior in daily life (Li 2006).

There are also other general virtues that Confucian teaching promotes, such as sincerity (誠), harmony (和), filial piety (孝), gratitude (報答), kindness/generosity (厚道), magnanimity (寬宏大量), warm-heartedness (情), humility (謙虛), referential yielding (謙讓), being slow to speak but quick to act [on virtues] (訥於言, 敏於行), moral exemplarity (以身作則), and considerateness (替人著想). Finally, for more defined domains of life, such as learning, the Confucian model stresses specific virtues such as diligence (勤學), self-exertion (發憤), endurance of hardship (刻苦), perseverance (恒心), concentration (專心), and respect for teachers (尊師). These virtues are believed especially effective in addressing routine difficulties and challenges.

Each of these virtues has been subject to further philosophical elaboration and artistic/literary expressions and renditions throughout history (Li 2012). They all merit careful discussion, but suffice it here to stress that the most important among these virtues is *ren* (仁) or becoming the most genuine, sincere, and humane person one can become (Tu 1985). Confucius discussed this consummate value at length with his students, emphasizing the process by which a person moves toward *ren*. In fact, the character 仁 occurs 105 times in the roughly fifty-five pages of fragmented passages comprised in the *Analects*.

However, merely seeing the goal of self-cultivation does not miraculously result in the realization of one's virtuous potential. Confucians were keenly aware that humans are commonly confronted with obstacles and challenges. To begin with, we all have natural tendencies that are often self-serving rather than altruistic (Dawkins 2006), willful rather than yielding to others; we are often tempted to do things we know are not good for us. In short, we are born raw stone. Despite our capacity to change, we struggle even when we firmly resolve to do so.

Furthermore, human lives are full of unanticipated encounters and entanglements that we cannot avoid. These unexpected and unwanted mishaps come our way often because we strive to achieve things that may interfere with others' pursuits in life. For example, in a zero-sum competition such as a tennis match, there is only one winner and by definition a corresponding, consequential loser. Our success as winners necessarily causes others to be losers. Sometimes, we do not enjoy amicable relationships with people in spite of our good intentions and efforts. Even with best intentions and preparations, we may still be rendered hopeless when sheer bad luck strikes because we happen to be at the wrong place at the wrong time, such as on the site of an earthquake. These are routine experiences in human life.

Moreover, even when we succeed, there is, counterintuitively, a negative winner effect (Robertson 2012). Psychological and neurological evidence indicates that success makes us happy and proud; we feel a rising sense of self due to surging dopamine in our brain. Unfortunately, such positive self-regard, as research has documented, tends also to make us overoptimistic, overconfident, more egoistic, harsher and less forgiving toward others' imperfections, and less cautious, empathetic, and receptive to other perspectives (Galinsky, Magee, Inesi, and Gruenfeld 2006; Lammers and Stapel 2009; Lammers, Stapel, and Galinsky 2010; Weick and Guinote 2010). An overinflated ego may be a liability in the end.

Nonetheless, Confucians did not think that humans are doomed by their crudeness, blemishes, and uncontrollable external challenges. Instead they believed that humans can face these challenges through self-cultivation as a personal journey of effectively addressing life's problems. Because challenges accompany life, self-cultivation must necessarily be a lifelong endeavor. To extend the metaphor of self-sculpting, one must have a vision of one's self-project. This vision is not to be finalized at the outset, but is instead to remain open to revision in response to changing conditions of life. Still, having a vision, any vision, for the long pathway is required as guidance along the way, especially when distractions and disturbances present themselves. In Confucian conviction, one holds onto one's vision and takes the first step, the second, and so on without stopping; an artwork will eventually emerge out of the raw stone of the self—the refined, virtuous self. This final achievement of self-cultivation is the *overcome self* of which Confucius spoke. Even when we do not ultimately achieve this final state, our self-overcoming endeavor is cause for admiration.

Practice of Self-Cultivation

Much could be said about the actual process through which children in CHCs are socialized into self-cultivation. Limited space does not permit a fuller account of this process. Still, I hope to highlight some central parts. To begin with, as the term unambiguously indicates, self-cultivation cannot be done by someone else, but must be done by oneself. However, the process is not individualistic. On the contrary, it requires and unfolds with concerted social support from early childhood throughout one's life.

Dual Frame for Practice

This self-cultivation practice follows a path with two mutually enforcing components. First, the child must be loved and cared for with utmost commitment, which involves not only all members in the immediate family but also extended kin. The childrearing role is never assigned solely to the mother or a single caregiver within the family. Grandparents, aunts and uncles, other adult relatives, and siblings and cousins all take part in ensuring a child's nurture and well-being. Such whole-family involvement is known as co-parenting (Fung 1999; Li, Holloway, Bempechat, and Loh 2008). Such total dedication to the child is often expressed in the notion of parental/family sacrifice. It is sacrifice because family members often must forgo food, pleasure, and personal pursuits to yield resources and time to children. Depending on the socioeconomic status of the family, parental sacrifice can take different forms (e.g., low-income parents buying cheap food to save money for their children to attend an afterschool program, while middle-class parents may forgo a vacation to accompany their children to piano lessons; Li et al. 2008). Confucian teaching refers to this dedicated care as "tender love" (慈愛). Children are the beneficiaries of such family tender love. It is believed that this foundation serves as a context rich in social and emotional significance that prepares children for their further development.

The second focus is on deliberate teaching for children to recognize, appreciate, and respond to the fact that their well-being owes much to their family's devotion and sacrifice. Therefore, children shall never take their family's dedication and sacrifice for granted because not all children receive such care and support. Instead, they are guided to develop a deep sense of gratitude to their family (報答父母養育之恩). This second focus is the well-known concept and practice of *filial piety* in CHCs. It is believed that when children have acquired the virtue of filial piety, they have obtained the moral foundation to further their social and moral development, as captured in the Chinese adage "all goodness is predicated on filial piety" (百善孝為先). This Confucian conviction rests on the belief that if children do not receive due love and care, they may not be able to develop adequate socioemotional competence to form the primordial but lasting parent-child bonds. How can a person who is not able to love and care for the closest people in the family ever form meaningful relationships with strangers, let alone serve them? With the solid socioemotional bonding established, children become, gradually, the benefactors to their family, which also prepares them for assuming the parental role for the next generation. Importantly, with the family in order, the person is believed then able to take greater responsibility to serve the community and beyond. Although Confucians articulated this conviction over two millennia ago, modern developmental science has accumulated clear evidence for this crucial early process of human development (Bowlby 1969; Stamoulis et al. 2015).

Four Interrelated Principles for Practice

Grounded in the dual frame of practice, a basic set of at least four interrelated principles guides the practice: (1) learn how to relate to each person in the family and extend this learning to those outside, along with understanding and embodying the moral duties for each role; (2) make everyday effort; (3) self-reflect and self-improve constantly and throughout life; and (4) provide unceasing social support.

Learn to Relate to Each Person and Embody Role Responsibilities

As a core task, every child learns how to relate to *all* family members. Because each member is different, assuming different roles and associated responsibilities, the learning for each is also different. For each person, the child must learn what each role is, independent of the child's particular relationship to that role—for example, one's mother and father for all of their children, not just oneself, the grandmothers and grandfathers for one's respective parents but also one's aunts and uncles, older siblings and younger siblings having the same parents and grandparents but differentiated by generation and age. Beyond the independent learning of these roles, the child must also learn how each role is relevant to *himself* or *herself*. In the Chinese family system, each role is differentiated by maternal and paternal lineage, with the paternal side assuming greater importance because most children carry their paternal names and are traditionally raised in the paternal family. These roles are further differentiated by generation, status, and age, and each role has a different address. Merely understanding the roles and relationships of this family system, even just correctly naming each, is quite complex for children to learn.

Moreover, and most importantly, each role is implicated with moral charge and responsibility, which accords the person in a given role authority, privileges, duties, and behavioral requirements (Ames 2011). Depending on the particular relationships, these responsibilities and privileges change. For example, parents have authority over children. Parents also enjoy the privilege from their children as the lower generation (e.g., in a social setting receiving honor before children). But parents also carry the moral duty to do their utmost to nurture and to "sacrifice" for their children. Children in turn need to accept parental care and instructions and do their best to honor their parents. However, parents are the lower generation to their own parents, their children's grandparents. Their duty to and behavioral requirements for their own parents are the same as those their children accord them.

Thus, within the family, children learn to understand what it means to be a child to his or her mother and father, to be a grandchild to his or her grandmother and grandfather, and to be a sibling to an older or younger brother and sister. Additionally, children also learn what it means to be a child to an aunt and an uncle and to be a cousin to an older or younger male and female cousin from both the maternal and paternal side. Learning to exercise authority, fulfill duties, and accept the privileges associated with these various roles is a formidable task. Before the child ever steps outside the family and kinship, he or she has already acquired this complex social understanding and ability to live the roles appropriate for the child's given age, gender, and generational status. Learning them well is undoubtedly a tremendous accomplishment. There is little wonder why Confucians stress the family as the nursery for one's moral and virtuous growth (Fung 1999; Li 2012; Li, Fung, and Chen 2014).

In Confucian self-cultivation, learning how to relate well to family members and how to live all the roles is only the *beginning*. The next step is what Confucians refer to as extending this basic social/moral sensibility to people outside the family (推己及人). The fundamental belief is that one can build further relationships with others in the community and beyond by applying the same virtues learned at home. For example, in school, teachers shall teach all students as if they were their own children with the same role-based care and duty. Similarly, children shall respect, honor, and learn from teachers as they do from family elders, thus the adage "a teacher for a day, a parent for life" (一日為師，終身為父, originally, teachers were all males, but now this adage refers to teachers of both genders). Likewise, school children should regard, care for, and help each other as they do for siblings and cousins.

Make Everyday Effort

Learning to self-cultivate in CHCs is not a matter of quick, sporadic, or efficient learning, but a daily, ongoing effort, just as the sculptor works constantly on the raw stone in order to produce a great artwork. It is also learning within the condition of spontaneous, therefore "messy," daily life. This real-life-based learning to relate to people is a complex process that requires constant effort over the course of a lifetime. Even just for the same person, say, a young brother to a sister, each time the sister interacts with the brother is a different situation. As a result, renewed effort is needed. While previous interactions may have been smooth, the next one may be rough. For instance, the ten-year-old sister must try to execute her sisterly responsibility by demanding that her younger brother clean up after himself. However, the six-year-old brother is annoyed, resisting. The sister feels upset and seeks her mother's arbitration. The mother reprimands the brother, making him clean up, but he does so resentfully. It is not hard to imagine that the two siblings will likely face difficult interactions down the road.

Although the sister and brother have had a shared life for six years, and probably also enjoy a reasonably good sibling relationship, each part of each event remains distinct. Each provides opportunities for both siblings to learn about each other and about themselves in their relationship. In this chain of events, there is plenty of room for both to think, feel, and behave differently and better if they are to make progress on the path of self-cultivation. The mother in each interaction also stands to improve herself. What would Confucian self-cultivation do to guide all of the parties in this encounter? First, the sister taking responsibility to guide the brother should be lauded for her sense of sisterly duty. However, reflecting the Confucian virtue of sibling love and responsibility (*ti* 悌), the way she went about expressing her charge could be improved, from the rough demand to kind persuasion (勸說). She could have, for example, offered to clean up together with the brother, and as a younger sibling, the brother could benefit from some assistance and modeling of desired behavior. On the other hand, the brother could respond with a promise for delayed clean-up and give plausible reasons for the delay, instead of rejecting the sister's urging altogether. Involving the mother in CHC families is acceptable. However, the mother could praise the sister for her due diligence to carry out her duty, but suggest a gentler way to approach the brother, who is only six. Instead of scolding the brother immediately, the mother could also inquire about the reason for the brother's resistance. This would afford an opportunity for him to reflect on his sister's basic charge for monitoring him and his responsibility to clean after himself. This would likely help the brother learn the duties of his role as a younger brother and a son to his parents. To prevent the sibling animosity from worsening, parents can also ask the siblings to apologize to each other and to seek better cooperation for the future.

As this example illustrates, much daily effort is encouraged for Confucian self-cultivation within the family alone. Learning to relate to each other by living different roles (often simultaneously), children gain increased understanding and skill. Daily, constant effort over time is the only way to progress given the opportunities for change within all roles along with their social and virtuous/moral implications.

Self-Reflect and Self-Improve Constantly

Confucian self-cultivation stresses the need for one to self-reflect and self-improve whenever one interacts with another. Confucians firmly believe that merely following moral precepts without reflection has the potential to keep virtues and morals external to the person. Acquisition of virtues and morals is the process of owning them for oneself. In the parlance of human development, this is the internalization by which the external virtues and morals become one's own (Rogoff 2003; Vygotsky 1978). Only thus will one be able to exercise true and appropriate moral sensibilities and judgment in social contexts and then act accordingly.

Internalization requires ongoing experience, self-reflection, and self-improvement in one's interactions with others. Continuing with the earlier example, it is not optimal simply to tell the sister how she could improve; it is better to give her a chance to reflect on her own thinking, feeling, and handling of the situation. For example, she could be asked, "Is there a better way to accomplish the moral charge of your sisterly role? What could you have done to motivate or persuade your brother to clean up after himself willingly and gladly?" Likewise, the brother could also be engaged in the discussion with the sister and asked, "Would you be more willing to clean up if your sister would help you at first?" As the adult, the mother could pause from rushing to chide the brother and self-reflect: *my daughter is exemplary in recognizing her duty to guide her brother, but because my son is only six, he might need more support. The way my daughter approached him was rather rough. Maybe I can help her think of a better way so that her help can influence her brother better?* All three parties stand to gain from self-reflection, and consequently they all would make progress on their self-cultivation pathways.

The basic idea of self-reflection leading to self-improvement has been echoed by Western thinkers throughout Western intellectual history. This is key to what Durkheim (1961) refers to as moral autonomy. People must freely desire and choose moral action instead of merely accepting the imposition from someone else, society, or other forces.

Provide Unceasing Social Support

As alluded to earlier, although self-cultivation is all about the self, the process is far from lonely. Confucian self-cultivation would be impossible if the child were left to struggle alone. Other than the fundamentally social nature of actual learning, the process itself requires unceasing support from the social world. Family adults are charged with guiding their children from early on, and later are joined by other social agents such as teachers, other adults in the community, and peers through adolescent years, and ideally throughout life. The social support system uses at least three routine approaches: modeling/exemplarity (以身作則), combining verbal instruction with embodiment (言傳身教), and emotional engagement followed by reasoning (動之以情, 曉之以理). For this section, I focus on these approaches within the family for illustrative purposes.

Modeling/exemplarity. This approach is frequently employed. For instance, in order to teach the core family virtue of filial piety, the mother often hands the first piece of food or the first bowl of rice to the child and asks her to give it to grandpa at the dinner table. This ritual is repeated for grandma and other elders in the descending age order at the table. All children are given such "tasks" to serve family elders. Parents also refill grandparents' bowls through mealtime and hand them the best pieces of food, ensuring that the elders are cared for with love and respect. These acts are deliberately done in front of children for three purposes: (1) to demonstrate the need to express filial piety not as an *abstract* idea but as a concrete day-to-day act, (2) to show the desired behavior and the manner in which the act is to be performed, and (3) to have children experience the effect of expressed filial piety on the elders. These and other virtuous acts are performed regularly so that there is little need to call members' attention to them verbally or to spell out their meanings. As recent research reveals, children's ritual/norm learning is best accomplished through modeling because the end goal is to express the ritual/norm itself rather than instrumental learning to achieve some other end (e.g., technical problem solving) (Legare, Wen, Herrmann, and Whitehouse 2015). Parents' modeling of virtuous/moral behavior is the most important learning of the former type. Such modeling also exerts the power of moral exemplarity (Bilgrami 2015), which displays the good intention (to honor the elder), its act in real time (concrete behavior), and its positive result (dignifying the elder by younger generation with their gratitude). Moral exemplarity is both easier for children to understand and more convincing for them to emulate.

Combining verbal instruction with embodiment. This approach is also deeply established in socialization. There is a very long and strong tradition in CHCs to mistrust verbal eloquence in achieving worthy ends. All three major spiritual schools of Confucianism, Daoism, and Buddhism denounce glibness and verbal argumentation, and instead value action before speaking (see Li 2012 for a more comprehensive discussion of this topic). Nevertheless, in teaching children about self-cultivation, some verbal instruction is unavoidable, especially when the child is learning a new skill or trying to comprehend the underlying philosophical principle of a virtue. Verbal explanation can help clarify confusion or misunderstanding. However, and importantly, Confucian self-cultivation stresses embodiment of what one is trying to impart. Even when the adult gives verbal explanation and instructions, he or she must still, ideally, live the virtue. The latter is believed necessary to achieve real impact because seeing the adult in action consistently and over time is much more compelling and concrete for children to learn.

A good example is teaching children how to yield to others. Referential yielding (謙讓) is an important Confucian virtue.[1] It is less about sharing or turn-taking (Damon 1988), however, than about letting the other have the desired end (tangible or intangible). This virtue is emphasized by Confucians because it is believed potent in helping children learn how to wean themselves from unbridled wants, unfair advantage, aggression, and selfishness. When young children play with other children, they commonly grab desirable toys from one another or just keep a toy to themselves, resulting in fighting. Parents usually intervene by first asking their own child to yield to the other child. They appeal to reasons that Confucianism uses to prioritize yielding. For example, older children should yield to younger children, advantaged children should yield to disadvantaged children, higher-achieving children to lower-achieving children, and so forth. Thus, a mother may say to her child "She is younger. Remember that your older brother yields his toys to you all the time?" Or: "She is a new child at school," or "she doesn't have as many toys as you." Upon hearing this kind of reasoning, some children may succeed in yielding, but others may still struggle. However, at home, parents commonly demonstrate yielding to each other (e.g., watching a favorite TV show). When this happens, parents may draw the parallel between the child's yielding virtue at school (e.g., "today you yielded your toy to John") and the spouse's yielding virtue at home (e.g., saying "your father yields his TV time to my favorite show, and mom appreciates that very much"). For the struggling child, parents also use this type of embodiment to show how yielding should be done. By and by, the struggling child is likely to learn how to yield willingly and gladly.

Emotional engagement followed by reasoning. Confucian self-cultivation does not prioritize rational thinking over emotional engagement. Confucians believe that both human capacities are important in the process of self-cultivation. They especially emphasize moral emotions such as empathy, sympathy, compassion, embarrassment, shame, and guilt (Li, Wang, and Fischer 2004). The approach is believed more effective than any form of punishment alone and is used more often for moral transgressions and the need to discipline the child (Fung 1999).

For example, the older brother (OB) commits a misdeed such as hitting his younger brother (YB). Depending on the severity of the incident, parents may need to stop OB first. Then they inquire about the cause that led to the physical aggression by OB. Upon learning that YB called OB an insulting name, the father sits down with both children. But instead of criticizing OB first, he may ask YB to put himself in the shoes of his brother who heard the insulting name. YB is asked to be the recipient of the hurtful name and to tell how he would feel. Now YB's human feelings have been aroused, the father will ask YB to see why OB wanted to strike back. At this point, the father turns to OB and says "your YB now sees that it was wrong for him to call you a name and understands why you felt a need to hit him. But now, pause to put yourself in the shoes of your YB and tell us how you would feel being hit. Seeing his father's fair inquiry and his brother's empathy and consequent remorse for insulting him, OB is much more willing to empathize with YB after being hit. OB is likely to admit YB's pain and hurt. The father seizes the moment to reason with OB: "Your brother should not have insulted you, but hitting him was also not a good way to help him learn to behave better toward you. Hitting him will make him angrier. Can you both see that this would lead to more and more animosity between you two? But you are brothers. We love you both, and you should also love each other." How about letting YB apologize first for calling you a name? When YB does so, the father will ask OB to apologize for hitting YB. To end the teaching, the father may reiterate that it feels bad to be hurt, both by words and by hitting, so you should not hurt each other. If you have problems, we can sit down to talk about them, or you can try on your own to put feelings for each other first and then to apologize to each other. Following this type of teaching, parents will watch and enforce such learning by requiring that both children follow through.

These four sets of principles for socializing children in Confucian self-cultivation aim at getting people to engage in the process rather than just think or talk about it. The more a child learns how to relate to others in the family and beyond, the more the child will understand the virtues and moral duties involved in each role and each relationship.

Socializing Children in Learning Virtues: Mother-Child Conversations

In this section I present empirical data that my team has collected on learning virtues that preschool children develop. We do not have data that bear directly on the two virtues of filial piety and yielding in the family, as discussed earlier. However, our data do contain references to a number of processes in self-cultivation: constant effort, self-reflection, self-improvement, parental social support, and emotional engagement followed by reasoning. As such, they provide clear examples for how children are fostered in the cultural tradition.

We collected these data for a three-year longitudinal study to examine how parents socialize their children in learning in and out of school. We followed three groups with 100 children and families each: European American middle-class, Chinese middle-class immigrant, and Chinese low-income immigrant. We started with children age four and repeated data collection when they were five and six. The three examples presented below came from our first wave of mother-child conversations about learning (MCCs) with children at four. We asked each mother in the comfort of her home to recall an incident that in her judgment showed her child's good learning attitude or behavior. The mother then spoke to her child about that incident in any way for however long she wished. We also asked the mother to talk to her child of an opposite incident that she identified as showing her child's poor learning attitude or behavior. The order of the two incidents was randomized to prevent order effect. Each MCC was recorded, transcribed verbatim, and double-checked for accuracy. The MCCs took anywhere between a few minutes to an hour. In order to highlight parental socialization for Confucian self-cultivation, I present excerpts on children's poor learning attitudes and behaviors: an excerpt typical of European American MCCs first, followed by two excerpts from two Chinese immigrant MCCs. Because our European American sample was middle-class, the Chinese immigrant excerpts also came from middle-class MCCs for comparability.

I chose to present three segments from poor learning rather than good learning attitude or behavior because virtues are more needed to *overcome* the self when the self is faced with challenges in learning. The particular analytical approach is discourse analysis that aims at the moment-to-moment unfolding in human communication (Schiffrin 1994). Drawing particularly on speech act theory and research (Gumperz 1982), I show how mothers guide children to think about their past and future learning. The first excerpt comes from Jack's MCC, a European American boy at four addressed by his mother (all children's names are pseudonyms. M stands for mother and C for child. Numbers to the left indicate the turns, referred to as T).

. . . .
1. M: You like it [writing]?
2. C: But sometimes it gets frustrating.
3. M: Yeah, what part about it gets frustrating?
4. C: Um, writing the dots.
5. M: Writing the dots?
6. C: Writing on them.
7. M: Oh, I know when you have the lines with the dotted line in between you have to fit your letters perfectly in that space.
8. C: They're like this [showing].
9. M: Yeah. That's, that's hard trying to fit it right in that space. Yeah, I could understand that. It's, is it much easier when you just write on a blank piece of paper?
10. C: Yes.
. . . .

11.	M:	. . . do you still wanna practice?
12.	C:	Uh, yes.

. . . .

13.	M:	Yes? Okay. When do you not wanna practice?
14.	C:	Now.
15.	M:	Now? (Laughs) so you don't wanna practice now? Why? 'Cause you're busy doing something else?
16.	C:	Yeah.
17.	M:	What are you doing?
18.	C:	Doing my puzzle.
19.	M:	Okay, you're doing your puzzle?

. . . .

20.	M:	Okay. Do you do it [practice] at school at all?
21.	C:	Yes.
22.	M:	Yes. Is it better at school? Is it better at home? Is it harder at school?
23.	C:	It's harder at school.
24.	M:	Oh, why's that?
25.	C:	'Cause it just is harder at school cause they make it dots.
26.	M:	'Cause they make you do it with the dots.
27.	C:	Yes.

. . . .

28.	M:	Okay, yeah so fitting it in that space is . . . what is frustrating in writing?
29.	C:	Yeah.
30.	M:	Stating what you're feeling?
31.	C:	Yes.
32.	M:	Correctly? Okay.

When hearing that Jack finds writing sometimes frustrating, his mother probes for the reason (T3). Then they discuss the technical difficulty for Jack to write his letters on the dotted line (T4–8). His mother shares her empathetic understanding and offers another, perhaps easier, way to write letters on blank paper (T9). Next, she moves on to ask Jack if he still wants to practice his writing (T11, a possible reference to a learning virtue, viewed from the Confucian perspective; Li 2004), and he affirms (T12). However, the mother also asks when Jack does not want to practice, as if she is trying to give Jack two choices (T13). Sure enough, Jack takes "now" as his answer (T14). His mother seems to be surprised and amused at the same time and wants to know why (T15). But without giving Jack a chance to respond, she suggests: "Cause you're busy doing something else?" (same T). Jack replies that he is doing his puzzles, which seems to be a reasonable excuse for him not wanting to practice his letters at the moment. For the next set of turns, the mother continues to probe for practice, but instead of focusing on practice itself, she leads Jack to attend to where his practice becomes harder (i.e., at home or at school, T22). Again, Jack names dotted lines as a stumbling block at school (T23–27). The remaining turns make it clear that the mother is actually not probing about any learning virtue but Jack's need to *know* and to *express* his negative emotions correctly about learning the particular skills of writing his letters on the dotted line.

It seems that the mother's goal of this MCC segment is to help the child get in touch with his frustration about learning, rather than how to *overcome* his frustration. Research on European American maternal socialization documents this type of affective elaboration with children (Wang 2001). Accordingly, this effort is intended to instill positive views and feelings about the self.

The next excerpt is from a Chinese immigrant mother with her boy Matt (translation from Chinese into English by the author):

. . . .
1. M: . . . What did you learn in your dance class?
2. C: Uh . . . I don't know.
3. M: Why don't you know?
4. C: Uh . . . I'm also. . . . I don't understand.
5. M: Don't understand? Because you didn't learn; that's why you don't understand; is that true?
6. C: Uhh . . . not really.
. . . .
7. M: Why did you say that you shook? You really did that?
8. C: Mhm-mhm.
. . . .
9. M: Was it that the posture that your teacher taught you, or was it that you felt shaking just by watching them dance?
10. C: By watching them dance.
11. M: Oh! Not because the teacher asked you to make a posture that made you shake?
12. C: No.

13.	M:	OK, do you feel it hard to learn how to dance?
14.	C:	Yes.
15.	M:	Yes. Because you are afraid of the difficulties?
16.	C:	Yes.
17.	M:	OK, then what was the real reason for you not to want to learn?
18.	C:	[Loudly] I am afraid of the difficulties! [Softly] afraid of the difficulties—
19.	M:	—It's not OK to fear difficulties! . . . You should not be afraid of them, do you agree?
20.	C:	Yes.

. . . .

21.	M:	Will you be afraid of them next time?
22.	C:	[Softly] Not anymore.
23.	M:	It won't count just to promise. You need to show it in action.
24.	C:	Mhm-mhm.

. . . .

25.	M:	The more you fear something, the more difficult it becomes, you forgot that?
26.	C:	[Silence, 3 secs.]
27.	M:	Has Mommy not talked about this?
28.	C:	Mhm-mhm.

. . . .

29.	M:	You should take the courage to face it. The more courageous you are, the further away the scary thing will move from you, see that?
30.	C:	Yes.

. . . .

31.	M:	Next time, you should not stop learning just because it's hard, OK?
32.	C:	Yes.
33.	M:	It should be that the harder something gets, we will be more determined to learn. That's a real ability, right? Don't you hope to have ability?
34.	C:	Mhm-mhm.

. . . .

Matt complained earlier (not shown) that he shakes when his mother takes him to his dance class. He says that dancing is just for girls because he has never seen any boys dance on TV or in preschool. His mother told him that that is not true. Besides, dancing is like sports, a good form of exercise for children. In the beginning of this segment, his mother probes what he has learned in his dance class, but he does not know (T1–2). When asked why, he says he does not understand dance (T3–4). His mother seizes the moment and inserts a different cause "because you didn't learn" (T5). But Matt denies that (T6). Next, his mother asks about the reason for his claim that he shakes when he goes to the dance class. She also utters a doubtful expression, but Matt insists on his claim (T7–8). His mother finds out that Matt shakes at merely watching other kids dance, not even after trying to make the postures/movements that might put his physical strength to test (T9–12). Seeing that her son fears the mere idea of dance more than the actual learning, she asks if he *feels* it hard to learn how to dance (T13). Matt admits this (T14).

His mother then makes a conceptual move by turning away from the specific learning of dance to facing difficulties in learning as a general problem from which Matt appears to suffer (T15). Matt agrees (T16). His mother urges Matt to acknowledge that he is afraid of difficulties, which is the real reason that blocks his willingness to learn (T17). Matt cooperates and states his problem (T18). His mother simply rejects her son's unfounded fear of difficulties by appealing to the virtue highly valued by Confucianism: perseverance in learning—that is, not backing down in the face of difficulties (T19). With a strong moral tone, she also asks for her son's agreement, which he gives (T20). His mother drives this virtue further by putting Matt in a plausible real situation: next time (T21). Being only a four-year-old child, Matt seems to pick up the difference, and thus softens his agreement: to "not anymore" be afraid (T22). However, his mother does not drop the topic but urges him to move from verbal promise to action, practice and embodiment, which meets Matt's acceptance (T23–24). To solidify the virtue, his mother reiterates a new causal link by saying that the more he fears something, the more difficult it becomes. Apparently, this must have been a familiar teaching, hence the rhetorical question at the end, "you forgot that?" Matts concurs (T25–28).

In the next section, his mother goes a step further by teaching Matt how to overcome his fear: take courage to face it; she generalizes the perspective but in a very clear metaphor that the more courage he has, the further the scary thing moves away (T29). Matt seems more convinced (T30). His mother sets up the next time: Matt "should not stop learning just because it's hard" (T31). After seeing Matt's inching up with agreement (T32), his mother follows up with an even stronger virtuous contingency "we will be determined to learn more the harder something gets" (T33). Notice the pronoun "we" instead of "you" that his mother uses all along. This kind of "we" usage is common among CHC parents. Undoubtedly, "we" signals the commitment of parental support (Li, 2012). His mother does more in this turn by claiming this determination to learn more when things get harder as a real ability, thus turning the conventional understanding of ability as residing inside the person to something the person develops by exercising this kind virtue. To bring Matt more on board with this virtue, she rhetorically asks him, "Don't you hope to have ability?" The segment ends with Matt's alignment with his mother's persuasion for self-cultivation.

Similar to the European American mothers, this Chinese mother also begins acknowledging a negative emotion associated with learning a particular skill. However, the two mothers quickly diverge. Jack's mother probes for the cause of his frustration for learning how to write letters on dotted lines at school and stresses his need to identify and articulate his feeling. Being able to express one's emotions is an important developmental and learning goal because this skill enables children to get their needs met (Grove 2013). It is thus a common socialization focus among European American parents (Chao 1996; Wang 2001). Matt's mother aims at helping him address and then overcome his fear of learning, a central goal of developing virtues for self-cultivation. Not only does she acknowledge Matt's fear, she also guides him in seeing the cause of his fear: giving up in the face of challenges. She further sets up plausible situations for Matt to consider by breaking his unfounded fear with new causal contingencies.

The final excerpt comes from a Chinese mother talking to her daughter, Ellen, about her poor learning attitude/behavior. Again, M = mother, and C = child.

. . . .
1. M: A few days ago, do you remember . . . Paula was teaching us her English class. But you said "No, I want to listen to the trumpet song." You didn't go to the class but got mad at Mommy the whole time, right?
2. C: What happened?
3. M: Uh, you didn't pay attention to the whole class, wasn't that true? You were mad at Mommy.
. . . .
4. M: Ellen . . . let's think for a moment. Do you think that if you are in a good mood you'd go to class?

5.	C:	Yeah.
6.	M:	Do you find Paula's class nice and interesting? Is it that you can learn English? . . . You didn't know how to speak English, and now you have learned to speak well. And Paula often asks you to go to the board to tell which letters begin words, and you are very happy doing that, right? . . . . But that day you were mad at Mommy, and then you skipped the class? Or was it that you didn't like Paula's class, and you just pretended to be mad at Mommy?
7.	C:	I was mad . . . so I didn't go to class.
8.	M:	If you weren't mad, you'd go?
9.	C:	(Nods).

. . . .

10.	M:	Uh, then do you think that when you are mad you can't learn? Is that not so? It is such a pity, see it?
11.	C:	Yes.
12.	M:	What would you do if you get mad again?
13.	C:	I don't know.

. . . .

14.	M:	That day Mommy played the song for you then, didn't I? You need to tell me ahead of time. You can't wait until the teacher tells kids to go back to class; then you say "I want to listen to the trumpet song," right? . . . It'd be too late.
15.	C:	. . . That was not right.
16.	M:	That was not right. Uh, OK, then you would not be mad, right?
17.	C:	Right, right.

. . . .

18.	M:	Then, uh, later even when you get mad, you still need to go to class. Would you stay mad instead of going to class? What would you do?
19.	C:	Uh, go to class.
20.	M:	Go to class first. OK, for the thing that makes you unhappy you can tell Mommy after class, would that be OK?
21.	C:	(Nods).
22.	M:	OK, that is a great idea. Uh, would you really remember that?

23. C: Mhm-mhm.

. . . .

24. M: Because while you stay mad, the class is over, do you see it?
25. C: (Nods).
26. M: Such a pity, see it?
27. C: (Nods).
28. M: OK . . . you can't stop going to class because you were mad.
29. C: Right.

. . . .

The mother recalls this incident with the child at the beginning of this MCC to establish Ellen's lack of attention in her English class (and later we are told that Ellen actually skipped the class). Because concentration and attentiveness are important virtues in Confucian learning (Li 2004), Ellen's lack of them is a problem for her mother. She immediately juxtaposes her problem next to the interfering effect of her emotional disturbance: anger at her mother for not playing her favorite song at a time she wanted to hear it (T1–3). Instead of grilling her, her mother pauses to let Ellen think for a moment if she would attend the class when in a good mood (T4). Ellen agrees she would (T5). Her mother then recounts that Ellen has good reasons to like Paula's class that are contradicted by Ellen's skipping the class. Her mother is careful not to impose her own interpretation of the situation. So she asks if Ellen did not like the class and just pretended to be mad at her mother as a trick to skip the class (T6). Ellen admits that she was truly mad, leading her to skip the class (T7). Her mother ascribes her anger as the cause of missed learning, again with Ellen's concurrence (T8–9).

After the interfering effect of Ellen's anger on learning has been established, her mother moves to discuss the lost opportunity to learn, which she calls a pity and invites Ellen to share that perspective, which Ellen does (T10–11). Now, seeing that her daughter shares her view, the mother probes for a plausible and similar future situation (T12), but Ellen does not know (T13). Her mother recounts the situation of deciding on the spot to want something that is for sure to interfere with her class and lets Ellen draw the negative consequence herself, which she does (T14–15). Repeating Ellen's own words "that was not right," her mother then asks for the very self-disciplined response she has been building all along: "You would not be mad, right?" (T16), which Ellen eagerly affirms (T17).

Her mother next sets the choices of getting mad / staying mad and going to class for Ellen to choose (T18). Ellen chooses the latter (T19). But her mother does not dismiss her legitimate feelings of unhappiness, and she proposes a solution for Ellen to tell her after class. Ellen agrees (T20–21). Obviously, her mother is pleased with her choice and praises her for this "great idea." But her mother also presses for Ellen's commitment to remembering her choice. Ellen now concurs more readily (T22–23). Her mother strengthens her reasoning that Ellen would miss the learning opportunity while staying mad, again a pity (T24 and 26). Her mother ends the segment with the conclusion that Ellen's going to class is not something that can be excused by how mad she feels (T28–29). Ellen completely aligns with her mother's guidance in the last few turns (T25, 27, and 29).

Ellen's mother, too, begins to acknowledge her negative emotion, as did the other two mothers. Like Matt's mother, but unlike Jack's mother, Ellen's mother takes a similar approach to guide Ellen toward overcoming her mad (less good) self in order for her to choose a better self in learning. The mother engages her in step-by-step reasoning. However, this reasoning is not driven by cognition, as the Western learning tradition tends to emphasize (Li, Fung, Rae, Bakeman, and Wei 2014), but by the need to self-cultivate with virtues.

Conclusion

In this chapter I have drawn the parallel between the artist's work of shaping a raw stone into a great sculpture and Confucian social and moral self-cultivation, which Confucians themselves often likened to the process of refining raw stone into beautiful jade ware. I stated that Confucian self-cultivation rests on the conviction that humans have the capacity to engage in purposeful learning to mold their own development. I further indicated that such learning is not only an expression of our capacity, but a culturally inscribed norm of personal development.

In the Confucian view, self-cultivation is not only possible, it is necessary for everyone. This belief stems from the conviction that the human self is not some essential being, self-contained, innate, and context-neutral, but is instead particular, porous, malleable, and interrelational. The relationality and malleability of this self-view accords the person a tremendous degree of agency to resolve and follow through with self-cultivation. But self-cultivation does not start with the individual alone or with unconditional love and care only from the parents. It includes the entire family and extended kin. At the same time, children are taught to recognize, appreciate, and respond to the fact that they are the beneficiaries of their family's nurturance and sacrifice. Children ought never take their family's dedication and sacrifice for granted. Instead they are taught to practice filial piety to regard their family with deep gratitude and to become benefactors to their family in mutual love and devotion. Filial piety thus is taken as the most important foundation for children's further moral and virtuous development because only through its practice are they readied to extend their self-cultivation from the family to the larger community.

Confucian self-cultivation emphasizes learning how to relate to each family member, understanding the particularities of each relationship along with its moral duty. More important is embodiment—that is, practicing the virtues rather than just thinking and verbalizing them. Everyday effort is needed to sustain practice, as are constant self-reflection and self-improvement. However, children are not left to struggle with the process alone. Instead, family, community, school, and the larger society provide continuous support, guiding the children each step of the way. This support system uses many approaches, but three are most central: (1) modeling/exemplarity, (2) combining verbal instruction with embodiment, and (3) emotional engagement followed by reasoning. The socialization examples of mothers conversing with their preschool children about learning demonstrate how these approaches are used in real time to guide children toward self-cultivation. Each child has the potential to become a better person if he or she can learn how to overcome him- or herself. A raw stone can be turned into a great sculpture if the artist has that vision and persists to the end with unceasing effort.

Notes

This paper was first written for the workshop "Learning and Self-Transformation from a Confucian Perspective," held May 5–7, 2016, at the University of Zurich, Switzerland. The title and content have been revised.

1. See Gan Chunsong, Chapter 3 in this volume.

References

Ames, Roger T. 2011. *Confucian Role Ethics: A Vocabulary*. Hong Kong: The Chinese University Press.

Ames, Roger T., and David L. Hall. 2001. *Focusing the Familiar: A Translation and Philosophical Interpretation of the Zhongyong.* Honolulu: University of Hawai'i Press.

Ames, Roger T., and Henry Rosemont Jr. (1998). *The Analects of Confucius: A Philosophical Translation.* New York: Ballantine.

Bell, Daniel A. 2008. *China's New Confucianism: Politics and Everyday Life in a Changing Society.* Princeton, NJ: Princeton University Press.

Bilgrami, Akeel. 2015. *Gandhi, the Philosopher.* Published by the Philosopher and Culture Center, Berggruen Institute. admin.berggruen.org//uploads/document/filename/898/Bilgrami.pdf

Bowlby, John. 1969. *Attachment and Loss, Vol. 1: Attachment.* New York: Basic Books.

Chao, Rruth K. 1996. Chinese and European American Mothers' Views about the Role of Parenting in Children's School Success. *Journal of Cross-Cultural Psychology* 27: 403–423.

Damasio, Antonio, and G.B. Carvalho. 2013. The Nature of Feelings: Evolutionary and Neurobiological Origins. *Nature Reviews Neuroscience* 14(2): 143–152. doi:10.1038/nrn3403

Damon, William. 1988. *The Moral Child: Nurturing Children's Natural Moral Growth.* New York: Free Press.

Dawkins, Richard. 2006. *The Selfish Gene.* New York: Oxford University Press.

Durkheim, Emile. 1961. *Moral Education: A Study in the Theory and Application of the Sociology of Education.* New York: Free Press.

Fung, Heidi. 1999. Becoming a Moral Child: The Socialization of Shame among Young Chinese Children. *Ethos* 27: 180–209.

Galinsky, Adam D., Joe C. Magee, M. Ena Inesi, and Deborah H. Gruenfeld. 2006. Power and Perspectives Not Taken. *Psychological Science* 17: 1068–1074. doi:10.1111/j.1467-9280.2006.01824.x

Giordano, Peter J. 2014. Personality as Continuous Stochastic Process: What Western Personality Theory Can Learn from Classical Confucianism. *Integrative Psychological and Behavioral Science* 48(2): 111–128. doi:10.1007/s12124-013-9250-2

Giordano, Peter J. 2015. Being or Becoming: Toward an Open-System, Process-Centric Model of Personality. *Integrative Psychological and Behavioral Science* 49(4): 757–771. doi:10.1007/s12124-015-9329-z

Grove, Cornelius N. 2013. *The Aptitude Myth: How an Ancient Belief Came to Undermine Children's Learning Today.* New York: Rowman and Littlefield.

Gumperz, John J. 1982. *Discourse Strategies.* New York: Cambridge University Press.

Han, Hyong-Jo. 2016. Lixue (理學 ihak) the Lost Art: Confucianism as a Form of Cultivation of Mind. *Educational Philosophy and Theory* 48: 75–84. doi:10.1080/00131857.2015.1087300

Harkness, Sara, and Charles M. Super. (Eds.) 1996. *Parents' Cultural Belief Systems: Their Origins, Expressions, and Consequences.* New York: Guilford.

Heine, Steven. J., Shinobu Kitayama, and Darrin R. Lehman. 2001. Cultural Differences in Self-Evaluations: Japanese Readily Accept Negative Self-Relevant Information. *Journal of Cross-Cultural Psychology* 32: 434–443. doi:10.1177/0022022101032004004

Ivanhoe, Philip J. 2000. *Confucian Moral Self-Cultivation* (2nd ed.). Indianapolis: Hackett.

Kato, Morimichi. 2016. Humanistic Traditions, East and West: Convergence and Divergence. *Educational Philosophy and Theory* 48: 23–35. doi:10.1080/00131857.2015.1084216

Kaufmann, Walter A. 1956. *Existentialism from Dostoevsky to Sartre*. Cleveland: The World.

Kitayama, Shinobu, and Hazel R. Markus. 1994. *Emotion and Culture: Empirical Studies of Mutual Influence*. Washington, DC: American Psychological Association.

Kwak, Duck-Joo. 2016. Ethics of Learning and Self-Knowledge: Two Cases in the Socratic and Confucian Teachings. *Educational Philosophy and Theory* 48: 7–22. doi:10.1080/00131857.2015.1084217

Lammers, Joris, and Diederik A. Stapel. 2009. How Power Influences Moral Thinking. *Journal of Personality and Social Psychology* 97, 279–289. doi:10.1037/a0015437

Lammers, Joris, Diederik A. Stapel, and Adam D. Galinsky. 2010. Power Increases Hypocrisy: Moralizing in Reasoning, Immorality in Behavior. *Psychological Science* 21: 737–744. doi:10.1177/0956797610368810

Legare, Cristine. H., Nicole J. Wen, Patricia A. Herrmann, and Harvey Whitehouse. 2015. Imitative Flexibility and the Development of Cultural Learning. *Cognition* 142: 351–361. doi:10.1016/j.cognition.2015.05.020

LeVine, Robert A. 1990. Enculturation: A Biosocial Perspective on the Development of Self. In D. Cicchetti and M. Beeghly (Eds.), *The Self in Transition: Infancy to Childhood* (pp. 99–117). Chicago: University of Chicago Press.

Li, Chenyang. 2014. The Confucian Conception of Freedom. *Philosophy East and West* 64(4): 902–919. doi:10.1353/pew.2014.0066

Li, Jin. 2006. Self in Learning: Chinese Adolescents' Goals and Sense of Agency. *Child Development* 77(2): 482–501. doi:10.1111/j.1467-8624.2006.00883.x

Li, Jin. 2012. *Cultural Foundations of Learning: East and West*. New York: Cambridge University Press.

Li, Jin. 2016. Inexhaustible Source of Water: The Enduring Confucian Learning Model [有源之水難涸也: 百折不衰的儒家學習模式]. *Education Research Monthly* 2: 33–41.

Li, Jin, Heidi Fung, and Eva C.-H. Chen. 2014. Taiwanese Parent-Child Conversations for Moral Guidance: Uncovering the Ubiquitous but Enigmatic Process. In C. Wainryb and H. Recchia (Eds.), *Talking about Right and Wrong: Parent-Child Conversations as Contexts for Moral Development* (pp. 71–97). New York: Cambridge University Press.

Li, Jin, Lianqin Wang, and Kurt W. Fischer. 2004. The Organization of Chinese Shame Concepts. *Cognition and Emotion* 18(6): 767–797. doi:10.1080/02699930341000202

Li, Jin, Susan D. Holloway, Janine Bempechat, and Elaine Loh. 2008. Building and Using a Social Network: Nurture for Low-Income Chinese American Adolescents' Learning. In H. Yoshikawa and N. Way (Eds.), *Beyond Families and Schools: How Broader Social Contexts Shape the Adjustment of Children and Youth in Immigrant Families* (pp. 7–25). New Directions in Child and Adolescent Development Series. R. W. Larson and L. A. Jensen (Series Eds.). San Francisco: Jossey-Bass.

Li, Jin, Heidi Fung, Roger Bakeman, Katherine, Rae, and Wanchun Wei. 2014. How European American and Taiwanese Mothers Talk to Their Children about Learning. *Child Development* 84: 1–16. doi:10.1111/cdev.12172

Lightfoot, Cynthia, Michael Cole, and Sheila R. Cole. 2018. *The Development of Children* (8th ed.). New York: Worth.

Martin, Raymond, and John Barresi. 2006. *The Rise and Fall of Soul and Self: An Intellectual History of Personal Identity*. New York: Columbia University Press.

Robertson, Ian. 2012. *The Winner Effect: How Power Affects Your Brain*. London: Bloomsbury.

Rogoff, Barbara. 2003. *The Cultural Nature of Human Development*. New York: Oxford University Press.

Rosemont, Henry Jr. 2003. Is There a Universal Path of Spiritual Progress in the Texts of Early Confucianism? In W. M. Tu and M. E. Tucker (Eds.), *Confucian spirituality*, vol. 1 (pp. 183–196). New York: Crossroad.

Schiffrin, Deborah. 1994. *Approaches to Discourse: Language as Social Interaction*. Malden, MA: Blackwell.

Searle, John R. 2014, October 9. What Your Computer Can't Know. *The New York Review of Books*. www.nybooks.com/articles/2014/10/09/what-your-computer-cant-know

Stamoulis, C., R. E. Vanderwert, C. H. Zeanah, N. A. Fox, and C. A. Nelson. 2015. Early Psychosocial Neglect Adversely Impacts Developmental Trajectories of Brain Oscillations and Their Interactions. *Journal of Cognitive Neuroscience* 27(12): 2512–2528. doi:10.1162/jocn_a_00877

Sun, Anna. 2015. Confucianism as a World Religion: Contested Histories and Contemporary Realities. Princeton, NJ: Princeton University Press.

Sun, Qi. 2008. Confucian Educational Philosophy and Its Implications for Lifelong Learning and Lifelong Education. *International Journal of Lifelong Education* 27: 559–578. doi:10.1080/01411920802343269

Taylor, Charles. 1989. *Sources of the Self: The Making of the Modern Identity*. Cambridge, MA: Harvard University Press.

Tu, Wei-Ming. 1979. *Humanity and Self-Cultivation: Essays in Confucian Thought.* Berkeley, CA: Asian Humanities Press.

Tu, Wei-Ming. 1985. *Confucius Thought: Selfhood as Creative Transformation.* New York: SUNY Press.

Wang, Qi. 2001. "Did You Have Fun?" American and Chinese Mother-Child Conversations about Shared Emotional Experiences. *Cognitive Development* 16: 693–715. doi:10.1016/S0885-2014(01)00055-7

Wang, Qi. 2001. Cultural Effects on Adults' Earliest Childhood Recollection and Self-Description: Implications for the Relation between Memory and the Self. *Journal of Personality and Social Psychology* 81: 220–233. doi:10.1037//OO22-3514.81.2.220

Weick, Mario, and Ana Guinote. 2010. How Long Will It Take? Power Biases Time Predictions. *Journal of Experimental Social Psychology* 46: 595–604. doi:10.1016/j.jesp.2010.03.005

Wong, David B. 2004. Relational and Autonomous Selves. *Journal of Chinese Philosophy,* 31(4): 419–432.

Wu, David Y. H. 1996. Chinese Childhood Socialization. In M. Bond (Ed.), *The Handbook of Chinese Psychology* (pp. 143–154). Hong Kong: Oxford University Press.

Yue, Nan. 2009. 陳寅恪與傅斯年 [Chen Yinke and Fu Sinian]. Taipei, Taiwan: Yuan-Liou Publishing.

Vygotsky, Lev S. 1978. *Mind in Society: The Development of Higher Psychological Processes.* Cambridge, MA: Harvard University Press.

Chapter 5

Human Beings and Human Becomings
Creative Transformation of Confucianism by Disengaged Reason

Kwang-Kuo Hwang

In an international conference on *Confucianism, Democracy and Constitutionalism: Global and East Asian Perspectives*, the well-respected sinologist Roger T. Ames argued on behalf of resisting the temptation to frame explorations of connections signaled in the conference title by first defining Confucianism. "Framing our question as 'What is Confucianism?' in analytical terms tends to essentialize Confucianism as a specific ideology," he argued and should be seen, at best, as "a first step in evaluating the content and worth of a holistic and thus fundamentally aesthetic tradition that takes as its basic premise the uniqueness of each and every situation, and in which the goal of ritualized living is to redirect attention back to the level of concrete feeling" (Ames 2013, 20–21). The question we should be asking, instead, is how "Confucianism" has functioned historically and been transformed within the specific conditions of ever-evolving Chinese culture.

Creative Transformation

Ames's stress on Confucian responsiveness reminds me of the concept of *creative transformation* proposed by Lin Yusheng—a process of reorganizing and/or reconstructing "some (but not all) symbols, thoughts, values, and behavioral patterns by multiple models of thinking (多元思考模式), so that the reorganized symbols, thoughts, values, and behavioral patterns may become a beneficial resource for reform and change, while maintaining cultural identity during the process of change" (Lin 1989, 388).

In an article entitled "The Sociological Analysis of Creative Transformation," Yeh Chizheng (1990) identified three types of crisis that emerged in the consciousness of Chinese intellectuals in response to the incursions of foreign powers during the "century of humiliation" that China suffered in the latter part of the Qing Dynasty: survival crisis, system crisis, and identity crisis. Thus, after being defeated in the Opium War (1839–1842), a series of reform programs were proposed to save the nation from subjugation and ensure its survival. Following the collapse of Qing Dynasty in 1911, the survival crisis was replaced by a general loss of confidence in China's own cultural traditions, as evidenced during the May 4th movement of 1919. The concept of *creative transformation* emerged in response to an identity crisis that began to manifest in the 1980s after the gradual dissolution of the cultural system crisis that had begun in the early twentieth century. Hence, Ames's emphasis on how "Confucianism" has functioned historically, generation after generation, is apposite. Yet, framed in terms of analytic dualism (Archer 1988), the argument can be made that the *morphostasis* of a cultural system must, in fact, be specified prior to any elaboration of its *morphogenesis*. There is a sense in which what is changing must be specified prior to assessing the nature of the specific changes taking place.

Accommodation of Western Culture

Indeed, the necessity of elaborating Confucian morphostasis as well as its morphogenesis can be viewed as a conscious aim of an international community of intellectuals in our contemporary age of globalization. Hence, the need to return to and answer the question: "What is Confucianism?"

This question can be answered by using such imaginative terms as Lin's *multiple models of thinking* or Ames's *systematic philosophy*. Nevertheless, in attempting to answer this crucial question, I would like to cite Yingshi Yu's (1982) conclusion after his reflection on related issues: "Cultural reconstruction must be established on the foundation of a comprehensive understanding of both Chinese and Western cultures. This is exactly the fundamental work which should be accomplished by us, but in fact, we never do it seriously."

It seems to me that "a comprehensive understanding of both Chinese and Western cultures" means an adjustment of the Chinese cultural system to accommodate some crucial components of Western Culture—a demanding task for Chinese intellectuals over the next generation. The difficulty of this work can be explained in terms of the essential differences between Chinese and Western cultures.

Contemplation for Beings

The most significant feature of Western culture can be illustrated in the context of Heidegger's (1927/1962) masterpiece *Being and Time*, in which he indicated that in the tradition of Western philosophy, Being has been regarded as the invariant essence behind the changing phenomena. The title of his book was purposely aimed at stressing the temporality of a particular Being, that is, Human Being. Since the age of Plato, most Western philosophers have concentrated their speculations on the characteristics of beings in this world as well as their usages. Descartes assumes a dualistic attitude to assess and measure objects in nature. This way of thinking implies a misunderstanding of Being. It regards Being as a state of reality that can be observed objectively and ignores a fundamental question first proposed by Aristotle, namely, "What is Being?"

In considering this question, we are thinking about various beings, but not Being itself. In order to understand the meaning of Being, it is necessary to contemplate the existence of a particular being that exists for its own sake, not for becoming anything else. Thus, Heidegger refers to human being as *Dasein*. All human beings were thrown into this world without intentional choice of their own. We all must begin life with what we were endowed with at a point when so-called autonomy had no role to play at all. We enter existence with an awareness that we must strive to be different from what we are, rather than remaining as we are in the situations into which we find ourselves thrown. In this case, *Dasein* has to reflect on not only its own existence, but also its relationships with other beings. It must assume responsibility for what it has done in its past history, to anticipate future consequences for all possible actions in advance, and to work out a feasible course of action to be undertaken now.

Understanding the meaning of death is the only way to transform inauthentic existence into authentic being. Being-toward-death makes everything lose its original value. It forces us as individuals to think about the meaning of our own existence and to seek authentic presence. Reconsidering temporality enables *Dasein* to realize that one's existence is essentially nihility, denoting one's eternal home to which one can eventually return.

Moral Topography of Self

Following Heidegger's line of reasoning, Charles Taylor (1988) argues that *self* exists in a moral space where one must question what kind of person one must be, how one should make moral judgments, and so on. Each of us must find our unique position in such a space where we can each formularize our own perspectives. This is what Heidegger means in claiming that *Dasein* is existing "in question."

The moral topography of the self advocated by Taylor (1988) can be described concretely by my mandala model of self (figure 5.1). In this figure, *self* is located in the center of two bidirectional arrows: the top of the vertical arrow points at person, and the bottom points at individual. The left end of the horizontal arrow points at wisdom or knowledge, and the right end

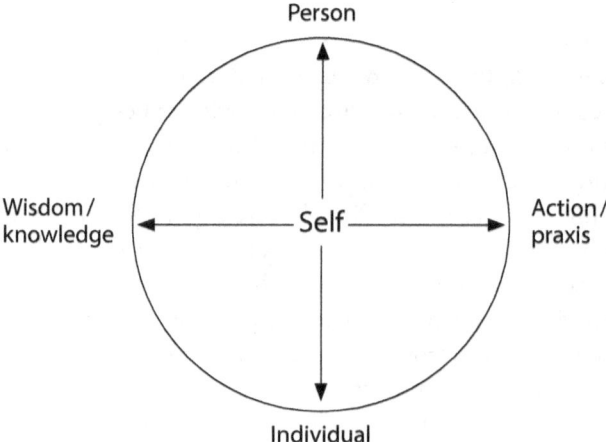

Figure 5.1. The prototype of the self as a mandala.

points at action or praxis. All four concepts are situated outside the circle but within the square. The organization of these five concepts means that one's *self* is being affected by several forces from one's psychological field.

Trinity of Personality Structure

Based on her intensive review on anthropological literature, Grace G. Harris (1989) indicated that the *person/self/individual* structure of personality can be found in every culture. But, the meanings of these three terms differ greatly across Western academic disciplines.

As a biological concept, the *individual* regards the human being as member of the human species, motivated to pursue some resources to satisfy biological needs akin to those of other creatures. *Person* is a sociological concept of the agent-in-society who takes a certain position in the social order and plans a series of actions to acquire certain goals. *Self* is a psychological concept. As the locus of experience, *self* is able to take various actions in different social contexts and engage in self-reflection when blocked from goal striving.

Inwardness of Self-Reflection

In his monograph *Sources of the Self: The Making of Modern Identity*, Charles Taylor (1989) articulates a three-axis moral framework within which individuals evaluate moral values. The first axis refers to a sense of inwardness, the second to a sense of connectedness, and the third to expressive dignity. In this section I will begin by referring to the first axis of inward self-reflection in the making of personal identity.

Anthony Giddens's structuration theory suggests that the self as agency is endowed with two important capabilities, *reflexivity* and *knowledgeability* (Giddens 1984, 1993). *Reflexivity* means that the *self* is not only able to monitor its own actions but also able to give reasons for actions. *Knowledgeability* means that the *self* is able to memorize, store, and organize various types of knowledge, and make them a well-integrated system of knowledge.

From the perspective of Eckensberger's (1996, 2012a, 2012b) action theory, when actors face unsolvable problems in the lifeworld, they may engage in agency-oriented reflections and ask questions such as: What goals do I really want? How important is a particular outcome of action for me? What does some moral principle mean to me?

Two Types of Identity

Answers to the above questions may converge and result in the duality of self. First, self as a subject is able to integrate behaviors that distinguish it from others; this is the basis of one's sense of *self-identity*. In addition, self has the ability to reflect on itself and therefore knows the self's relationship with other objects in the world. Therefore, one may regard oneself as part of a particular social group and acquire a sense of *social identity*.

Both *self-identity* and *social identity* have their unique significance in Taylor's (1988) ontological hermeneutic. In his discussion of the making of modern identity, he emphasizes the importance of inwardness as well as depth of agency-oriented self-reflection. Normally, people care for external things like wealth, power, success, and pleasure. The call for care of oneself, however, invites giving less concern to things in the external world and turning inward to direct concern toward one's own moral condition. This injunction calls one to a reflexive stance, but not a radically reflexive one.

Radical Reflexivity with Disengaged Reason

Taylor (1988) makes a clear distinction between these two types of reflexivity. Because my major concern here is the creative transformation of Confucianism by epistemological means, I will discuss the issue of *radical reflexivity* first and leave the concept of self-reflection in general to when we turn to address social identity.

The lifeworld, as I know it, is there for me, is experienced by me, or thought about by me, or has meaning for me. In contrast, the theoretical models offered in the scientific microworlds of our advanced natural sciences attempt to offer a "view from nowhere" and can be constructed only in the most "objective" language by one who identifies oneself as a scientist employing the *disengaged reason* advocated by Cartesian dualism (see figure 5.1).

In our moral dealing with things, we disregard this disengaged dimension of experience and focus on the things experienced. But, we can also turn and make it our object of attention, engaging in awareness of our awareness, experiencing our experience, focusing on the way the world is for us. This is what I call taking a radical stance or adopting the first-person standpoint. In the following section I will explain how I construct a series of culture-inclusive theories by radical reflexivity with disengaged reason.

Epistemological Strategy for Cultural Analysis

When I began devoting myself to the social science indigenization movement in the 1980s, I soon realized that the fundamental barrier for Chinese social scientists to make genuine research breakthroughs is a lack of comprehensive understanding of progress in Western philosophy of science, which is the essential ethos of Western civilization. It has become one of my profound beliefs that, in order to overcome the difficulties encountered in the work of theoretical construction, non-Western Indigenous Psychologists must understand not only their own cultural tradition, but also Western philosophy of science.

Confucian Relationalism

Based on the principle of "one-mind, many mentalities" (Shweder et al., 1998), I have argued (Huang 2009, 2012) that the epistemological goal of indigenous psychology is to construct a series of theories that represent not only the universal mind of human beings, but also the particular mentality of people in a given society. To this end, I have developed a theoretical model, Face and Favor, which represents the universal mind for social interaction, and which is particularly useful in analyzing the inner structure of Confucianism in relation to Western ethics.

Multiple Philosophical Paradigms

Here I would like to present my epistemological strategy of using multiple philosophical paradigms in constructing culture-inclusive theories of psychology. As summarized in figure 5.2, this involves bringing the philosophies of *constructive realism* and *critical realism* into conversation with the differentiation between the *scientific microworld* and the *lifeworld* (Wallner 1994), emphasizing the importance of *generative mechanisms* (Bhaskar 1975, 1979) in discovering the deep structure of the universal mind. Let me begin the elaboration of my strategy with a brief description of the philosophy of constructive realism.

Scientific Microworld and Lifeworld

In constructive realism, reality divides into three categories: reality itself (*wirklichkeit*), lifeworlds, and microworlds (Wallner 1994). *Reality itself* is

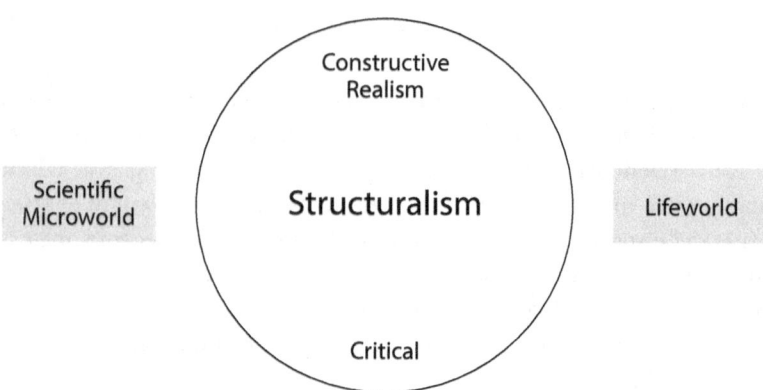

Figure 5.2. Epistemology strategy for transforming traditional wisdom into objective knowledge.

something that cannot be understood by human beings. Human beings can understand only the worlds they have constructed with language, which include *lifeworlds* constructed by cultural groups in their long-term history of development, and *microworlds* constructed by individual scientists.

Chinese Wisdom versus Western Philosophy

The separation of the knowable world into lifeworlds and microworlds is very useful for social scientists in dealing with the challenges encountered by indigenous psychologists. Here, we may take as an illustrative example the essential difference between the knowledge of traditional culture utilized by Chinese people in their lifeworld and the Western knowledge for constructing a scientific microworld.

In his book, *Un sage est sans idèe: ou l'autre de la philosophie*, French philosopher François Jullien (1998) indicated that Chinese traditional thought—including Daoism, Confucianism, and Buddhism—are fundamentally different from that of Western philosophy. The teachings of Confucian, Daoist, and Buddhist sages, he suggests, should be called expressions of wisdom rather than of philosophy. Western philosophy is deduced using dialectical reasoning based on certain *a priori* concepts. The term *a priori* has its origins in the ancient Greek word *axiom*, which Heidegger named the principle of ground. It is used as the first principle for deduction. On the contrary, Chinese traditional wisdom emphasizes "no speculation, no absolute definitude, no inflexibility, no selfishness." There are no prior concepts, no fixed positions, and no individual self. All concepts proposed by the sages can be regarded as statements existing on the same plane, rather than as prior or posterior.

Because Western philosophy is deduced via dialectical reasoning on the basis of certain prior concepts, philosophies can be developed on the basis of different presumptions. Therefore, there is a history of development in Western Philosophy. The explanations for certain things in a given domain made by different philosophers are often progressive, evolving step by step. In contrast, there is no history of wisdom. Nobody can write a history of the development of wisdom. A sage may say different things from different perspectives, but what he says represents an entire self-contained unit of wisdom, which could be interpreted again and again.

In order to think dialectically, Western philosophy requires a clear definition for each core concept so that one can use them to recognize the external world exactly. Philosophers can use various methods to examine the correctness of a proposition about objects in a given domain in order to approach the so-called "truth." By contrast, sage wisdom is expressed in the form of sayings without fixed definitions. These can remind people to see through the "Dao" (way) of ordinary things or events that is otherwise frequently taken for granted. An individual may be inclined to ignore the Dao because his or her sights are so obscured by prejudice that it is possible to see only one side of the issue. A sage's words of wisdom may enable us to become aware (*wu*, enlighten) of the entirety of things or events rather than learning a new framework for knowing the world.

Two Types of Naturalism

For the sake of advocating that the constitution and value of moral goods are intrinsic to human existence, Taylor (1988) differentiated two types of naturalism that emerged in Western history. *Radical naturalism* holds that all human values can be reduced to laws of nature that preclude qualitative distinctions among moral goods. In contrast, *projectionist naturalism* insists on the irreducibility of human identity to laws of nature. People orient to the world within frameworks that guide their action. Such orientations are formed with a subjective strong evaluation within a universe of values. To provide the best account of human life, consideration must be accorded to the qualitative distinctions in moral goods to which particular individuals or cultural communities may adhere.

In terms of Taylor's (1988) typology, both Confucianism and Daoism advocate for a projectionist naturalism. As Laozi has said in the *Daodejing*:

> In the cosmos, there are four Greats,
> Man is one of the four
> Man follows the laws of the Earth
> The Earth follows the laws of Heaven
> Heaven follows the laws of Dao
> Dao follows the law of Nature (*Daodejing*, ch. 25)

As pre-Qin Confucians explained the orderly sequence of the hexagrams in the *Yijing*: "Heaven and Earth exist; all [material] things exist. After all [material] things existed, there came male and female. From the existence of male and female there came husband and wife. From husband and wife there came father and son. From father and son there came ruler and minister. From ruler and minister there came high and low. When [the distinction of] high and low existed, the arrangements of propriety and righteousness came into existence" (*Yijing*, Ten Wings).

In the *Yijing*, human beings are conceptualized as one of the myriad things in the world. The universe was composed of Heaven and Earth, corresponding to *Yang* and *Yin*. When males and females came into existence creating a social world, their unification gave birth to a second generation, providing grounds for constructing social relationships between father and son, and sovereign and subordinates. The arrangement of social relationships between oneself and others (the Way of Humanity) therefore corresponds to the Way of Heaven.

The Confucian cosmology of naturalism manifests three main characteristics. First, it assumes that the universe itself has infinite capacity for procreation. The endless flow and changes of the "myriad things in the universe" are caused by the encounter and interaction between Heaven and Earth. This understanding is not like the Christian view in the West, which sets aside a divine entity that surpasses the universe and created everything in it. Second, it assumes the change of all things in the universe to be cyclic: "The way of Heaven and Earth is characterized by its consistent change. Everything is going forth and coming back, its end is followed by a new beginning. The sun and the moon are always moving and shining in the sky, the four seasons are changing to foster the harvest, and the sages are consistently practicing their way to change the world. The nature of everything in the universe is revealed by watching its consistent change" (*Yijing*, Ten Wings, Appendix I).

The third assumption in this cosmology is that all things in the universe have endless vitality: "The grand virtue of Heaven and Earth is to breed in an endless succession." *Wei Chi* (未濟), the last hexagram in the *Yijing* , emphasizes that "from an end there comes a new beginning." The ideas of circularity such as "when things are at their worst, they will surely mend" and "adversity, after reaching its extremity, is followed by felicity," are readily apparent in this cosmology (Fang 1981).

Inspired by natural phenomena such as the alternate illumination of the sun and the moon, the cycle of the four seasons, the gush of water from deep pools, and the ceaseless vibrant flow of rivers and streams, Confucian scholars of the pre-Qin period made the following insights: "To total sincerity there belongs ceaselessness." "Without sincerity, there would be nothing." "It is only he who is possessed of the most complete sincerity and authenticity that can exist under heaven, who can transform." Based on these insights, Confucian scholars concluded that the attainment of sincerity with authenticity is the Way of Humanity (*Zhongyong*, ch. 20–25). The order and reason within the human heart correspond to the order and reason in nature (Liu 1989/1992). Once total sincerity with authenticity is achieved, the nature of human beings and the Way of Humanity, which derive from the Way of Heaven, will emerge. Therefore: "Heaven exists within humans. As humans bring out their internal virtue, they bring to light the Way of Heaven. Hence, although a human's life is limited, it may be channeled into the infinite and participate with Heaven and Earth" (Liu 1989/1992).

Confucians believed that the Way of Humanity as revealed by their sages has a spiritual essence corresponding to the Way of Heaven. As biological organisms, individuals are destined by their congenital conditions. However, as human beings with moral awareness, they are able and obligated to practice the Confucian Way of Humanity, which corresponds to the Way of Heaven. Each person is endowed with the heavenly-ordained mission of applying the Way of Humanity through the mind of benevolence, a key component of the Confucian ethical system.

The Problematic Situation

To summarize, in contrast to the Western tradition of seeking Being behind Becoming, Confucians have minimal interest in seeking the invariant Being behind the world of constantly Becoming. The Confucian cultural tradition was originated from *Yijing,* the *Classic of Change,* which provides Chinese people a kind of cosmology (Yu 2005), but not an ontology in the Western sense. It is essentially a kind of projectionist naturalism.

The pre-Qin Confucian interpretation of *Yijing* transformed it from a book of divination into a book for self-cultivation with its concentration on seeking for the *immanent transcendence of inner sageliness* (內聖), as advocated by contemporary New Confucianism in Hong Kong and Taiwan. Thus, the problematic situation becomes: how can a culture oriented towards *immanent transcendence* adjust itself to accommodate Western culture's striving for *external transcendence* (Hall and Ames 1998)?

This problematic situation can also be restated in terms of advocacy for establishing an autonomous tradition of social science in Confucian culture: Confucian ethics and morality has long been the transcendental formal structure for sustaining the lifeworld of Chinese people. If, and only if, we are able to construct theoretical models to expound what Confucian ethics and morality are, will we then be able to construct a series of culture-inclusive theories to constitute the scientific macroworld of Confucian Relationalism. This will then answer Ames's question regarding how Confucianism has functioned historically within the specific conditions of an ever-evolving Chinese culture in pursuit of making the most of present circumstances.

Critical Realism

As I indicated in figure 5.2, my epistemological strategy to solve this problem utilizes the philosophy of critical realism advocated by Bhaskar (1945–2014). Bhaskar (1975) differentiated the objects of scientific knowledge into an intransitive ontological aspect of unchanging real objects, and a transitive epistemological aspect of changing cognitive objects. The transcendent *noumena* of real objects are intransitive and exist independently of any human description, while the cognitive objects of knowledge are artificial products of human beings, including assumptions, laws, models, theories, methodologies, and techniques of research. All these are fallible products of human knowledge, and the philosophy of critical realism thus advocates for an epistemological relativism.

Bhaskar advocated three steps for the progress of Western philosophy of scientific discovery: the tradition of classical empiricism (including positivism with its ontological stance of radical empiricism) as the first step;

the neo-Kantian school with the epistemology of transcendental idealism as the second step; and his own transcendental realism as the third step (Bhaskar 1975). (See figure 5.3.)

The term transcendental was used to denote the fact that his philosophy is supported by the so-called transcendental argument, which means the inference from an observed phenomenon to a lasting structure, or the inference from a particular real event to a more basic or a more fundamental generative mechanism that makes the event possible. In terms of Bhaskar's philosophy, transcendental argument is a kind of retroductive argument which requires a scientist to retroduce the "structure on the condition for originating a phenomenon" from "a description of that phenomenon" (1975, 30–36).

Face and Favor Model

In chapter 4 of my book *Foundations of Chinese Psychology: Confucian Social Relations* (2012), I explained how I constructed the model of Face

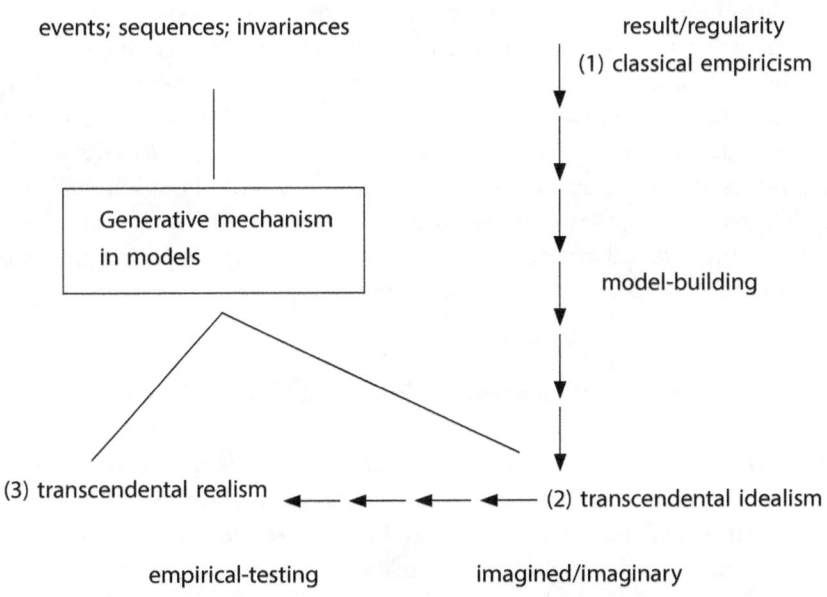

Figure 5.3. Philosophies for scientific discovery (adopted from Bhaskar 1975, 174).

and Favor for depicting the universal mechanism of social interaction. In my theoretical model of Face and Favor (Hwang 1987), the dyad involved in social interaction was defined as *petitioner* and *resource allocator*. When the resource allocator is asked to allocate a social resource to benefit the petitioner, the resource allocator would first consider: "What is the *guanxi* (relationship) between us?"

In figure 5.4, within the box denoting the psychological processes of the resource allocator, the shaded rectangle represents various personal ties. It is first divided into two parts by a diagonal. The shaded part stands for the affective component of interpersonal relationships, while the unshaded part represents the instrumental component.

The same rectangle denoting *guanxi* (interpersonal relationships) is also divided into three parts (expressive ties, mixed ties, and instrumental ties) by a solid line and a dotted line. These parts are proportional to the expressive component. The solid line separating expressive ties within the family and mixed ties outside the family indicates a relatively impenetrable psychological boundary between family members and people outside the family. Different distributive justice or exchange rules are applicable to these two types of relationships during social interactions. In expressive ties, the need rule for social exchange should be adhered to and people should try their best to satisfy the other party with all available resources. In mixed ties, following the *renqing* rule, when individuals want to acquire a particular resource from someone with whom they have instrumental ties, they tend to follow the equity rule and use instrumental rationality. That is, the *renqing* rule in Chinese society is a special case of the *equality rule* which emphasizes that once an individual has received a favor from another, she is obligated to reciprocate in the future. (Hwang, 1987) I have proposed that this Face and Favor model is a universal model applicable to different cultures. Is there any evidence to support my argument?

Structuralism: Elementary Forms of Social Behavior

In *Structures of Social Life*, Fiske (1991) expounded on four relational models or methods that human beings use to organize their social domains. Manifestations of these four elementary forms of relations can be found in various situations, works, activities, domains of action, substantial problems and attitudes—a fact which implies that these structures are produced from the same psychological schemata, or the deep structure of the universal mind.

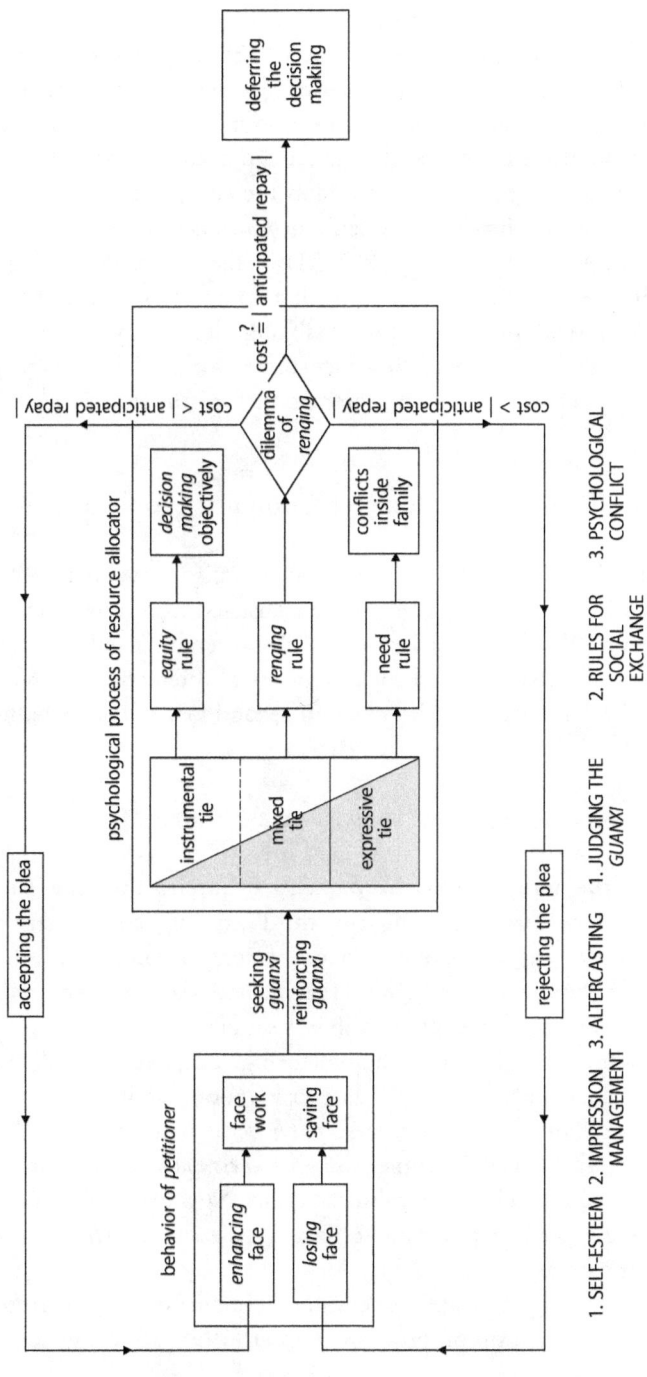

Figure 5.4. A theoretical model of Face and Favor (adopted from Hwang 1987, 948).

Sundararajan (2014) compared Fiske's (1991) four elementary forms of relational models with my Face and Favor model (Hwang 1987). It shows that the three relational models of *communal sharing, equality matching*, and *market pricing* correspond with the expressive tie, the mixed tie, and instrumental tie, as well as the three rules of exchange for the dyad of those relationships, namely, the need rule, the *renqing* rule, and the equity rule in the Face and Favor model. The relationship between the *petitioner* and *resource allocator* implies the power distance (Hofstede 2001) or the authority ranking (Fiske 1991) within the dyad of interaction. Such a comparison shows that Fiske's (1991) model provides a system for classifying elementary forms of social relations in human society, while my Face and Favor model was constructed as a universal mechanism of social interaction for human beings.

Confucian Ethics for Ordinary People

Viewed from the philosophy of constructive realism (Wallner 1994), the core concepts in these two models can be translated from one model to the other. Therefore, the Face and Favor model was constructed to reflect the deep structure of universal mind for interpersonal interactions. It represents an *inescapable framework* of Taylor's (1989) second axis of connectedness for describing selves in terms of moral beliefs.

Inescapable Framework and Inescapable Horizon

Furthermore, the term *inescapable framework* implies that the Face and Favor has been constructed along the third axis of expressivism, which conceptualizes the expressive component of interpersonal relationship as the origin of inner morality. Taylor (1988) cited George Herbert Mead's works to indicate that concept of self is formulated in one's interactions with significant others. Minds of human beings originate in dialogue, not monologue. When people are in dialogue with one another, their shared cultural language will constitute an *inescapable horizon*. In his book *The Ethics of Authenticity*, Taylor (1992) argues that the *inescapable horizon* means the historical cultural heritage for social interaction. Now our problem becomes how to analyze a particular culture heritage by the *inescapable framework* of Face and Favor model?

The epistemological strategy of cultural hermeneutics can be expounded with the analytical dualism proposed by Archer (1995, 1996), which should not be confused with the philosophy of dualism. Archer (1996) indicated that social structure, culture and agency are not separate entities, but it is necessary to treat them as analytically separable. The analytical distinctions enable us to understand the substantial differences between them, to examine their interplay, and to maintain the respective analytical distinction between material interests and cultural ideas in social life.

Analytical Dualism

Instead of listing representative samples of cultural artifacts without further investigation, Archer (1995) proposed the concept of cultural system and highlighted its distinction from sociocultural interaction in her analytic dualism. Compared with social structure where units of analysis such as roles, organizations, institutions are easily identified, she indicates that the concept of culture and its properties tends to be grasped rather than analyzed. This lack of development in the concept of culture can be attributed to "the myth of cultural integration" that might be traced back to early anthropology (Archer 1995, 333).

The myth perpetuates a view that culture is shared by the community at the social-cultural level (S-C), which results in the evasion of cultural meanings at the cultural system level (CS) in social theorizing (Archer 2005). When culture and agency are conflated, it is very hard to make analytical distinctions between the "parts of culture" and the "parts of people." This fallacy of conflation hinders the analysis of their interplay and prevents the investigation on the foundation of cultural dynamics (Archer 1996). Moreover, there is no objective knowledge about of internal cultural dynamics available to explain social change. Accordingly, sources of change are said to be externally located (Archer 2005). Therefore, Archer advocated that an analytic distinction be maintained between CS and S-C.

Hermeneutics for Morphostasis

A cultural system comprises all ideas proposed as knowable at a particular time, each of which may be either true or false. It is constituted by the collection of existing intelligibilia, which contains all things capable of being grasped, known, understood or deciphered by someone. "By definition the cultural intelligibilia form a system, for all items must be expressed in a common language (or be translated in principle) since it is a precondition of their being intelligible" (Archer and Elder-Vass 2012, 95).

Archer and Elder-Vass (2012) proposed that a reasonable theoretical approach to study culture and structure should include both diachronic and synchronic analysis. The former would examine how certain ideas came to wide spread at a certain period of time, who advocated them, what challenges these ideas have encountered both in the past and at present, and why. The latter would aim to understand what sustains morphostasis or cultural reproduction rather than morphogenesis or cultural transformation over time (cf. Archer 1996, 290).

Confucian Ethics

Following this strategy, in chapter 5 of *Foundations of Chinese Psychology* (Hwang 2012), I explained how I analyzed the classics of pre-Qin Confucianism with reference to the *Face and Favor* model in light of the method of hermeneutics. This analysis revealed that pre-Qin Confucianism consisted of four major parts: Confucian conceptions of destiny; Confucian ethical system of benevolence, righteousness, and propriety for ordinary people; Confucian ethics for scholars and benefiting mankind with the Way of Humanity; and Confucian theory of self-cultivation with the Way of Humanity.

Confucians of the pre-Qin period defined two kinds of ethics for arranging interpersonal relationships, namely, ethics for ordinary people and ethics for scholars. The former should be followed by everyone, including scholars. Here, I will concentrate on Confucian ethics for ordinary people.

Among classical works of pre-Qin Confucian sages, the following passage in the *Zhongyong* best depicts the relationships among the three core concepts of benevolence (*ren*), righteousness (*yi*), and propriety (*li*) in Confucian ethics for ordinary people:

> Benevolence (*ren*) is the characteristic attribute of personhood. The first priority of its expression is showing affection to those closely related to us. Righteousness (*yi*) means appropriateness, respecting the superior is its most important rule. Loving others according to who they are, and respecting superiors according to their ranks gives rise to the forms and distinctions of propriety (*li*) in social life. (chapter 20)

The notion of loving others according to who they are and respecting superiors according to their rank indicates an emphasis on the differential order of interpersonal relationships. The above passage not only demonstrates the interrelated relationships among the three concepts of benevolence (*ren*), righteousness (*yi*), and propriety (*li*), it also implies the dimensions along which pre-Qin Confucians assess role relationships in social interaction (see figure 5.5).

Structuralism and Isomorphism

Specifically, pre-Qin Confucians propose that, when interacting with other people, one should first assess the relationship between the other party and oneself along two cognitive dimensions: intimacy/distance and superiority/

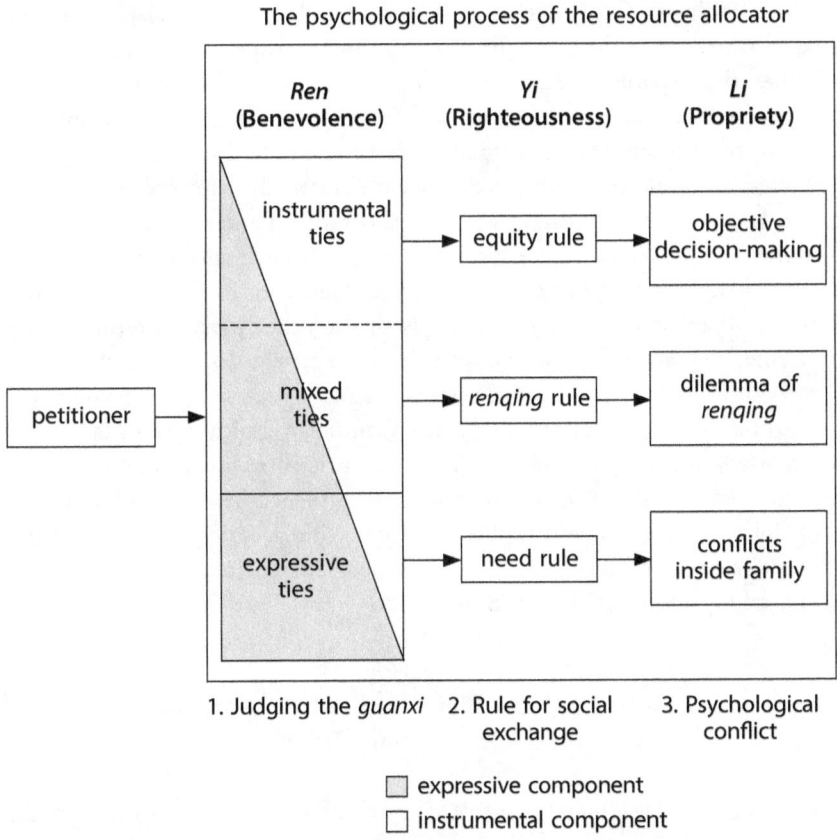

Figure 5.5. The Confucian ethical system of benevolence-righteousness-propriety for ordinary people (adapted from Hwang 1995, 233).

inferiority. The former pertains to the closeness of the relationship, while the latter indicates the relative superior/inferior positions of the two parties involved. Once the assessment is done, favoring people with whom one has a close relationship can be termed benevolence (*ren*), respecting those for whom respect is required by the relationship is called righteousness (*yi*), and acting according to social norms is propriety (*li*).

This proposition of *Zhongyong* has important implications for comparison with justice theory in Western psychology, which divides the concepts of justice in human society into two broad categories: procedural justice and distributive justice. Procedural justice refers to the process that should be followed by members of a group to determine methods of resource distribution. Distributive justice is a particular method of resource distribution that is accepted by group members (Leventhal 1976, 1980).

According to Confucian thought, procedural justice in social interaction should comply with the principle of respecting the superior. The person who occupies the superior position should play the role of resource allocator. The resource allocator should then adhere to the principle of favoring the intimate in choosing an appropriate rule of resource distribution or social exchange. It should be emphasized that Confucian ethics for ordinary people has an isomorphic relationship with my theoretical model of *Face and Favor* (Hwang 1987). When the petitioner asks the resource allocator to give out the resource under his/her control in a way beneficial to the petitioner, the resource allocator is likely to interact with the other party in terms of the *need* rule, *renqing* rule, and *equity* rule, respectively. In the psychological process of the resource allocator, the judgment of *guanxi*, rule for exchange, and explicit behavior correspond to the Confucian ethical system of benevolence (*ren*) with righteousness (*yi*) and propriety (*li*) for ordinary people: the judgment of *guanxi* corresponds with benevolence (*ren*), rule of exchange with righteousness (*yi*), and explicit behavior with propriety (*li*). All of these concepts represent substantial rules to be considered in Confucian culture before taking corresponding actions.

Reciprocal Ethics: Five Cardinal Relationships and Differential Order

Confucians consider the relationships between father and son, sovereign and subordinate, husband and wife, elder and younger brother, and friends to be the most fundamental relationships in society, which are termed the five cardinal relationships (*wu lun*). According to Confucianism, each relationship among the five implies an adequate style of interaction in accordance with the relative superior/inferior positions as well as with the intimacy/distance of the relationship. In fact, it is along these two dimensions that Confucian scholars of the pre-Qin period evaluated the role characteristics of these five relationships and proposed the most appropriate ethics for each of them, For example, Mencius maintained that, "Between father and son, there should be affection; between sovereign and subordinate, righteousness; between husband and wife, attention to their separate functions; between elder brother and younger, a proper order; and between friends, friendship."

Although the interaction between each of the five cardinal relationships should be based on benevolence (*ren*), the values and ethics emphasized in these relationships differ due to their various role functions. Thus in the *Liji*, ten things of righteousness are specifically defined in keeping with a differential order within the five sets of roles involved. In accordance with the ten things of righteousness (*yi*), father, elder brother, husband, the elderly, or ruler should make decisions in line with the principles of kindness, gentleness, righteousness, kindness, and benevolence, respectively. And son, younger brother, wife, junior, or minister, should follow the principles of filial duty, obedience, submission, deference, loyalty, and obedience.

Moral Topography of Confucianism

According to Taylor's (1988) moral topography, human beings are self-interpreting animals who living in a web of significance. In his book *Relational Being: Beyond Self and Community*, Gergen (2009) classified two categories of morality. The first-order morality has nothing to do with good or evil; it consists of implicit values of any long-lasting pattern of interpersonal relationships which are meaningful in one's particular ways of life. An individual may use them to integrate various ideas of personhood to formulate his *self-identity* or *social identity* in a particular social group.

In the case of conflicts in values, beliefs, or practices when two cultural groups encounter one another, reflection with cultural awareness may transform the implicit first-order morality into the explicit second-order morality which can be represented as norms, rules, or principles. Taylor's (1985) ontological hermeneutics indicated that such reflection is always made on the basis of one's *inescapable horizon* constituted by his/her previous cultural experience. I would like to demonstrate the aforementioned argument by my advocacy for the creative transformation of Confucianism.

THREE GUIDING PRINCIPLES

Confucius spent fourteen years touring various kingdoms trying to convince rulers of the merits of his teachings, but nowhere did he receive much attention. He returned to his home state of Lu at the age of sixty-eight and began to write annotations for *Yijing* with some of his disciples. However, one of his close disciples, Zi Gong, said: "The Master's discourses about human nature and the way of Heaven cannot be heard."

Another young disciple of Confucius, Zeng Shen, who was only twenty-seven years old when Confucius passed away, was very bright and able to propose one principle of unification to run through all Confucian teachings. He authored *The Great Learning* (大學) after the death of Confucius. It depicted "three guiding principles" (三綱領), "eight entries" (八條目), and "six steps"(六步驟) for Confucian self-cultivation, using only roughly five hundred Chinese characters and became one of the most important classics of pre-Qin Confucian thoughts. The "three guiding principles" are that the way of great learning consists in manifesting one's bright virtue, in loving the people, and in resting in the perfect goodness.

CONFUCIAN NATURALISM

The traditional commentary made by Zeng Shen with a careful consideration of Confucian teachings explained the meaning of "resting" as follows:

> The *Book of Odes* says, "The people stay comfortably only in a state where there is security."
>
> The *Book of Odes* says, "The chirping birds rest only in the wooded part of the hill."
>
> The Master said, "When it rests, it knows where to rest. Can a person possibly be unequal to a bird?"
>
> The *Book of Odes* also says, "How was King Wen! He rested in clear, shining reverence. As a ruler, he rested in benevolence; as a

minster, he rested in reverence. As a son, he rested in filial piety; also a father, he rested in loving compassion. In his interaction with the following people, he rested in trustworthiness."

Benevolence, reverence, filial piety, loving compassion, and trustworthiness are the self-evident "bright virtue" for dyadic interaction with another party when one is playing various social roles. The aforementioned commentary explains the meaning of "resting in perfect goodness" by using the metaphor of "chirping birds rest only in the wooded past of the hill." This is what I mean by Confucian naturalism.

As recorded in the first part of Gaozi, Mencius had several rounds of debate with Gaozi about the nature of human being. Gaozi was a naturalist who insisted that "life is what we call nature," and argued that "the desire for appetite and lust is part of human nature . . . which is neither good nor bad." Mencius strongly opposed this position with a famous theory which advocated for a Heavenly-endowed original human nature of becoming toward Goodness. Once he even criticized Gaozi directly: "Your words would certainly lead all people to disregard benevolence and righteousness as calamities" (*Mencius, Gaozi*, part I, ch. 1).

Four Origins

In his dialogue with Gongdu Zi, the disciple cited examples for supporting various sayings about human nature that emerged after the death of Confucius. He asked Mencius: "The philosopher Gaozi says, 'human nature is neither good nor bad,' some others say 'human nature may be made to practice good, and it may be made to practice evil,' some others say 'the nature of some is good, and the nature of others is bad.' Now, you say 'the nature is good.' So, are they all wrong?"

Mencius proposed his famous "four origins"(四端) in responding to Gongdu Zi:

> When I say human beings are inherently good, I am talking about their most fundamental qualities of feeling. If someone does evil, it is not the fault of their natural endowment. Everyone has the feeling of concern for the wellbeing of others. Everyone has the sense of shame and disgust at their own evil. Everyone has the sense to treat others respectfully. Everyone has the sense to judge right and wrong. The feeling of concern for the wellbeing

of others is Benevolence. The sense of shame and disgust is Righteousness. The sense to treat others respectfully is Propriety. The sense to judge right and wrong is Wisdom. Benevolence, Righteousness, Propriety and Wisdom are not melded into us from outside. They are our original endowment. You have not really thought them through yet!

Hence it is said: "If you strive for it, you will attain it; if you ignore it, you will lose it." Men are different in their extents of actualization. Some are double, some are five-fold, and some manifest it to an incalculable degree, because some are not able to fully develop their natural endowments. (*Mencius, Gaozi,* part I, ch. 6)

Cultural Interpretation

In addition to the positive statements, Mencius also argued for the essential nature of the "four origins" by means of more assertive mode of negative statements (See *Mencius, Gongsun Chiu,* part I, ch. 2). Many Confucian scholars have tried to elucidate the meaning of Confucian naturalism by drawing a distinction between it and the popular naturalism held by Gaozi and others. In doing so, they are trying to add a second level of cultural interpretation for Confucian naturalism.

Confucian ethics and morality are transcendental frameworks for sustaining the lifeworlds of Chinese people. Confucian scholars of any generation must be able to elaborate and transform them from the first-order implicit wisdom into the second-order explicit knowledge for educating the current young generation on the basis of their academic horizons. The traditional system of Chinese education was replaced by a Western style of education along with the abolishment of the Chinese civil service examination system in 1905. Yet, it remains an urgent need for Chinese scholars to figure out a modern epistemological strategy to successfully undertake a creative transformation of Confucianism for the present day.

Scientific Interpretation

In this chapter I have presented an epistemological strategy for analyzing the Confucian cultural tradition by means of the radical reflexivity of Western philosophy of science. This strategy enables us to construct culture-inclusive theories of Confucian ethics for ordinary people that present the "four origins" of benevolence, righteousness, propriety, and wisdom as norms, rules, or principles for interpersonal interaction, along with a mandala model of self that indicates how individuals may work out courses of action by engaging in wise and strong evaluations of the normative requirements of being an acceptable person in a particular situation. Therefore, we may make the third level of scientific interpretation for Confucian relationalism of the four origins and represent them in accordance with Western reductive naturalism.

Because Confucian ethics and morality certainly will manifest everywhere in the daily life of Chinese people, such an epistemological strategy may enable the construction of a series of culture-inclusive theories in various fields of social science. It is expected that this approach to the creative transformation of Confucian with radical reflexivity may help the Chinese academic community establish an autonomous tradition of social science on the basis of Confucian humanism in the near future.

References

Ames, R. T. 2013. Confucian Role Ethics and Deweyan Democracy: A Challenge to the Ideology of Individualism. Paper presented at the International Conference on Confucianism, Democracy and Constitutionalism: Global and East Asian Perspectives. Institute for Advanced Studies in Humanities and Social Sciences, NTU, Taiwan.

Archer, M. S. 1995. *Realist Social Theory: The Morphogenetic Approach*. Cambridge: Cambridge University Press.

Archer, M. S., and D. Elder-Vass. (2012). Cultural System or Norm Circles? An Exchange. *European Journal of Social Theory* 15: 93–115.

Archer, M. S. 1996. *Culture and Agency: The Place of Culture in Social Theory* (Revised edition). New York: Cambridge University Press.

Archer, M. S. 1998. Addressing the Cultural System. In M. Archer, R. Bhaskar, A. Collier, T. Lawson, and A. Norrie (Eds.). *CR: Essential Readings* (pp. 503–543). London: Routledge.

Archer, M. S. 2005. Structure, Culture and Agency. In M. D. Jacobs and N. W. Hanrahan (Eds.), *The Blackwell Companion to the Sociology of Culture* (pp. 17–34). UK: Blackwell Publishing.

Bhaskar, R. A. 1975/1997. *A Realist Theory of Science*. London: Verso.

Bhaskar, R. A. 1979/1998. *The Possibility of Naturalism* (3rd ed.) London: Routledge.

Eckensberger, L. H. 1996. Agency, Action and Culture: Three Basic Concepts for Cross-Cultural Psychology. In J. Pandey, D. Sinha, and D.P.S. Bhawuk (Eds.), *Asian Contributions to Cross-Cultural Psychology* (pp. 72–102). New Delhi, India: Sage.

Eckensberger, L. H. 2012a. Culture-Inclusive Action Theory: Action Theory in Dialectics and Dialectics in Action Theory. In J. Valsiner (Ed.), *The Oxford Handbook of Culture and Psychology* (pp. 357–402). New York: Oxford University Press.

Eckensberger, L. H. 2012b. The Invention of Indigenous Psychologies: Indicator for an Ongoing Crisis of Psychology. Paper presented at the International conference on New Perspectives in East Asian Studies, June 1–2, 2012, Institute for Advanced Studies in Humanities and Social Sciences, National Taiwan University, Taipei.

Fiske, A. P. 1991. *Structures of Social Life: The Four Elementary Forms of Human Relations*. New York: The Free Press.

Gergen, K. 2009. *Relational Being: Beyond Self and Community*. Oxford: Oxford University Press.

Giddens, A. 1984. *The Constitution of Society: Outline of the Theory of Structuration*. Berkeley: University of California Press.

Giddens, A. 1993. *New Rules of Sociological Method: A Positive Critique of Interpretative Sociologies* (2nd ed.). Stanford, CA: Stanford University Press.

Harris, G. G. 1989. Concepts of Individual, Self, and Person in Description and Analysis. *American Anthropologist* 91: 599–612.

Heidegger, M. 1927/1962. *Sein und Zeit, 15*. Tübingen: Max Niemeyer. *Being and time*. Translated by J. Macquire and E. Robinson. Oxford: Basil Blackwell.

Hofstede, G. 2001. *Culture's Consequences: International Differences in Work Related Values*. Thousand Oaks, CA: Sage.

Hwang, K. K. 1987. Face and Favor: The Chinese Power Game. *American Journal of Sociology* 92: 944–974.

Hwang, K. K. 1995. *Knowledge an Action: A Social-Psychological Interpretation of Chinese Cultural Tradition* (Chinese). Taipei: Sin-Li.

Hwang, K. K. 2000. The Discontinuity Hypothesis of Modernity and Constructive Realism: The Philosophical Basis of Indigenous Psychology. *Hong Kong Journal of Social Sciences* 18: 1–32.

Hwang, K. K. 2011. The Mandala Model of Self. *Psychological Studies* 56(4): 329–334.

Hwang, K. K. 2012. *Foundations of Chinese Psychology: Confucian Social Relations*. New York: Springer.

Hwang, K. K. 2013. *Logic of Social Sciences* (Chinese). Taipei, Taiwan: Psychological Publishing Co.

Jullien, F. 1998. *Un sage est sans idée ou l'autre de la philosophie*. Paris: Seuil.

Leventhal, G. S. 1976. Fairness in Social Relationships. In J. Thibant, J. T. Spence, and R. T. Carson (Eds.), *Contemporary Topics in Social Psychology* (pp. 221–239). Morristown, NJ: General Learning Press.

Leventhal, G. S. 1980. What Should Be Done with Equality Theory? In K. J. Gergen, M. S. Greenberg, and R. H. Willis (Eds.), *Social Exchange: Advance in Theory and Research* (pp. 27–55). NY: Plenum Press.

Lin Yusheng 1989. What Is Creative Transformation? In *Political Order and Plural Society* (Chinese). Taipei: Linking Publishing.

Liu, S. X. 1989/1992. A Perspective on the Relationship between Humans and Nature: A New Explanation of the Unification of Heaven and Human Beings." In *Confucianism and Modernization* (Chinese). Beijing: Chinese Radio and Television Pub. Co.

Shweder, R. A., J. Goodnow, G. Hatano, R. Le Vine, H. Markus, and P. Miller. 1998. The Cultural Psychology of Development: One Mind, Many Mentalities. In W. Damon (Ed.), *Handbook of Child Psychology (Vol. 1): Theoretical Models of Human Development*. New York: John Wiley & Sons.

Sundararajan, L. 2014. Indigenous Psychology: Grounding Science in Culture, Why and How? *Journal for the Theory of Social Behaviour.* doi:10.1111/jtsb.12054

Taylor, C. 1988. The Moral Topography of the Self. In S. B. Messer, L. A. Sass, and R. L. Woolfolk (Eds.). *Hermeneutics and Psychological Theory: Interpretative Perspectives on Personality, Psychology and Psychopathology* (pp. 298–320). London: Rutgers University Press.

Taylor, C. 1989. *Sources of the Self: The Making of the Modern Identity.* Cambridge, MA: Harvard University Press.

Taylor, C. 1992. Modernity and the Rise of the Public Sphere. *The Tanner Lectures on Human Values* 14: 203–260.

Taylor, C. (1985). Interpretation and the Sciences of Man. In C. Taylor, *Philosophy and Human Sciences: Philosophical Papers II*. Cambridge: Cambridge University Press.

Wallner, F. 1994. *Constructive Realism: Aspects of a New Epistemological Movement.* Wien: W. Braumuller.

Ye Chizheng. 1990. The Sociological Analysis of Creative Transformation." In *Social Logic of Institutionalization* (pp. 193–223; Chinese). Taipei: Tungta Publishing.

Yu Yingshi. 1982. On Issues about the Chinese Cultural Reconstruction. In *Historical Science and Tradition* (p. 16; Chinese). Taipei: China Times Publishing.

Chapter 6

The Idea of Freedom within the Confucian Conception of Human Relations, Viewed through the Lens of Chen Yinke's Mourning Poems for Wang Guowei

Tang Wenming

After Wang Guowei 王国维 (1877–1927) drowned himself in Kunming Lake at the Summer Palace in Beijing in 1927, Chen Yinke 陈寅恪 (1890–1969) composed a seven-word, eight-line poem (*qilü* 七律) entitled "Elegy for Wang Guowei" (*Wan Wang Jing'an xiansheng* 挽王静安先生), which he followed up with a couplet grieving Wang's death. Afterward, Chen felt that he "had not said it all, and so I went on to write a long rhapsody," bearing the title "Lament for Wang Guowei, Accompanied by a Preface" (*Wang Guantang xiansheng wanci bing xu* 王观堂先生挽词并序).[1] Two years later, when the Research Institute for National Studies at Tsinghua University erected a monument in the campus garden to commemorate Wang, Chen composed his "Memorial Inscription for Wang Guowei's Monument at Tsinghua University" (*Qinghua daxue Wang Guantang xiansheng jinianbei ming* 清华大学王观堂先生纪念碑铭). As is well known, the most popular and influential part of this series of poems is the phrase "spiritual independence and freedom of thought" (独立之精神, 自由之思想) from the "Memorial Inscription."[2] This expression, as Li Shenzhi 李慎之 described it back in 1999, "has long since come to denote the academic spirit and value orientation held in common and pursued by all Chinese intellectuals."[3] Although grounds are sufficient for interpreting this phrase as simply an expression of personal integrity or an intellectual pursuit on an academic level,[4] a comparative reading of all of Chen's mourning poems is bound to raise some doubts concerning this interpretation.

An obvious fact very few have attended to is that the "Memorial Inscription" and the "Lament" employ clearly distinct expressions in evaluating the event of Wang Guowei's death. Moreover, lacking further analysis, it remains hard to discern any sort of continuity between these different expressions. Especially if we read "spiritual independence and freedom of thought" as a description of the pursuit of academic integrity, as we are accustomed to do, the discrepancy between them becomes even more glaring. Perhaps one might argue that interpretations and appraisals of one and the same event can vary according to the circumstances and the historical context, and little can be said against this. But we would be guilty of a lack of rigor if we remain at this level of analysis instead of approaching Chen Yinke's evaluation of Wang's death in a more concrete manner and trying to understand the relation between these two texts separated by around two years' time.

Perhaps the first thing I should emphasize here is that in the context of the "Memorial Inscription," the expression "spiritual independence and freedom of thought" does not simply appear as Chen Yinke's blanket description of Wang Guowei's academic pursuits, but rather is closely tied to the event of Wang's death and woven into the text as a whole. This is why Chen writes that "his death revealed the independence and freedom of his will, it had nothing to do with private feelings of gratitude or resentment or with his own personal fame." Consequently, we must confront the following problem: if "spiritual independence and freedom of thought" is straightforwardly and reductively interpreted as expressing the pursuit of a form of personal integrity on an academic level, then we have to provide an analysis of the sort of academic and intellectual pressures Wang Guowei was exposed to that drove him to suicide. It seems we might find an answer to this question in the following explanation, which was widely circulated at the time: it was only after Wang received news that the scholars Ye Dehui 叶德辉 (1864–1927) and Wang Baoxin 王葆心 (?–1927) had been shot by revolutionary partisans in Hunan province that he was driven to suicide. Strictly speaking, however, in the context of the present analysis, regardless of how it is phrased, this answer misses the main point. After all, what matters is not so much whether the execution of Ye and Wang can adequately account for Wang Guowei's suicide, but rather that this event plays no role whatsoever in Chen Yinke's interpretation and appraisal of Wang's death.

If we take these reasonable objections into account, it becomes quite clear that although the "Lament" uses disparate modes of expression, it nevertheless presents us with a relatively unambiguous outlook. By contrast, although the formulations used in the "Memorial Inscription" seem straightforward enough, it remains a riddle what this text is trying to convey. If Wang's suicide was the manifestation of a kind of freedom, exactly what sort of freedom are we dealing with here? The preceding analysis should suffice to make it clear that the "Lament" and the "Memorial Inscription" have to be considered in relation to each other and that it is necessary to reflect on the continuity between these two texts in order to provide an adequate solution to this enigma.

The most obvious point of commonality between these two texts is their use of the term "sacrificing oneself" or "dying for" (xun 殉). But what, in the end, was it that Wang Guowei sacrificed himself for? As is well known, this was a much-debated question at the time, one that Chen Yinke's texts of mourning were clearly intended to address. Moreover, the answer he articulated in these texts became widely known and accepted. Nevertheless, although it would be exaggerated to say that the views he put forward in his texts of mourning were later completely distorted, at the very least they came to be interpreted in rather one-sided fashion under the influence of the image of Chen Yinke painstakingly crafted by Chinese academics ever since the nineties of the previous century.

The most frequently quoted passage from the "Lament" is probably the following:

> Whenever a culture begins to decline, those who have been shaped and transformed (hua 化) by this culture (wenhua 文化) will suffer anguish. The more a person embodies his own culture, the stronger his suffering will be. At the height of such suffering, it can come to a point of no return where only suicide still offers a way to find peace of mind for oneself and to accomplish what is right.

Given its popularity, most interpreters have turned to this passage to provide the following general summary of Chen's appraisal of Wang's death: what Wang sacrificed himself for was Chinese culture. To a certain extent, we can speak of a clear opposition between the idea of sacrificing oneself for Chinese culture on the one hand, and the then widespread ideal of being buried with the Qing dynasty on the other. However, we should not overstate this contrast, as is evidenced by the fact that in the "Elegy for Wang Guowei," written on the day of Wang's death, Chen states that "our culture and the Divine Land of China has lost a part of itself" (文化神州丧一身). In other words, Chen consistently viewed Wang as someone entrusted with the fate of Chinese culture as a whole. The more subtle and at the same time more important point is that we would be greatly mistaken if we were to infer from this phrase that Chen opposed the idea of sacrificing oneself for the Qing.

After the popular passage quoted in the above, Chen goes on to argue that a definition of our culture is contained in the notion of the "three bonds and the six connections" (*sang gang liu ji* 三纲六纪) found in the *Comprehensive Discussions in the White Tiger Hall* (*Bai hu tong* 白虎通),[5] which refers to the realm of the highest abstract ideals, much like what Plato called *eidos*. As far as the bond between the ruler and the servant is concerned, we can say that when a ruler resembles the incompetent emperor Li Yu 李煜 (937–978), his servant will expect him to become someone like Liu Xiu 刘秀 (5 BCE–57), who restored the Han dynasty. In terms of the connection between friends, if someone behaves like the treacherous Li Ji 郦寄, his friend will still treat him with the loyalty of Bao Shu[ya] 鲍叔[牙]. The way Wang sacrificed himself and the humaneness he thereby accomplished both refer to the universality of abstract ideals, and not to particular people or things.

This passage too has been quoted often and has mostly been used to provide a "definition of Chinese culture." In the context of the "Lament," however, this passage undoubtedly implies that Chen Yinke interpreted Wang Guowei's death within the framework of the notion of sacrificing oneself for the sake of the relation between ruler and servant. This notion obviously appears in the main text of the "Lament" as well, where we come across the phrase "through his death he serenely sacrificed himself for the sake of the weightiest of relations between human beings" (一死从容殉大伦).

As the main current of Chinese culture, Confucianism always attached great value to interpersonal relations, with the connections between ruler and servant, father and son, and husband and wife counting as the "weightiest of relations between human beings," which is precisely what the "three bonds" are concerned with. However, because the relationship between ruler and servant was a lot less stable than that between father and son and husband

and wife in ancient Chinese society, the former was often referred to as the "weightiest relation" (*da lun* 大伦) in the relevant texts. A relatively early example can be found in a passage from the *Analects* where Zilu criticizes hermits for forsaking the bond between ruler and servant: "Proper relations between elders and juniors cannot be discarded—how, then, can one discard the rightness that obtains between ruler and minister? To do so is to wish to keep one's hands from getting dirty at the expense of throwing the weightiest of human relations into chaos."[6] In comparison to the idea of dying for one's culture, which appears to be very lofty but ultimately remains somewhat nondescript, the notion of sacrificing oneself for the weightiest of human relations is much more concrete and, accordingly, also a lot more clearly defined.[7] However, since the bond between ruler and servant has been consistently subjected to harsh criticism ever since the modern era, most of those who wish to express their respect for Wang Guowei's character and scholarship have not been inclined to argue that he sacrificed himself for the sake of this bond, and have preferred to honor him by saying he died for Chinese culture.

The occurrence of the phrase "sacrificing oneself for the weightiest of human relations" in the "Lament" suffices to make it clear that although Chen also emphasized that Wang had died for the sake of Chinese culture, he was not opposed to the idea of sacrificing oneself for the Qing dynasty. Rather, we could say that Chen's analysis constitutes a deeper engagement with this idea. As such, it counts as an attempt to probe into its spiritual essence by departing from the empirical observation that Wang had effectively been buried with the Qing. In this respect, we are also confronted with the importance of properly interpreting the rhetoric of a "sphere of abstract ideals," which we encounter both in the "Lament" as well as in the "Memorial Inscription." Although the relation between ruler and servant could be said to constitute an abstract ideal, when a person sacrifices himself for this relation by committing suicide, something He Lin 贺麟 (1902–1992) later captured in the expression "remaining faithful to one's ideals to the very end," then such an act is undoubtedly related to the actual conditions characterizing the relations between ruler and servant in which the person in question finds himself, as well as to certain concrete events tied up with these relations.[8] Chen's stress on the importance of the "sphere of abstract ideals" was obviously motivated by the fact that in the context of his time, the idea of Wang having died for the Qing dynasty might have cast a shadow over Wang's integrity and damaged his reputation. However, the notion of sacrificing oneself for the Qing was actually not only propagated by infamous diehard conservatives such as Luo Zhenyu 罗振宇 (1866–1940), but also met with the approval of many of Wang's colleagues at Tsinghua University, such as Liang Qichao 梁启超 (1873–1929) and Wu Mi 吴宓 (1894–1978) at the Research Institute for National Studies, as well as the president of the university Cao Yunxiang 曹云祥 (1881–1937) and many others.[9] In sum, Chen Yinke's notion of sacrificing oneself for culture was not a reaction against, but rather a further development of, the idea of dying for the Qing. As for the other ways in which the idea of dying for one's culture is expressed in Chen's texts, we should bear in mind that apart from the notion of "sacrificing oneself for the weightiest of human relations" analyzed in the above, where the essential meaning of this idea presents itself most clearly, we also come across phrases such as "sacrificing oneself for the way" (in the "Lament") and "dying for the truth" (in the "Memorial Inscription").

Having clarified the "essential ideals the humane sages of past and present died for," we can now return to the question raised above. If it can be argued that Wang Guowei's act of sacrificing himself for the sake of the bond between ruler and servant counts as the expression of a certain type of freedom, then how should we understand the relation between this bond (as well as other human relations in which there is no equality between the two parties involved, such as those between husband and wife and father and son) and such freedom? In short, how should we understand the notion of freedom contained within the Confucian conception of interpersonal relations?

The main difficulty we face in raising this question is not so much that of providing an answer, but rather that many of us are fundamentally incapable of imagining that the Confucian view on human relations might even contain a notion of freedom. Especially when it comes to the unequal human relations corresponding to the "three bonds," most people can think only of domination and find it impossible to imagine any sort of freedom being involved here. People who hold this opinion are certainly in for a big surprise, as soon becomes clear if we examine a bit more closely Chen Yinke's description of Wang Guowei sacrificing himself for the sake of the relation between ruler and servant as an instance of freedom.

To begin with, the fact that Wang Guowei voluntarily died for this relation implies that there must have been an inner psychological force stemming from his own will at work here. In other words, as soon as we follow Chen in approaching Wang's death as his own rational choice, instead of as the result of some kind of spiritual or psychological disorder, we can derive a form of self-determined freedom from his suicide.[10] Nevertheless, we would be overhasty to already conclude at this point that the notion of "freedom" in the "Memorial Inscription" can only be read in this way. Perhaps something else can be factored into our analysis of the act of dying for the relation between ruler and servant that is also related to the idea of freedom, namely, Wang Guowei's voluntary identification with this relation. In 1927, he no longer had any external obligation to abide by the traditional Confucian normative requirements related to the bond between ruler and servant. In other words, Wang's identification with this bond as well as the practical actions resulting from such an identification were purely the result of his own aspirations. From this point of view, it could be argued that in this voluntary identification, where a close relation between the self and a particular dimension of society is established and put into practice, we see the embodiment of a certain type of freedom. The idea that Wang's suicide was his own way of expressing his resistance against external forces and thus also entailed a quest for freedom is probably a lot more straightforward.

From the perspective of the sociology of knowledge, we can say that the conception of freedom in our spiritual lifeworld comes from the West, which entered into the modern age earlier than China. According to Axel Honneth's (b. 1949) overview, up to this day, three completely different conceptions of freedom as centered around individual autonomy emerged in the moral discourse of modern Western societies.[11] The first conception of freedom was introduced by Thomas Hobbes (1588–1679), namely, negative freedom, or what Isaiah Berlin (1909–1979) would later call "the freedom of the moderns" as opposed to "the freedom of the ancients." Historically speaking, the emergence of the idea of negative freedom was closely related to the specific condition of religious conflicts and religious wars in the West during the sixteenth and seventeenth centuries and mainly implied that individuals should be able to establish their own behavioral goals without any external constraints. For example, Hobbes argued that "a free person" is someone who "is able to do anything allowed to him by his abilities and reason according to his own will without being subject to external interference."[12] Honneth does not hold this conception of freedom in high regard, and argues that the main reason it lived on in Western intellectual history was that it managed to perpetuate a crucial idea, namely that of "securing a protected free-space for egocentric action, unimpeded by the pressures of responsibility towards others."[13] In other words, "if individuals in their endless particularity had not been able to constantly appeal to the idea of negative freedom, Hobbes's theory would never have had a future."[14]

The theory of justice (or ideas concerning social order in the state) corresponding to the negative concept of freedom was that of the social contract. Such social contract theories grounded in a negative conception of freedom have a fundamental flaw, or at least face a specific difficulty. Honneth indicates that it is intrinsically impossible to arrive at a theory of justice concerned with communal life purely on the basis of a negative concept of freedom. Social contract theory must provide an answer to the enigmatic question of how a connection can be established between this concept of freedom on the one hand and theories of natural law on the other, specifically by turning the latter into the "external boundary" of the former and reaching the theoretical goal it sets itself by reconciling these two aspects with each other. Bringing this difficulty to light obviously entails a critique of the negative concept of freedom and the corresponding theory of justice. Because the negative concept of freedom "focuses entirely on the 'external' liberation of action," individual freedom does not "entail an ability," more precisely, the ability "to select the aims it wishes to achieve in the world."[15] Rather, within the contractual theory of justice grounded in negative freedom, "the right socially accorded to individual freedom is thus reduced to a sphere in which all subjects pursue their own, occasionally egocentric and even idiosyncratic aims. It extends neither to the formulation of law nor to any interaction with fellow legal subjects."[16]

The significance of the second type of freedom, which Honneth calls "reflexive freedom," can to a large extent be understood by departing from the shortcomings of negative freedom.[17] Jean-Jacques Rousseau (1712–1778) was the first to isolate and highlight reflexive freedom in a theoretical manner. In Rousseau's view, it is only when a subject's intention to perform a certain act genuinely stems from its own will that an act can qualify as free. The introduction of reflexive freedom was initially meant to address possible conflicts or clashes between will and desire. In other words, if the actions of an individual do not stem from his true intentions but remain completely at the mercy of his desires, then we cannot argue that such actions count as an embodiment of his freedom, even if they never encounter any external constraints. Providing a normative pattern for the motivations behind a person's actions is what reflexive freedom is all about, which also makes it clear why this conception of freedom is summarized in the word "reflexive." Rousseau's internally oriented approach of the concept of freedom would be developed in two different directions by later thinkers. The first interpretation starts out from the formal aspect of rational reflection and is epitomized by Immanuel Kant (1724–1804), in whose work inner freedom becomes tied up with transcendental philosophy and is developed into a theory of moral autonomy. The second orientation departs from the actual content of rational reflection. The representative figure here is Johann Gottfried Herder (1744–1803), who emphasizes that people can discover their true inner self, that is to say, their own authenticity, by reflecting on themselves with utmost sincerity and thereby becoming able to embark upon the path toward genuine self-realization.

Theories of justice related to the concept of reflexive freedom also displayed significant differences resulting from these distinct orientations. The Kantian idea of moral autonomy led to a procedural theory of justice: "the procedure of individual self-determination is transferred to a higher stage of the social order once it is viewed as a shared process of will-formation."[18] By contrast, the type of reflexive freedom that understands freedom as self-realization developed into two different theories of justice: the first type is relatively individualized and is represented by John Stuart Mill (1806–1873), who stressed that society must ensure that individuals are able to discover and realize their own true selves in the course of their lives without ever experiencing any restrictions. The crucial point in Mill's theory is his introduction of the "harm-principle" as a basic guarantee that individuals can dispose over the space necessary for self-realization. The second type is more collectivist in orientation and is represented by Hannah Arendt (1906–1975), who advocated a liberal republicanism where democratic deliberation functions as a collective form of self-realization.

Honneth indicates that the reflexive mode of freedom and its concomitant conceptions of justice are clearly preferable to negative freedom and its theories of justice because of the importance the former attaches to procedures of subjective interaction and the emphasis it places on a spirit of cooperation within the social system. However, in his view, reflexive freedom still fails to turn the social conditions which actually make the realization of freedom possible into a constitutive part of freedom itself and does not sufficiently take these conditions into account in its theorization of freedom. It is precisely this criticism that allows us to understand why a third type of freedom came to be introduced.

Georg Wilhelm Friedrich Hegel (1770–1831) was the first thinker in history to put forward this third form of freedom, which Honneth, following Frederick Neuhouser's terminology, summarizes as "social freedom." For Hegel, freedom should not be understood only as the absence of external constraints, nor should it be restricted to inner self-determination, but rather ought to be genuinely realized within the objective system of social life. In other words, whereas negative freedom is unable to reach into the inner depth of freedom, reflexive freedom cannot accommodate its objective dimension. Only a concept of social freedom allows us to overcome these flaws by approaching the system of social life as the objective settling place where freedom can come into its own. To borrow the methodological triad and the triadic categories often used by Hegel, we can say that if negative freedom denotes the "possibility" of freedom and reflexive freedom counts as the "necessity" of freedom, then social freedom constitutes the "actuality" of freedom. It is only by means of this third stage that we can arrive at a genuine unity between the previous two stages of freedom.

In this respect, it should be stressed that we would be sorely mistaken in following the common assumption that Hegel's idea of social freedom implies that individuals endowed with a free will of their own will ultimately have to approach their own compliance with the objective system of social life as the true fulfillment of their freedom. Although the notion of social freedom put forward by Hegel is indeed logically predicated on that of reflexive freedom, it does not primarily manifest itself as a quest for freedom understood as increased reflexivity and self-determination, but rather as a requirement directed at objective reality, that is, at the objective system of social life, or in other words, as an expectation that the system of social life should be able to meet the requirements of freedom and conform to the norms of freedom. It is only then that a system of social life can rationally function as a genuine settling place where individual freedom can be fulfilled. Honneth's concept of a "normative reconstruction" of the system of social life can be used to convey what Hegel means, although he has another motive for introducing this concept, namely, to confront the theoretical task specific to the post-Hegelian period and the contemporary situation, in which Western society is still trying to free itself from Hegel's philosophy of spirit.

As a form of social analysis, normative reconstruction at the same time provides a method for designing a theory of justice. In this regard, we have to begin by identifying those forms of social life that have a universal value and are of the utmost importance for realizing human freedom. Hegel calls these "ethics" (*lunli* 伦理) in order to differentiate them from a type of "morality" that remains at the level of the inner life of individuals. In concrete terms, ethics consists of three dimensions, namely, the family, civil society, and the state. A large portion of the *Outlines of the Philosophy of Right* is concerned with providing a normative reconstruction of these three elements on the basis of the idea of freedom. Accordingly, friendship and love come to function as important examples drawn from intimate everyday experience that serve to unfold such a reconstruction, which revolves around the category of the mutual recognition between equals grounded in individual freedom.[19]

In short, a reconstruction of the family, civil society, and the state can be accomplished through the mutual recognition between equal individuals. Put differently, even though the modes of recognition proper to the family, civil, and the state are different, they all must be grounded in relations of equality between free individuals. In turn, logically speaking, after such a system of social life has been normatively reconstructed, it can provide free individuals with the proper normative requirements. In other words, "individuals can only experience and realize freedom if they participate in social institutions characterized by practices of mutual recognition."[20] It is precisely by departing from the idea of a mutual recognition of free and equal individuals that Hegel manages to "unite the basis for freedom with its realization."[21] As such, this idea was both a new version of liberalism, but would later also become an important intellectual resource for communitarianism. I should add here that if we consider Hegel's use of the concept of "ethics" (*lunli* 伦理) and the enormous influence exerted on the Chinese intellectual context by the Confucian tradition with its focus on the principles (*li* 理) governing human relations (*renlun* 人伦), I would be more inclined to summarize the Hegelian conception of freedom as a "freedom of the principles behind human relations" (*lunli ziyou* 伦理自由). Additionally, it goes without saying that the logic of normative reconstruction can entail a critical dimension and serve as a resource for engaging in critique. We probably need only push the logic of normative reconstruction a bit further to encounter Marx, specifically the young Marx.

After this brief overview of the concept of freedom and the related conceptions of freedom in Western intellectual history, let us return to the problem we started out from in the above. A series of external factors undoubtedly played a role in driving Wang Guowei to suicide. In this respect, his actions can be analyzed as constituting a search for freedom in the face of adverse external pressure, so that death comes to count as an act of defiance. In other words, the concept of negative freedom is not entirely irrelevant in this context. That being said, if we pursue our analysis by bearing in mind that Chen Yinke uses the sentence "through his death he showed his independent and free will" in describing Wang's suicide in the "Lament," we might say that Chen interprets Wang's death mainly as an expression of an inner freedom of the will or of freedom understood as self-determination. This would mean taking reflexive freedom as our central interpretative concept. However, if we bring the Lament's crucial appraisal of Wang having "serenely sacrificed himself for the sake of the weightiest of human relations" into the equation, we are bound to discover that we would be mistaken in merely interpreting Chen's evaluation of Wang's death on the level of free will. Arguably, the concept of free will can provide a convincing account that Wang Guowei's suicide stemmed purely from his own genuine aspirations, but it fails to explain why he died for the sake of the relation between ruler and servant. It goes without saying that, in Wang's case, the realization of his own freedom could not go without a resistance against possible outside pressures and required inner, rational reflection as a determination of will grounded in such reflection. But this is still not the whole story. The most rational and adequate interpretation can only be that Wang considered the kind of freedom he was after only to be truly attainable by putting the relation between ruler and servant into practice. This means that we can arrive at a satisfying interpretation of the reason why Chen Yinke described Wang's death as an expression of "spiritual independence and freedom of thought" only by means of the Hegelian concept of ethical freedom.[22] One additional comment might be in order here. The merit of the interpretation proposed here is not only that the notion of ethical freedom can explain the central idea of "realizing subjective freedom within objective interpersonal relations" (for which Hegel used the expression "preserving oneself within the other"), but also that ethical freedom does not entail a dismissive attitude toward negative and reflexive freedom, but rather can overcome their respective deficiencies by sublating them at a higher level.

Surprising as this solution will in all likelihood appear to most interpreters, it is precisely through the concept of ethical freedom that we are able to resolve the problem of the textual discontinuity between the "Lament" and the "Memorial Inscription."[23] If we retrace our steps and return to the Confucian theory of human relations, we encounter the well-known fact that the "weightiest of human relations," those between father and son, husband and wife, and ruler and servant were traditionally considered to something "no-one under heaven and on earth can escape from." In other words, these relations do not merely refer to the circumstances of actual daily life, but also constitute the most important factor allowing human beings to shape their own personal identity within everyday existence. To borrow Aristotle's terminology, there is no doubt that the Confucian understanding of human relations conveys the following understanding in its own manner: human beings are by nature ethical, that is to say, relational, animals. In this context, "ethics" (*lunli*) obviously compromises crucial domains of existence such as the family, civil society, and the state.[24] As to the question whether these relations aren't already completely out of touch with modern society and run contrary to its most basic ideas, Hegel would seem to have already provided an answer to this question, as I argued above. In my view, we can find a very similar answer in Chen Yinke's evaluation of Wang Guowei's death.[25]

What Hegel does is precisely to approach the "weightiest of human relations" that ancient society attached so much importance to as the objective domain that compromises the most important human modes of existence and is endowed with universal value, while engaging in a normative reconstruction of these relations on the basis of the modern concept of individual freedom. In doing so, he goes on to introduce a set of rational restrictions on the modern outlook on freedom, which apply both to a negative form of freedom that remains at the level of an absence of external constraints, as well as to reflexive freedom as concerned with inner reflection, thereby ultimately integrating them into his concept of ethical freedom. Although Hegel's undertaking was deeply influenced by Aristotle, his point of departure still remained the modern conception of individual freedom. What we should probably point out here is that in confronting the actual modes of existence in modern society and under the influence of studies in political economy, Hegel also considered the market to be an objective system of mutual recognition between free and equal individuals and attempted to provide a normative reconstruction of the market by describing it as a "system of needs."

This synthesis of the way of life in the ancient Greek polis with a modern theory of freedom implies that Hegel put forward a comprehensive program for reconciling past and present in confronting the problem of modernity. I am convinced that, in the context of his own encounter with modernity in China, Chen Yinke would have approved of Hegel's methodological approach of establishing a connection between past and present. The expression "spiritual independence and freedom of thought" in the "Memorial Inscription" provide us with an important clue in this respect. For instance, as many others have already noted, we can find a further elaboration of this expression in Chen's late works "On the Ballad *The Karmic Bonds of Rebirth*" (*Lun Zaisheng yuan* 论再生缘) *and An Alternative Biography of Liu Rushi* (*Liu Rushi biezhuan* 刘如是别传). In his depictions of the female poet Chen Duansheng 陈端生 (1751–ca. 1796), who wrote the ballad *The Karmic Bonds of Rebirth*, and the famous courtesan and poet Liu Rushi 柳

如是 (1618–1664), it becomes apparent that Chen is hardly sparing in using terms such as "independence" and "freedom." Additionally, he clearly refers to the "three bonds" in a critical manner and mentions "conflicts between the system of society and individual emotions." Although I cannot offer a detailed analysis at this instance, I would still like to make the general point that in Chen Yinke's later works, which are sometimes described through the verse "all that is left to do in writing books is singing the praises of female beauty," there remains a clear concern with interpersonal relations. "Singing the praises of female beauty" actually comes down to rethinking the problem of gender relations in the face of modernity. For a tradition such as the Confucian one, which puts a great deal of stock in the spiritually transformative dimension of the family, the problem of gender relations is obviously of supreme importance and is thus related to the notion of the "weightiest of human relations." Moreover, as I have indicated above, Hegel too approaches love as an exemplary instance of relations of equal and mutual recognition between free individuals in modern society. Needless to say, the kind of patriotism embodied by the figure of the Ming loyalist Liu Rushi was also one of the main reasons why Chen considered her to be "one of the most ideal personalities realized in everyday life of the last four hundred years." As a matter of fact, in a diary entry by Wu Mi following a meeting with Chen on the first of September 1961, Wu already pointed out that "Yinke's researches into the life-experiences and writings of 'female beauties' are actually a means to inquire into the actual conditions of politics (the distinction between Chinese and barbarians) and morality (integrity) at the time. There must be a profound sense in what he is doing, it is certainly not just a matter of carefree sophistication."[26] According to the traditional Confucian conception, the so-called "distinction between Chinese and barbarians" essentially revolves around the question of whether or not interpersonal relations function as universal values within human existence. Likewise, moral integrity can be realized only within these relations.

To this day, the project of connecting the past and the present contained in Chen Yinke's historical researches has been left unfinished and will remain highly significant for us in the future. Especially on a philosophical level, this project has not really been seriously initiated. In the thirties and forties of the previous century, He Lin pursued Chen's train of thought in his own work, but with only very limited results. Moreover, after the establishment of the People's Republic in 1949, his efforts in this direction were interrupted. In sum, a normative reconstruction of the "five relations" grounded in the modern concept of individual freedom is still one of the most pressing issues we have to confront.[27] If we are to truly embark on this project, we will have to avoid the following two possible misconceptions: the first of these would be to provide a conservative defense of the traditional Confucian conception of interpersonal relations while completely ignoring the modern concept of individual freedom, which would come down to refusing to provide a normative reconstruction of these relations grounded in the mutual recognition between equal individuals. A second mistake would consist in propagating the modern idea of individual freedom in an exaggerated manner, which would lead to a lopsided understanding of freedom that remains at the level of negative or reflexive freedom, thereby rendering us incapable of coming to terms with the profound significance of ethical freedom. If the first mistake could be said to be recognized by most interpreters, which means that it might not be the real problem after all, the second mistake requires a constant vigilance on our part to avoid letting it slip from view.[28] Additionally, a normative reconstruction of human relations also has the ability to serve as resource for critical theory. Accordingly, if this Hegelian normative reconstruction is related to a specific theory of society, it can also be extended into the domain of the social sciences.

Notes

This chapter was translated by Ady Van den Stock (Ghent University, Belgium).

1. Chen Yinke 陈寅恪, "Lament for Wang Guowei, Accompanied by a Preface" (*Wang Guantang xiansheng wanci bing xu* 王观堂先生挽词并序), in *Writings of Chen Yinke: the Collected Poems, followed by the poems compiled by Tang Yun* (*Chen Yinke ji, shiji, fu Tang Yun shicun* 陈寅恪集, 诗集, 附唐篔诗存). Beijing: Sanlian shudian (2009, 12–17). Apart from the main text, this volume also contains a number of statements by Chen recorded by his wife Tang Yun 唐篔 (1898–1969), as well as his student Jiang Tianshu's 蒋天枢 (1903–1988) afterthoughts and comments. In what follows, the abbreviation "Lament" will be used for this text without any additional footnotes.

2. Chen Yinke 陈寅恪, "Memorial Inscription for Wang Guowei's Monument at Tsinghua University" (*Qinghua daxue Wang Guantang xiansheng jinianbei ming* 清华大学王观堂先生纪念碑铭), in *Writings of Chen Yinke, Second Volume of the Collected Drafts from the Jinming Manshion* (*Chen Yinke ji, Jinming guan conggao er bian* 陈寅恪集, 金明馆丛稿二编), Beijing: Sanlian shudian 2009, 246. Abbreviated to "Memorial Inscription" in what follows without any additional footnotes.

3. Li Shenzhi 李慎之, "Spiritual Independence and Freedom of Thought—on Chen Yinke as an Intellectual" (*Duli zhi jingshen, ziyou zhi sixiang—lun zuowei*

sixiangjia de Chen Yinke 独立之精神，自由之思想——论作为思想家的陈寅恪), *Huangdan chunqiu* 炎黄春秋 (1999, vol. 12).

4. Tr. note: see Tang's comments in footnote 24.

5. Tr. note: See *Baihutong shuzheng* 白虎通疏证, Beijing: Zhonghua shuju (1994, *juan* 8, 373): "What are the three bonds? Those between ruler and servant, father and son, and husband and wife. The six connections refer to [the various relations between] paternal uncles, older and younger brothers, clan members, maternal uncles, teachers, and friends." (三纲者何谓也? 谓君臣、父子、夫妇也。六纪者，谓诸父、兄弟、族人、诸舅、师长、朋友也).

6. [Tr. note: *Analects* 18:7; translation quoted, with modifications, from Edward Slingerhand, *Confucian Analects, with Selections from Traditional Commentaries*, Indianapolis: Hackett (2003, 218).] For a detailed analysis of the different attitudes displayed by hermits and Confucianists toward the problem of ordinary human relationships and of the importance of the bond between ruler and servant in Confucianism, see my "The Existential Ideals of Hermits and the Political Concerns of Confucianists," in *The World of Life and the World of Thought* (*Shenghuo shijie yu sixiang shijie* 生活世界与思想世界), volume 11 in the series *Thought and Culture* (*Sixiang yu wenhua* 思想与文化), edited by Yang Guorong 杨国荣, Shanghai: Huadong shifandaxue chubanshe (2011).

7. In the second part of the chapter "Discourses of Yue" (*Yueyu* 越语) in the *Discourses of the States* (*Guoyu* 国语), the following statement is attributed to Fan Li 范蠡: "I have heard that a person who acts as a servant must console his ruler when he is grieved and will die when he is dishonored" (臣闻之，为人臣者，君忧臣劳，君辱臣死).

8. It is obvious that when He Lin later wrote his "A New Investigation into the Concept of the Five Relations" (*Wu lun guannian xin jiantao* 五伦观念新检讨) in clear opposition to what had become the mainstream since the New Culture Movement, this was due to the fact that he had been greatly influenced by Chen Yinke. To put it more simply, He Lin's text counts as a philosophical exposition of the viewpoints introduced in Chen's "Lament." [Tr. note: for a detailed discussion of He's text, see the author's "Reconsidering the Concept of the Five Relations: A Rereading of He Lin's *A New Investigation into the Concept of the Five Relations*" (*Wu lun guannian de zai jiantao – zaidu He Lin 'Wu lun guannian xin jiantao* 五伦观念的再检讨——在读贺麟《五伦观念新检讨》), in Tang Wenming 唐文明, *Proximate Concerns: Cultural Politics and the Future of China* (*Jin you: wenhua zhengzhi yu Zhongguo de weilai* 近忧: 文化政治与中国的未来), Shanghai: Huadong shifandaxue chubanshe (2010, 67–80).]

9. The following three points deserve further attention: first, if the word "family of the Han" (*hanjia* 汉家) in the opening verses of the "Lament" ("It has been ten years since disaster struck the family of the Han") is taken as referring to the Qing dynasty, this implies that Chen interpreted Wang Guowei's approach to the distinction between "barbarians and Chinese" in the following manner: although

those in power belonged to the Manchu race, the Qing dynasty was still part of the main Chinese lineage, simply because it upheld Confucianism. As is well known, this approach has its origins in the *Spring and Autumn Annals* (*Chunqiu* 春秋), more specifically in the notion that "when the barbarians enter into China, they will be Sinicized." Second, after pointing toward the import of the idea that Wang "serenely sacrificed himself for human relations through his death," Chen pays particular attention to portraying Wang as a scholar, which is not at all inconsistent with his previous train of thought. Third, in a footnote Chen himself indicates that the overarching theme of the entire poem is described in the following lines: "Alas! The troops they had trained became traitors and they were overrun. Empress Dowager Xiaoding wept bitterly. Then there rose up a servant who was the backbone of the demons and the head of the rebels [Tr. note: this quote from Du Fu's 杜甫 "A Song for the Arab Sword" (*Dashi dao ge* 大食刀歌) most likely refers to Yuan Shikai 袁世凱 (1859–1916)], who supplanted the lineage of the widow and her orphaned son." This makes it clear that the description of Wang's suicide in the "Lament" is closely tied to the demise of the Qing empire.

10. In the "Lament" is a verse that reads "But when both worthies and fools pronounce judgement on life and death, they should not confuse a short and a long life with wrong and right." Wu Mi and Jiang Tianshu both indicate that this was meant as a refutation of Lu Maode's 陆懋德 (1885–ca.1961) text "Why Wang Guowei Ought not to Have Killed Himself" (*Wei Wang xiansheng bu ying zisha* 谓王先生不应自杀), which suffices to make clear that Chen was suspicious of any sort of critique of Wang's suicide.

11. See Axel Honneth, *Freedom's Right: the Social Foundations of Democratic Life*, New York: Columbia University Press (2013, ch. 1). To date, Honneth's work is the best available on the history of liberalism, both in terms of its approach of conceptual history and of the actual practices surrounding the concept of freedom, as well as in its combined attention for normative and critical theory. Unfortunately, so far it has escaped the attention of Chinese scholars. My understanding of the concept of freedom in the current text draws primarily on the views Honneth articulates in this book.

12. Tr. note: See Thomas Hobbes, *Leviathan*, edited by A.P. Martinich, Toronto: Broadview Press (2005, part 1, ch. 14, 98).

13. Honneth, *Freedom's Right*, 23.

14. Honneth, *Freedom's Right*, 23.

15. Honneth, *Freedom's Right*, 28.

16. Honneth, *Freedom's Right*, 27–28.

17. This does not mean, however, that reflexive freedom developed out of negative freedom. Actually, as Honneth clearly points out, whereas the concept of negative freedom is modern through and through, the intellectual origins of reflexive freedom can be traced back to ancient society.

18. Honneth, *Freedom's Right*, 37.

19. After discussing the "bond between ruler and servant" in the passage concerning the "three bonds and the five connections" from the "Lament" quoted above, Chen Yinke touches on the "connection between friends," as if he is merely giving an example in passing. Perhaps there is something more to this than meets the eye. In ancient times, the idea already existed that the relation between ruler and servant is actually derived from the bond between friends, although there are important differences between their respective normative requirements. However, maybe what Chen wanted to argue for is remolding all relations in which there is no equality between the parties concerned on the basis of the relation of friendship.

20. Honneth, *Freedom's Right*, 49.

21. Honneth, *Freedom's Right*, 49.

22. In Confucian discourse, theories concerning the heart-mind and human nature (*xin xing* 心性) directly point toward the concept of freedom. In this text, I focus on discussing freedom within the Confucian conception of human relations without providing a further analysis of how this problem is related to these two theories. Since in the intellectual framework of Song-Ming Confucianism, human relations are the most central and significant element of the concept of "heavenly principle" (*tianli* 天理), the problem of the relation between heavenly principle on the one hand and the heart-mind and human nature on the other actually corresponds to that between human relations and freedom in a very crucial and important sense. This allows us to grasp the significance of the fact that Song-Ming Confucianists put forward the idea that "human nature is the same as principle" (*xing ji li* 性即理) and "the heart-mind is identical to principle" (*xin ji li* 心即理) (I cannot discuss the differences between these two theses in greater detail here). In other words, ethical freedom, as the freedom of human relations, is really a crucial problem within Song-Ming Confucianism. From a slightly different angle, we could also say that freedom can only be absorbed into and realized within interpersonal relations by bringing the fundamental relation between heavenly principle and the heart-mind and human nature to light.

23. As for the reason I still consider the interpretation of the phrase "spiritual independence and freedom of thought" as an expression of personal integrity or a pursuit of intellectuals on an academic level to be well founded and reasonable, I would argue that apart from the fact that academic freedom can be rationally derived from the notion of ethical freedom, we should also take into account something much more straightforward. In "A Reply to the Academy of Science" (*Dui kexueyuan de dafu* 对科学院的答复) from 1953, a reply that was recorded by his student Wang Jian 汪籛 (1916–1966), Chen Yinke elaborates on the idea of academic freedom by building on the text of the "Memorial Inscription." One of the objective reasons that allowed him to do so was that the "Memorial Inscription" was primarily addressed to the community of teachers and students at Tsinghua University.

24. Formulated in the language of the "five relations": the ties between father and son, husband and wife, and between siblings correspond to the domain of the

family; the bond between friends to that of society, and the relation between ruler and servant to that of the state. Moreover, while Aristotle mainly refers to political life in claiming that "human beings are political animals by nature," in contrast, the Confucian idea that "human beings are relational animals by nature" would seem to express the equal importance attached to the familial and political life of human beings.

25. Those who misinterpret the relation between ruler and servant as one of outright subordination might argue that if we follow Chen's line of reasoning, we can conclude that the fact that Wang sacrificed himself for this relation is an expression of his "voluntary enslavement." Such a view is actually based on a misunderstanding of the relation between ruler and servant. The expressions "letting the ruler be a ruler" (*jun jun* 君君) and "letting the minister be a minister" (*chen chen* 臣臣) [Tr. note: see *Analects* 12:11] do not merely entail a normative expectation toward the servant, but also toward the ruler. In other words, the ruler and the servant each have a way (*dao* 道) of their own. Chen Yinke was clearly aware of this and would obviously disagree with such a misinterpretation. Additionally, Hegel's Christian background made him deny people the right to commit suicide, although he did defend the legitimacy of dying "in the service of the Idea" and even argued that the act of suicide "may . . . be regarded as an act of courage." [Tr. note: The reader should note that Hegel immediately goes on to add "but only the false courage of tailors and servant girls."] See G.W.F. Hegel, *Outlines of the Philosophy of Right*, translated by T.M. Knox, Oxford: Oxford University Press (2008, section 70, 82–83).

26. Quoted in Wu Xuezhao 吴学昭, *Wu Mi and Chen Yinke* (*Wu Mi yu Chen Yinke* 吴宓与陈寅恪), Beijing: Sanlian shudian (2014, 431).

27. The continuing relevance of a normative reconstruction of the relation between ruler and servant would, in a nutshell, involve reconstructing it as the relation between the state and its citizens.

28. Although a novel understanding of human relations from the perspective of negative and reflexive freedom may at first sight also seem to qualify as a normative reconstruction, the result of such a reconstruction may actually turn out to be a deconstruction of these relations. This means that although I propose providing a normative reconstruction of human relations on the basis of the modern concept of individual freedom, such relations should still be broader in scope than those involved in the mutual recognition between equal and free individuals. This is precisely where the significance of ethical freedom as a form of freedom within human relations is to be located. Otherwise, there would be no point in talking about ethical freedom to begin with. On a related note, although this approach has certain Hegelian characteristics, some crucial aspects of Hegel's project of normative reconstruction are totally unacceptable from a Confucian standpoint. Apart from the fact that such a normative reconstruction cannot be grounded in a Hegelian philosophy of spirit, there are also some serious problems with Hegel's normative

reconstruction of the family. In brief, Hegel was aware of the disintegration of the traditional family, but his normative reconstruction was not based on the traditional conception of the family, but rather on a new conceptualization, in which marriage comes to constitute the axis, if not the totality, of family life. This point of divergence with Hegel is where we should start out from in our future efforts, while bearing in mind that nothing clearly indicates that either Chen Yinke or He Lin had already come to this realization.

Chapter 7

Life as Aesthetic Creativity and Appreciation
The Confucian Aim of Learning

PEIMIN NI

Xu Fuguan 徐复观, a major representative of contemporary new Confucianism, believes that the Chinese aesthetic spirit reflected in both Confucianism and Daoism aims at dissolving biological functions and letting subjectivity emerge. Once the dichotomies of subject and object, self and society, and human and nature are overcome in the process of transformative cultivation, humans can roam in the transforming and nourishing process of heaven and earth. That is what "overcoming the self," "no ego," "no self," and "losing myself" mean. The emergence of subjectivity is both the completion of the person's humanity and the unification of the subject and the myriad objects. Therefore, one of the most striking differences between Chinese culture and Western culture is that, at the fountainhead of Chinese culture, there were no dichotomies between subject and object and between individual and community (Xu 1983, 132). In this regard, Confucianism and Daoism carry the same spirit.

However, Xu takes Daoism, and Zhuangzi in particular, as the best representative of the Chinese aesthetic spirit. He believes that the Confucian aesthetic spirit is filtered through morality, whereas in Daoism, especially in Zhuangzi, the unity between life and art is more direct. Confucian subjectivity appears more as a moral subjectivity, and Daoist subjectivity appears to be more an aesthetic one (Xu 1983, 82).

This view reflects a common assumption that the primary concern of Confucianism is morality. Aesthetic activities and enjoyment is valuable for Confucians only because it serves the function of contributing to the utility of moral education and moral transformation, or in a moderate version of the view: aesthetic enjoyment is secondary in importance in comparison with morality. Feng Youlan says, in his famous *A Short History of Chinese Philosophy*, that "The Confucianists took art as an instrument for moral education" (Feng 1948, 23). Li Zehou also holds such a view. He says that Confucians "emphasize the human efforts and external function of art," whereas Daoists "emphasize nature, or the independence of beauty and art. . . . If we say that, because of its narrow pragmatic utilitarian framework, the former often lead to the limitation, damage, and destruction to art and aesthetic experience, then the latter offers exactly the strong impact needed for breaking and negating the framework and limitation" (Li 1981, 54). Following the same view, Ye Lang says in his book the *History of Chinese Aesthetics*: "Why does Confucius value art and artistic experience? Because he thinks that art and artistic experience can perform positive functions in social life." "He thinks that aesthetic experience and art have profound influences on human spirit, and hence they can perform a special function in people's cultivation of themselves toward the spiritual realm of becoming human-hearted" (Ye 1996, 31, 32). The view is shared by Western scholars in Eastern philosophy as well. For instance, Stephen J. Goldberg, in his essay "Chinese Aesthetics" in *A Companion to World Philosophies*, writes, "One of the ways of seeking moral perfection, of becoming an authoritative person (*ren*), is through the practice of art as a means of self-cultivation" (Goldberg 1997, 226).

In this chapter I want to argue that the received view is questionable. It seems to me that the highest aim of Confucian learning is an aesthetic ideal rather than a moralistic one. In other words, the fundamental aim of Confucianism is to reach a state of aesthetic enjoyment and creativity. Morality is either part of the highest aim, in which it is part of the aesthetic beauty, or a means for arriving at the aesthetic beauty and enjoyment. In saying this, I do not mean to deny that, in the process of personal development, the practice of art can also be a means for moral cultivation. The relationship between morality and artistic life can be mutual/reciprocal. What I want to argue is merely that the ultimate aim of Confucian learning is more aesthetic than is moral.

I

I will begin with the observation that the received view is hard to square with what is known as the Zeng Dian *qixiang* 曾点气象 or Zeng Dian spirit as described in 11.26 of the *Analects*. The passage records a conversation between Confucius and his four close disciples, Zilu, Zeng Xi (aka Zeng Dian), Ran You, and Zihua. The Master said, with an obvious intention to create a relaxed atmosphere and to encourage the students to speak up their mind, "Though I may be a day or so older than you, do not think of that. You often say, 'No one recognizes my worth.' If someone were to recognize your worth, what would you do?" Following the Master's invitation, the four students expressed their wishes. Zilu said that his wish was to govern a state that is in trouble and to bring it back to a sure direction. Ran You's wish was to rule a small territory and to bring prosperity to the people within three years. Zihua stated his wish modestly: that he wanted to serve diligently as a minor officer and do his job well. Only Zeng Dian, after plucking a final note on his zither to bring the music to an end and setting his instrument aside, said that he would choose something different from the rest. Here is how Zeng Dian expressed his wish:

> In late spring, when the dresses of the season are made ready, I would like to take along five or six young men and six or seven boys, to bathe in the Yi River, enjoy the breeze at the Rain Altar, and then return home singing.

From the received view, one would expect that the Master would endorse the first three disciples' wishes, for they all expressed willingness to serve the state or the community, whereas Zeng Dian's wish appeared to be nothing but for personal enjoyment. However, the Master surprisingly said that he endorsed Zeng Dian's wish!

Let us take a closer look at Zeng Dian's wish and the manner in which he expressed it. He wanted to go out at the end of the spring, a season when it is warm enough to wear light spring clothes for some outdoor recreation. It is also the time when everything is actively growing and taking its own course of reviving. Zeng Dian seems to be seeing the ideal of Confucian learning to be reaching a state when there is no need to be busy doing things, no need to have moralistic ambition, but spontaneous participation in the revival of everything, enjoying and celebrating the transformation of heaven and earth. In the case of the other three disciples, they all showed signs of *yi* 意, conjecture (or, following Arthur Waley's translation, "taking things for granted") and *bi* 必, demanding certainty, which the Master abstained from (*Analects* 9.4). The recorder of the conversation carefully noted the way Zeng Dian brought up his point, as the manner is itself part of the message: he did not anxiously wait for his turn. Even when the other three finished their remarks and he was asked by his Master "What about you, Zengxi?" he kept playing his music to the end and then put aside his zither and rose up to make his own statement. Song dynasty Confucian Cheng Hao 程顥 says that this very relaxed manner is actually the spirit of the ancient sage kings Yao and Shun, because what they wanted to achieve is nothing but letting everything to take their own proper course.[1] The manner itself demonstrates the ideal hinted at in section 15.5 of the *Analects*, where Shun is said to be governing in a nonassertive manner (*wuwei*, or action of nonaction).[2]

Of course this interpretation of the Confucian ideal can easily slip into Zen or Daoism. The problem of Zen and Daoism, in the eyes of the Confucians, is the lack of practical wisdom in seeing the value of *ren* and *li*. But the passage reminds us that, on the other hand, those who take *ren* and *li* seriously often fail to transcend the daily routines and have the vision of Zeng Dian, hence falling short of seeing the aesthetic aim of Confucian learning.[3]

We can see the same point through reading many other passages in the *Analects*. Passage 7.6, for instance, places "*you yu yi* 游于艺," or sojourn in the arts, as the highest ideal, above other stages of practice, such as "Set your will on the way. Have a firm grasp on virtue. Rely on humanity." Reading the passage as a process of cultivation, we can see that setting one's sights or will on the way that one hopes to walk, getting a firm grasp on virtue, and relying on humanity are all conceived as means or stages for reaching the final ideal state of sojourning in artistic creativity, in which one needs no more efforts and focus on the *dao*, the virtues, and humanity, a stage that reminds us of passage 2.4 of the *Analects*, where Confucius is said to be able to follow his heart's will freely and contently, without overstepping the lines. It also reminds us of the statement in the *Book of Zhongyong*, where harmony is described as the ability to "hit right on the mark all the time" (*Zhongyong*, ch. 1). Following the received view about Confucianism we mentioned before, people often take the "lines" and the "marks" as moral norms and moral standards, as if the aim of Confucian cultivation is to set self-constraints so that one would never want to deviate from them. It is, however, much more reasonable to take Confucianism not as pre-supposing any external constraints or norms to limit people's freedom, but to the contrary, as advocating certain constraints and norms so as to lead people to freedom. From the point of view of "sojourning in the arts," the lines or norms are *gongfu* methods, just like basic rules of how to hold the brush and write the strokes are taken to be necessary for becoming a calligraphy artist. The norms are by no means the end purpose; they are ways to write well that calligraphy artists in the past learned from their own practice experiences. True calligraphy artists are not those who follow basic rules rigidly without ever crossing the line. For them, basic rules are not external constraints that limit what they can do, but guidance that would lead them to the right direction, until they become master artists and are able to put aside the rules. Confucius says, "There are some with whom we may pursue learning, but not go along in pursuing the Way. There are some with whom we may go along in pursuing the Way, but not take a stand together. There are some with whom we can take a stand together, but not jointly exercise discretion (*quan* 权)" (*Analects* 9.30). This is a process of gradual improvement. Here the highest stage, *quan*, is the *gongfu* or art of being able to hit the mark constantly without rigid adherence to rules.

Similarly, passage 8.8 of the *Analects* puts "*cheng yu yue* 成于乐," finding fulfillment or consummation in music/enjoyment, as a result of getting inspiration from the *Book of Songs* and taking a stand from observing ritual proprieties. The word for "*yue* 乐," music, is also the word for "*le*," enjoyment. In this context it is actually more appropriate to read it as "*le*," because the three sentences in a row indicate stages of personal development, from getting inspiration or motivation to taking a stand and finally reaching fulfillment or consummation. For Confucius, "knowing that it cannot be done and yet doing it" (*Analects* 14.38) is at its best when one "takes pleasure" in doing it (*Analects* 6.20). When Duke of She asked Zilu about Confucius, and Zilu did not answer, Confucius said: "Why did you not say that he is a man who in his eager pursuit would forget his meals, in his joy forget his worries, and does not notice the approach of old age?" (*Analects* 7.19). The word "forget" is a strong indication of the pure non-utilitarian aesthetic ideal. These passages reflect that the ideal of Confucian learning is not in morality, not being moral for the sake of being moral. It is the opposite—morality is valuable because of its utilitarian function of leading to the aesthetic ideal (which is itself non-utilitarian, and it works best when not done for the sake of utility). Once the ideal is achieved, there is no need to worry about morality. One simply follows the will of the heart-mind without overstepping the line and enjoys the freedom. "When the Way is under heaven, the common people will not dispute [about state affairs]" (*Analects* 16.2). The saying reminds us of the Confucian ideal to have no litigation, in contrast with having a strong administrative and legal order (*Analects* 12.13).

These texts all show that Confucius' highest ideal is not morality, or more accurately, not the Kantian kind of morality that is for the sake of being moral. His highest ideal is an artistic life. For him, the value of morality lies in its utilitarian function of generating aesthetic ideals, ideals that are themselves beyond utility. It is better to conceive what he teaches as artistic styles of life, and not as merely moral norms. When we think of an ideal personality that Confucius wants to cultivate, we should not come up with an image of a rigid adherer of moral rules but a lively person who is able to follow his or her heart's wishes and hit the proper target all the time. Of course in order to reach that goal, one would have to begin with mimicking exemplars and follow basic protocols. The relevance of nuances of Confucius' way of greeting guests, and so on, as they are recorded in Book 10 of the *Analects* and the importance laid on following good models all make perfect sense here.

The same can be said about Mencius's vision. Though Mencius does not talk much about art and beauty, from the perspective of cultivating an artistic life, the whole book of *Mencius* can be considered a work about aesthetics. Passage 7B:25 of *Mencius* summarizes the vision well:

> Hao-sheng Pu-hai asked, "What sort of a man is Yueh-cheng Tzu?"
>
> "A good man," said Mencius. "A true man."
>
> "What do you mean by 'good' and 'true'?"
>
> "The desirable is called 'good.' To have it in oneself is called 'true.' To possess it fully in oneself is called 'beautiful,' but to shine forth with this full possession is called 'great.' To be great and be transformed by this greatness is called 'sage'; to be sage and to transcend the understanding is called 'divine.' Yueh-cheng Tzu has something of the first two qualities but has not quite reached the last four."

In this passage, "desirable" or "he who commands our liking" is called "good" or "excellent," and "excellence," when embodied, is considered "beautiful" or, in other words, an aesthetic ideal. The rest of the higher stages are all degrees of this aesthetic ideal: when the beauty shines with an ostensible gleam, it is "great"; when the great becomes transformative, it is "sagely"; and when the sagely arouses awe in a way that people don't know how it could be so, it is called "spiritual" or "divine." This reminds us of passage 9.11 of the *Analects*, which describes how Yan Hui finds himself unable to articulate the greatness of his Master. Indeed, it is hard to think of any better way than to put such greatness into aesthetic terms. He thoughtfully uses music and archery as metaphors to characterize the sageness of Confucius (*Mencius*, 5:B1). They both entail beauty, and in perfecting music and archery, one needs not only knowledge about what is good, but also the strength, skill, and sense of timing to perform well. In contrast, we find that according to Kant, moral goodness lies strictly in the goodness of the will, which has nothing to do with one's ability to carry out the will, whether the ability regards skill or strength.[4]

The recently discovered Guodian bamboo script "Wu Xing" also contains a theme, like a melody in a music, that appears repeatedly in the text: "Without human-heartedness there is no tranquility; without tranquility, there is no music/enjoyment, and the lack of music/enjoyment is an indication of having no virtue/virtuosity" (Wei 2005, 5, 8, and 17). The word *yue* 乐—music or enjoyment—strikes as a central notion in the text. This is fully in accord with the idea expressed in the *Book of Music*, as quoted by Sima Qian in his *Book of History*: "Virtue is the origin of one's nature; music/enjoyment is the flower of virtue." After all, the flower is what makes the plant beautiful and complete.

It is not a coincidence that the Confucian six arts are considered "arts." Unlike the way "art" is used nowadays to mean merely fine arts, traditionally in China as well as in the West, art is understood much more broadly. Life itself is the field of art, and liberal arts are the arts of living. The learning of the arts is a transformative and creative process in which the person becomes an artist of life and at the same time creates his or her life artistically. Ritual, for example, is the training of the body to be able to express oneself artistically in daily life. To sit, walk, eat, and talk in a proper manner is art. Refined by ritual propriety, a person will have the grace that enhances the natural beauty of the body profoundly. To the contrary, lacking proper manner, the natural beauty of a person will diminish dramatically, and in extreme cases, to nothing but what is of the flesh. An unsightly behavior is always opposed to ritual propriety, and a conduct in accord with ritual propriety is always elegant and aesthetically pleasing (see Ni 2002, 65).

In their book *Thinking through Confucius*, David Hall and Roger Ames show us another way in which the whole Confucian approach toward self-cultivation and the ordering of society can be considered aesthetic. In their view, the Confucian ideal is to achieve an aesthetic order. In contrast with logical or rational order, which enforces some external or transcendental rule or principle from without, the aesthetic order emerges as embodied rules and principles through self-cultivation and mutual coordination. In a logical/rational order, there is no creativity, but only consistency and continuity, whereas in an aesthetic order, individuals and communities are able to creatively interpret and re-interpret the rules and principles. In a logical/rational order, everyone is equal, because everyone is conceived abstractly as an agent, and hence they are substitutable with any other agent, whereas in an aesthetic order, individuals are concrete particulars, un-substitutable, and the inequality is a matter of deference to excellence.

Here we can return to Xu Fuguan's remarks about the Chinese aesthetic spirit in comparison with Western aesthetics. We have mentioned before that, in Xu's view, Zhangzi is the best exemplification of the Chinese aesthetic spirit. Having laid out the points above, we are now ready to read his statement with an awareness that the name "Zhuangzi" might be as well replaced by the name of "Confucius":

> The main difference between the aesthetic spirit displayed and understood by Zhuangzi and the one seen in Western aesthetic theorists is not that Zhuangzi obtained the complete and the ordinary aesthetic theorists obtained only the partial. It is rather that the difference between the complete and the partial derives from the fact that Zhuangzi obtained his understanding from his *cultivation in his life*, whereas ordinary theorists got theirs *from reasoning and generalizing* from their experiences in dealing with particular aesthetic objects and artworks. Because what they obtained are in both cases aesthetic spirits, they will coincide here and there unexpectedly. Yet since for Western aesthetic theorists, their aesthetic spirit did not sprout and generate from the root of humanity, as far as the entirety of life is concerned they would inevitably leave room uncovered in their understanding. It is therefore inevitable that what they obtain is partial. The situation is much better in Phenomenology. However, since the phenomenologists are unable to grasp *the calm and empty nature* of the heart-mind, they are only "riding the horse to look for

the horse": trying to grasp [the spirit] from its function. To explain this from our traditional ideas, they are still unable to see the substance: *the subjectivity of aesthetic spirit*. (Xu 1983, 132, italics mine)

The only thing that needs to be modified in the above quote if we replace "Zhuangzi" with "Confucius" is the phrase "the calm and empty nature of the heart-mind." For the Confucians, it is the moral subjectivity that shines through and beautifies everything it creates or encounters.

II

Now let us take a closer look at three main arguments behind the dominant view. They are (1), that not much in the Confucian classics deals with aesthetic experiences and arts; in contrast, there are abundant passages devoted to morality; (2) when Confucians talk about arts such as music, poetry, and aesthetic appreciation of nature, they often, if not always, emphasize moral implications and transformative functions of artistic experience for individuals and for society; and (3), the main Confucian aesthetic ideal, *zhonghe* 中和 (centrality and harmony), sometimes characterized as *wenrou dunhou* 温柔敦厚 (being gentle and tolerant), is apparently a moral ideal. In this section, I would like to analyze these arguments and show that they do not provide adequate support for the dominant view.

The first one is perhaps the easiest to reject. The mere fact that most of the teachings in Confucian classics are devoted to morality does not necessarily entail that morality is the ultimate aim of Confucian teachings. War is the subject of discussion in the *Art of War*, but it does not mean that the aim of the book is war. Karl Marx's *Capital* talks extensively about capital, but that does not mean its purpose is to gain capital. Confucians normally have a strong sense of anxiety about what to do (*youhuan yishi* 忧患意识), but this does not mean anxiety is their aim. Similarly, the fact that Confucian classics contain abundant teachings on morality does not entail that morality is the Confucian ideal. When people say that Confucian classics devote little to aesthetic appreciation, it is actually because they have a narrow conception of art—a conception that takes art to be confined only to what one can find in museums, galleries, theaters, and sidewalks of human life. They decorate life, and are created for the sake of entertainment. In the mind of Confucius and his followers, the six arts that Confucius taught—ritual, music, writing, arithmetic, archery, and charioting—are all arts, and they constitute the main path of human life rather than resting spots of life.

The second argument deserves more careful analysis. Let me first spend some time to articulate this argument and explain its premises with some detail. The argument is that when Confucians talk about the arts, their emphasis is always the moral implications and the transformative functions of artistic experience for individuals and for society, and not on artistic enjoyment. Despite the quotes we cited in the first section that show the opposite, the argument does seem to hold some water when we consider the Confucian classics at large.

With regard to poetry, the Master said "The *Songs* are three hundred in number. They can be covered in one expression: 'Oh, let there be no deviation' " (*Analects* 2.2). He also teaches that "Capable of reciting three hundred *Songs*, yet, when given charge of governmental affairs, unable to carry out the tasks, or when sent abroad as an envoy, unable to respond without assistance—though extensive in learning, of what practical use is it?" (*Analects* 13.5) Later this becomes *shijiao* 诗教, education with poetry. The notion first appeared in chapter "Jing Jie 经解" of *Li Ji* 礼记, the *Book of Rites*: "Confucius says: 'In entering a country, one can recognize the kind of education it has. If the people are gentle and tolerant, it is the result of education by poetry. . . . Those who are gentle and tolerant, but not dumb, are the ones deeply affected by poetry" (*Li Ji*, 273).

In talking about music, Confucius is well known for discriminating "Shao 韶" and "Wu 武," the former being "perfectly beautiful, and also perfectly good" and the latter being perfectly beautiful but not perfectly good" (*Analects* 3.25). He condemns the music from the state of Zheng because it is licentious (*Analects* 15.11) and it "confounds classic music" (*Analects* 17.18). The chapter on music in *Li Ji* emphasizes the harmonizing function of music: "Music is for the sake of unification, Ritual propriety is for differentiation. With unification people will be close to each other; with differentiation, people will respect each other. . . . When ritual propriety and appropriateness established, the superior and the inferior are properly positioned; with music and culture unifying, the upper and the lower parts of the society will be in harmony" (*Li Ji*, 207). "Ritual propriety regulate people's heart-mind, music harmonizes people's voices. . . . [with ritual and music] the way of king is complete" (*Li Ji*, 206). "Use music to govern people's heart-mind" (*Li Ji*, 219). "The music of a well governed society is peaceful and pleasant, with it the state is harmonious; the music of a chaotic society is resentful and angry, with it the state is troublesome; the music of a declining society is gloomy and yearning, with it the people are frustrated. The way of music is connected with the way of government" (*Li Ji*, 204).

In appreciation of natural beauty, Confucians invariably draw moral lessons from natural objects: Pine and cypress are beautiful because they endure harsh cold weather (*Analects* 9.28). Those who are *ren* 仁 (human hearted) love mountains, because mountains are steadfast; those who are wise love water, because water is active (*Analects* 6.23). Standing on the riverbank, the Master admires the unceasing persistence of the flow (*Analects* 9.17). Facing a hen-pheasant on the hill bridge that flew away when startled, and settled again after circling around by and by, the Master said, "How timely! How timely!" (*Analects* 10.27) This characteristic Confucian appreciation of nature in terms of moral virtue was developed into a theory called *bi de* 比德, "comparing virtues." The term first appeared in the *Xunzi*, where a conversation between Confucius and Zigong is recorded: when Zigong asked the Master why he values jade more than serpentine, "Is it because of jade's rarity and the commonness of serpentine?" The master says:

> Nonsense, Ci [Zigong]! Why would you say that! Why would exemplary persons despise something because it is common and prize something because of its rarity? Jade is what an exemplary person would compare his virtue with (*bi de*). It shines through warm, smooth texture, that is like *ren* (human-heartedness); it is tight, fully embodied, and has consistent vines, like wisdom; it is hard, strong, and would not bent, like appropriateness; it is sharp and not injurious, like proper conduct; and it would rather break but not subdue, like courage. (*Xunzi*, ch. 30; see Knoblock 1994, v. 3, 257)

Having acknowledged these facts, I would like to add some observations and analysis. First, the fact that aesthetic activities can have important moral functions does not mean that their values locate simply in these functions. We should distinguish the non-utilitarian feature of an aesthetic appreciation from an aesthetic activity's utilitarian function. The Statue of Liberty is a work of art, yet it can also serve as a landmark of New York City. We do not say that, simply because it serves the function of being a landmark, it ceases to be a work of art. Similarly, the Confucian way of life does not have to eschew its utilitarian functions in order to retain its aesthetic spirit. The unity between life and art entails a unity between utility and aesthetic appreciation, and in this sense the Confucian way of life is more characteristic of the Chinese aesthetic spirit, as we described before, than is Daoism—a spirit that makes no separation between life and aesthetics. When Xu Fuguan took uselessness as a necessary condition for a pure aesthetic spirit, he seemed to be using a nineteenth-century Western notion of "art for art's sake" (*l'art pour l'art*), which easily leads (or misleads, to be exact) to a conclusion that an activity can be more aesthetic if it is useless or disinterested. But the Statue of Liberty would not become more aesthetic if it were not taken as a landmark, nor would it otherwise be less aesthetic. The logic is simply invalid, not to mention that separation of utility and aesthetic is uncharacteristic of Chinese thought in general, and not just of Confucianism.

Similarly, the dominant view is largely based on an unwarranted assumption that we can make a sharp separation between moral and aesthetic values (granted that this assumption seems to be shared even by Confucius, as his evaluation of the music of "Shao" and "Wu" indicates). However, taking into consideration that any use of words involves abstraction, we must not let our use of words mislead us. As the Zen Buddhist saying puts it, one should not confuse the finger that points to the moon with the moon that it points to. When we conceptually separate what is morally good from what is beautiful, we are not entitled to say that in reality, good cannot be at the same time beautiful, or even beautiful exactly because of its being good. Although the music of "Wu" can be said to be not perfectly good but perfectly beautiful based on the conceptual separation of the two, if one were to consider moral goodness as part of the aesthetic value, it could be said to be not perfectly beautiful also. Confucius' remark should be taken as a way of making a contrast between "Shao" and "Wu," which needs a deliberate emphasis on the lack of the moral goodness aspect of the latter. Considering the performative function of language, analysis based merely on literal meaning of the words may not be appropriate here.[5]

It is quite natural and commonplace to consider moral goodness as a part of what makes an object beautiful. In evaluating works of Chinese calligraphy, for instance, people constantly bring in words about moral characters. Song dynasty scholar Su Shi writes that "A man without a righteous mind will inevitably show in his calligraphy some sign of obsequiousness or cruelty" (Su 1969, 2186 and 2206). His view came from a broader view first clearly stated by Zhang Huaiguan 张怀瓘 and Liu Gongquan 柳公权, both in Tang dynasty. Zhang says: "It takes several words for a sentence to convey an idea, but it takes only one written character for a piece of calligraphy to display a heart-mind" (Zhang, vol. 4). When Liu was asked by Emperor Mu Zong 穆宗 about the way to maneuver the brush, he answered, "When the heart-mind is upright, the brush will be upright" (Tao, vol. 5). This does not rule out the fact that sometimes aesthetic and moral categories can be so entangled in those evaluations that it becomes hard to say whether moral character was taken as part of aesthetics or aesthetics became subordinated by moral values. Cai Jing 蔡京, for example, was initially on the list of the four most accomplished Northern Song Dynasty calligraphers, but because of his notorious immoral reputation, his name was replaced by another calligrapher whose family name is also Cai—Cai Xiang 蔡襄. The story can be interpreted in two ways: (1) that moral value is superior to aesthetic value, and hence although Cai Jing's calligraphy was great, his moral status made him unqualified for the honor, or (2) that although his calligraphy was otherwise excellent, his immoral character showed up through the strokes and dampened its beauty. Although the first interpretation is more plausible in this particular case, people prefer to accept the second. This is like the mutual causation illustrated by the so-called "Newton's cradle"—once initiated, two balls may be set in a perpetual motion of causing one another to swing back and forth.

Looking at *bi de* 比德, comparing moral virtues, it seems plausible to take the Confucian aesthetics as a "moral account of beauty," a kind of aesthetic view that takes moral qualities as a feature of what is beautiful. In Western aesthetics, there is a "prospect-refuge" theory of landscape appreciation. According to this theory, our appreciation of landscape is fundamentally a biological reaction: we take pleasure in certain features of landscape because biologically we feel comfortable being in the kind of landscape (see Appleton 1996). Whether it is a plausible theory or not, it may be taken as an account of certain people's appreciation of landscape, that is, what would appear in the eyes of these people as beautiful. Similarly, we can say that the Confucian appreciation of beauty is from a moral perspective. This perspective does not entail that for Confucians there is only morality, but no beauty, or that they do not aim at enjoying what they consider to be beautiful. Instead, it suggests that for Confucians moral goodness is part of the beauty that they particularly appreciate. Not only do Confucians draw beauty from natural objects according to their own moral ideals, they believe that an exemplary person can also beautify nature with her own moral virtues. In considering going to live in a crude environment, the Master says, "were an exemplary person to live in it, what crudeness could there be?" (*Analects* 9.14). In other words, even if a natural environment is not beautiful, an exemplary person's moral integrity can beautify it.

The above point leads to my reply to the third argument of the dominant view, namely, that the main Confucian aesthetic ideal, *zhonghe* 中和 (centrality and harmony), typically taken as the principle behind *wenrou dunhou* 温柔敦厚 (being gentle and tolerant), is more a moral ideal than an aesthetic one, or that the Confucian aesthetic standard is derived from his moral standard. Ye Lang 叶朗 says in his *The History of Chinese Aesthetics* that the lines in the *Book of Songs*, "pleasing without being excessive, mournful without being injurious" is "Confucius' standard of aesthetic appreciation." It is so because "this kind of sentiment is in accord with the norms of ritual propriety." Confucius' "focal point is not the harmony of the music tones themselves, but that the sentiments expressed by the music must be regulated by ritual propriety, and be proper in its limit" (Ye, 36, 38). This "proper limit" is in turn associated with Confucius' notion of *zhongyong* 中庸, which was typically translated as "the doctrine of the mean." As a mean, the proper limit is to be neither in excess nor in deficiency, and is considered a *de* 德, or "virtue."

Though Ye's point implies a unity between moral virtues and aesthetic appreciation, he is reducing beauty to morality rather than the opposite. In his view, beauty is the means while moral virtues and orders are the ends. I have argued, however, that moral ideals are valuable to Confucius because they contribute to his aesthetic ideal. In other words, *zhonghe* and *wenrou dunhou* are valuable because they either contribute to aesthetic beauty, or are themselves characterizations of what is beautiful for Confucians. Actually *zhongyong* as a *de* 德, virtue, is never strictly a moral one. Aware of the possible misunderstanding, Ames and Rosemont translate it as "excellence" (Ames and Rosemont 1998, 110), which can be moral or amoral, and I translate it as virtue/virtuosity. *Zhong* 中 entails both the meaning of maintaining equilibrium, being impartial, and inside, which in application to humans, often means the heart-mind. The word *yong* 庸 has three basic interpretations: commonality or being ordinary; practicality, to use, or to employ; and constancy or being unchanging.[6] To bring these points together, "*zhongyong*" means constant conscientious practice in one's ordinary common life so that one can hit the proper target all the time. As a result of such practice, one attains *he* 和 or harmony in everyday life, and hence turning life itself into artistic activity. Taken as a principle of aesthetics, it requires creative aesthetic activity to be carried into one's entire life, including most ordinary and common activities. It also entails the ability of engaging in artistic creativity at ease, as if one were doing nothing extraordinary. One can be completely with oneself in doing these things artistically. "The Master was always gracious yet serious, commanding yet not severe, deferential yet at ease" (*Analects* 7.38) is a good description of this artistic way of life.

Even though *wenrou dunhou*, being gentle and tolerant, is sometimes taken to mean the same as *zhonghe*,[7] it has a special connection with the *Songs*. The expression is originated in the quote from *Li Ji* (the *Book of Rites*) that we cited earlier in this section. "Confucius says: 'In entering a country, one can recognize the kind of education it has. If the people are gentle and tolerant, it is the result of education by poetry. . . . Those who are gentle and tolerant, but not dumb, are the ones deeply affected by poetry." But the view that it is the same as *zhonghe* is contested by others as too simplistic. A scholar proposed that *wenrou dunhou* is more a specific artistic style than a general characterization of whatever that is beautiful according to Confucians (Zhang Guoqing 2002). Given the brief analysis of *zhong*, *yong*, and *he*, we can reasonably speculate that in endorsing *wenrou dunhou*, Confucians do not necessarily reject other styles of beauty. There is no reason to say that Confucians cannot accept the beauty of the poems by Qu Yuan 屈原, who writes with strong resentment, or that having expressed appreciation for *wenrou dunhou*, Confucians cannot at the same time appreciate Mencius's style of having strong *qi* 气, vital energy. A clue can be found in Confucius' own description of the value of the *Songs*: The Master says that "The *Songs* can lead to inspiration, can stimulate observation, can increase sociability, and can express dissatisfaction" (*Analects* 17.9). Here the word for "express dissatisfaction 怨" may also be translated as "to give expression to complaints," as D. C. Lao did. This is an indication that the Master does not exclude resentment as one legitimate style of art. Qing dynasty Wu Qiao 吴乔 says, "poetry educates people in *wenrou dunhou* style, it is not something that can be done in bold and powerful style." Yet Zhang Qianyi 张谦宜, also from the Qing dynasty, says that "Being bold and powerful yet still remains gentle and tolerant—only Du Fu was able to be like that" (see Zhang 16 for the quotes). In calligraphy, Yan Zhenqing 颜真卿 would be a comparable example. Again, even though it is difficult to be both gentle and tolerant and yet be bold and powerful, or both be gentle and tolerant and yet be rigorous, it does not mean that one cannot be bold, powerful, lofty, and strict and yet maintain a proper limit at the same time. In short, endorsing *wenrou dunhou* does not mean that Confucians would have to reject other forms of beauty.

In summary, I propose to view the ideal of Confucian learning as an aesthetic ideal, and I venture to say that Confucian aesthetics is more typical of the Chinese aesthetic spirit than Daoism because, by unifying moral virtues and orders with aesthetic beauty and appreciation, it best exemplifies the holistic and contextualized worldview characteristic of the Chinese way of thinking. Confucians view art as life, and they view life as art. To borrow an expression from John Dewey, Confucianism does not "museumize and pedestrolize" art. It neither limits art to what is displayed in museums and galleries, the so-called tuxedo art that only decorates our life, nor does it limit art to something that people do on the sidewalks of human life, detached from the ordinary and the mundane. Its aim is to transform the mainstream of human life into a field of artistic activity and to beautify all of human life, making art intrinsic to life. Indeed, what can be more aesthetic than this?

Notes

1. Zhu Xi, 朱子语类 [*Classified Conversations of Master Zhu*], in Siku Quanshu 四库全书, Masters Part, Confucianism section, vol. 40.

2. There are a number of alternative interpretations of this passage. One most clearly articulated by Cheng Shude 程树德 is that the Master was lamenting that given his age and the fact that there was no sage-king to employ him, he had no choice but to be like Dian (see Cheng 1990, 812). This explanation does not go well with the Master's initial question, which is about one's wish. Another interpretation was from Zhang Lùxiang 张履祥 (1611–1674), who held that the four disciples' aspirations show an ascending order, from bringing peace to the land, to letting people have sufficient material supplies, and then to using ritual propriety to teach people and to transform the society, and finally, to enjoying the kind of pleasure that Zeng Dian was talking about (see Cheng 1990, 816). This interpretation is roughly consistent with Cheng Hao's "Zeng Dian Spirit" interpretation.

3. Of course the fact that Zeng Dian is able to see the big picture or a higher ideal does not mean that he knows already how to reach the ideal. The importance of the message in 11.26 is in the Master's endorsement of the ideal, not in Zeng Dian's ability to reach the ideal, which is not touched on in the passage.

4. When one wants to attribute moral responsibility to a person, one has to assume that the person has the ability to do it. But this "ought implies can" thesis

is not about the goodness of the will. As the latter is unconditionally good, its goodness is not contingent on one's ability to carry it out.

5. It would be inconsistent if one were to, on the one hand, criticize Confucians and Chinese thinkers in general for the lack of conceptual clarity and rigorous logic, and on the other hand, try to understand their views by using strict logic and treat their language as if they were "ideal language."

6. Zhu Xi 朱熹: "*yong* means ordinary and constant (*yong, pingchang ye* 庸, 平常也)" (Zhu: 1). Cheng Yi 程頤: "Admitting of no change is called *yong*" (Legge 1971, 382). Zheng Kangcheng 鄭康成 "takes *yong* in the sense of *yong*, 'to use,' 'to employ,' which is first given to it in the dictionary [*Shuowen Jiezi*《说文解字》: 70], and is found in the *Shujing* I.i. par. 9" (Legge 1971, 382).

7. This view is mainly represented by Zhu Ziqing 朱自清, in the article titled Shi Jiao 诗教 "Education by Poetry," in his《诗言志辨》*Disputes on "Poem Expresses Will"* (Shanghai: Kaiming Shudian 开明书店, 1947).

References

Ames, Roger T., and Henry Rosemont, Jr. 1998. *The Analects of Confucius: A Philosophical Translation*. New York: Ballantine Books.
Analects. 2017. *Understanding the Analects of Confucius, A New Translation of Lunyu with Annotations*. Translated by Peimin Ni. Albany, NY: State University of New York Press.
Appleton, Jay, 1996. *The Experience of Landscape*. Chichester: John Wiley and Sons.
Cheng Shude 程树德. 1990. *Lunyu Jishi* 论语集释 [*Collected Commentaries of the Analects*], Beijing: Zhonghua Shuju 中华书局.
Feng Youlan [Fung Yu-Lan]. 1948. *A Short History of Chinese Philosophy*. New York: The Free Press.
Goldberg, Stephen J. 1997. "Chinese Aesthetics" in *A Companion to World Philosophies*, Eliot Deutsch and Ron Bontekoe (Eds.). Cambridge, MA: Blackwell.
Hall, David L., and Roger T. Ames. 1987. *Thinking through Confucius*. Albany, NY: State University of New York Press.
Knoblock, John. 1994. *Xunzi, A Translation and Study of the Complete Works*. Stanford, CA: Stanford University Press, 1994.
Legge, James. 1971. *Confucian Analects : The Great Learning, and The Doctrine of the Mean*. New York, NY: Dover Publications
Li Ji. 1987.《礼记》[*Book of Rites*]. Shanghai: Shanghai Guji Chubanshe 上海古籍出版社.
Li Zehou. 1981. *Meide Licheng* 美的历程 [*The Journey to Beauty*], Beijing: Wenwu Chubanshe 文物出版社.
Su Shi 苏轼. 1969. *Su Shi Wen Ji* 苏轼文集 [*Collected Works of Su Shi*], Beijing: Zhonghua Shuju 中华书局.

Tao Zongyi. 陶宗仪. *Shushi Huiyao* 艺术类，书画之属 [*Essentials of the History of Calligraphy*], Sikuquanshu 四库全书, Masters section 子部，艺术类，书画之属. Dizhi Cultural Publications, digital edition, in collaboration with the Chinese University of Hong Kong Press, 1999.

Tu Weiming. 1985. *Confucian Thought: Selfhood as Creative Transformation*. Albany, NY: SUNY Press.

Wei Qipeng 魏启鹏. 2005. *Jianbo Wenxian Wuxing Qianzheng* 简帛文献五行笺证, Beijing: Zhonghua Shuju 中华书局.

Xu Fuguan. 徐复观. 1983. *Zhongguo Yishu Jingshen* 中国艺术精神 [*The Chinese Aesthetic Spirit*]. 8th ed. Taiwan: Xuesheng Shuju 学生书局.

Xunzi《荀子》. 1994. Translation based on John Knoblock, *Xunzi, A Translation and Study of the Complete Works*. Stanford, CA: Stanford University Press.

Ye Lang. 1996. *Zhongguo Meixue Shi* 中国美学史 [*The History of Chinese Aesthetics*]. Taipei: Wenjin 文津出版社.

Zhang Guoqing. 2002. *Ru, Dao Meixue yu Wenhua* 儒、道美学与文化 [*The Aesthetics and Culture of Confucianism and Daoism*]. Beijing: Zhongguo Shehui Kexue Chubanshe 中国社会科学出版社.

Zhang Huai Guan 张怀瓘: *Wenzi Lun* 文字论 [*On Graphs and Words*], Sikuquanshu 四库全书, Masters section 子部，艺术类，书画之属，法书要录，卷. Dizhi Cultural Publications, digital edition, in collaboration with the Chinese University of Hong Kong Press, 1999.

Chapter 8

Confucianism on Human Relations
Progressive or Conservative?

STEPHEN C. ANGLE

Introduction

Human relations have always been central to Confucianism. I mean this in two senses, general and specific. Generally, all forms of Confucianism have stressed the importance of good relations within human families and larger societies. More specifically, the idea of "relation" (*lun* 伦) or "human relation" (*renlun* 人伦) has been a key part of Confucian theory and practice through the tradition's history, especially formulated as the "five relations" (*wulun* 五伦) made famous by Mencius. For modern critics of Confucianism, hierarchically conceived human relations are emblematic of all that is wrong with the tradition. In recent years as Confucianism has undergone something of a revival in China, in contrast, some conservative scholars have argued for a return to traditional human relations. The thesis of the present essay is that both these sides are mistaken. As philosophers reflect on the nature of human life today, we have much to learn from Confucian ideas of human relations, but only if human relations are understood in what I will call a "progressive" way.

This chapter is built around two complementary theses, one positive and one negative. The negative thesis is that conservative Confucian arguments for maintaining or restoring traditional relations are unpersuasive and in fact harmful to Confucianism's future. These conservative arguments reinforce the century-long negative attitude toward Confucianism that has dominated China ever since the May 4th era, and they display how out of touch from contemporary realities some Confucians can be. Faced with these conservative arguments, modern intellectuals are led to conclude that older male Confucians prefer to defend their status rather than critically reflect on the meaning of Confucianism today. The positive thesis of this chapter, in contrast, is that when properly understood, human relations are central to modern human life and are embraced by progressive Confucians. "Progressive Confucianism," as I understand it, is a commitment to the ongoing development of the Confucian tradition that emphasizes the importance of critically accepting the distinctive impacts of modernity on our diverse societies. Progressive Confucianism emphasizes the importance of developing virtue, but it does not confine itself to inner, personal cultivation: it recognizes the intimate relationship between social structures and public action, on the one hand, and personal development, on the other. Although progressive Confucians argue that many relations must be redefined around the idea of equality, they still accept many traditional Confucian insights into the importance of human differences and the value of deference.

In short, while progressive Confucianism has an important place for human relations, it does criticize one-sided or overly rigid understandings of these ancient ideas, both because such interpretations fail to capture crucial insights of Confucianism, and because they undermine the possibility of Confucianism's playing a positive role in the modern world.[1] I will argue for these conclusions in four steps. First, I look closely at the idea of "human relation," both in early texts and from a more analytical perspective. Second, I examine and critique several types of arguments that purport to show why the Confucian conception of relations supports conservative social arrangements today. Third, I look at two versions of the idea that relations and virtuous agency mutually constitute one another, and ask whether this idea can ground conservative conclusions. Finally, I synthesize what we have learned in the previous three sections and outline a progressive Confucian approach to human relations.

What Are Human Relations?

"Human relation" is an ancient term. It appears in the *Guanzi*, where we read "If [people] turn their backs on human relations and act as animals, within ten years [society] will be destroyed."[2] The most famous early mention of human relations is in *Mengzi*:

> The Way of the people is this: if they are full of food, have warm clothes, and live in comfort but are without instruction, then they come close to being animals. The sage [Shun] was anxious about this, so he appointed Xie to be Minister of Instruction, and instruct them about human relations: between father and children there is affection; between ruler and ministers there is righteousness; between husband and wife there is distinction; between elder and younger there is precedence; and between friends there is faithfulness.[3]

The first thing to notice from these two passages is that human relations are in some way distinct from our merely biological existence: human relations must be taught, and they can be abandoned. At the same time, we should not think of the roles that these relations specify as easy to put on and take off, like the roles an actor performs in a play.[4] Human relations are pervasively reflected in our social structures, they shape our psychological development, and they are based on various aspects of our biology. In many ways, the concept of human relation is similar to the modern conception of "gender." As a contemporary scholar puts it, "sex differences pertain to physiological features related to procreation and biological reproduction. Gender differences, on the other hand, represent the social interpretation of sex differences."[5] Indeed, "between husband and wife there is distinction" is precisely a (partial) definition of gender differences.

In order to properly understand and assess the arguments that will come in the next section of this chapter, it is crucial to be as clear as possible on which aspects of the concept of human relation are contingent or flexible, and which are not. In principle, we can distinguish the following five layers (most basic at bottom):

5. The specific rituals through which the specific parameters of specifically Confucian relations are taught and expressed

4. The specific parameters of specifically Confucian relations

3. The specific relations identified by Confucians

2. Relations of some kind

1. Human biology (humans as "animals" [*qinshou* 禽獸]) and cosmic functioning

Notice that level 1 already assumes that human biology cannot be conceptualized apart from cosmic functioning; whatever we are as animals is just one aspect of cosmic processes and is inextricably connected to these broader processes. Note also that I am taking processes of change and interaction, rather than unchanging "essences," as my basic category of analysis, in keeping with the fundamental orientation of Chinese thinking.

The first question we should ask about the five levels is: can level 1 exist without level 2? That is, is it possible to have mere biology (or mere cosmos) without relations? Detailed answers to this question depend on which thinker one asks, but if we define relations in general as systematic patterns of meaningful, valuable interrelationships, then the general response of the Confucian tradition has been to focus on a combination of levels 1 and 2. That is, we view the world through the lens of relations. Most basic of all are yin and yang, the relation between receptive and active roles that can be used, according to the *Yi Jing*, to understand all phenomena.[6] So level 2, "relations of some kind," appears to be necessary, and when the *Guanzi* and *Mengzi* speak of abandoning relations, they are thus referring to abandoning the distinctive human relations that make up level 3. What more can we say about level 3? As a recent book by Zhang Xianglong reminds us, some organisms employ asexual reproduction, so it seems difficult to apply role categories like "father-son" or "husband-wife" (or even simply "mother" as opposed to "father") to some entities. On the other hand, Professor Zhang also correctly points out that according to our best evidence, even early human gatherer-hunter societies had male-female pair bonds and some system of jointly caring for children.[7] It is also likely that they registered the distinction between elder and younger. We know too little to be able to draw any conclusions about political organization or about friendship, but at least it appears that some of the relations that Confucians emphasize may have been ubiquitous among all, or nearly all, humans. This is in keeping with the Confucian insight that such roles are critical to human society.

What about level 4, the specific parameters with which Confucians tell us these relations should be evaluated? It is intrinsic to the notion of "relation" that I am using that relations are loci of value and thus responsive to evaluation; indeed, the criteria for evaluation help to determine the identity of the relation. For example, consider two different criteria for relations between elder and younger: absolute loyalty and respect. We actually understand the role "elder" differently if it demands absolute loyalty rather than demanding respect. So the identity of level 3 relations depends on the criteria chosen to evaluate them. The question concerning level 4 is whether the criteria the Confucians use to evaluate relations—and thus, in a more specific way than I considered in the previous paragraph, the relations themselves—are contingent and even subject to revision. According to a number of passages in the *Mengzi*, the criteria seem to be unavoidable—even though people do not always live up to them. For example:

> . . . Among babes in arms there are none that do not know to love their parents. When they grow older, there are none that do not know to revere their older brothers. Treating one's parents as parents is humaneness. Revering one's elders is righteousness.[8]

Other passages emphasize that the reaction of reverence and righteousness to an elder is "internal," meaning it does not depend on learning external norms.[9] In other words, the *Mengzi* is saying that "parent as one to be loved and treated with humaneness" and "elder as one to be revered and treated with righteousness" are necessary human roles.

A somewhat similar case is made in a chapter of the *Li Ji* concerning the relation of husband and wife. Consider the following passage:

> The ritual of marriage is the beginning of a line that shall last for a myriad ages. The parties are of different surnames; thus those who are distant are brought together, and the distinction [to be maintained between those who are of the same surname] is emphasized. . . . The woman should be admonished to be upright and sincere. Faithfulness is requisite in all service of others, and faithfulness is the virtue of a wife. Once mated with her husband, all her life she will not change her feeling of duty to him and hence, when the husband dies she will not marry again. The man goes in person to meet the bride, the man taking the initiative and not the woman, according to the idea that regulates the relation between the strong and the weak. It is according to this same idea that heaven takes precedence of earth, and the ruler of the subject. Presents are interchanged before (the parties) see each other, this reverence serving to illustrate the distinction that should be observed between man and woman.

> When this distinction between husband and wife is exhibited, affection comes to prevail between father and son. When there is this affection, the idea of righteousness arises, and to this idea of righteousness succeeds the observance of ritual. Through ritual there ensues universal repose. The absence of such distinction and righteousness is characteristic of the way of beasts.[10]

In his discussion of this passage, Zhang Xianglong draws an intriguing connection between this account of "distinction" and the near-universal phenomenon of incest taboos among human societies. In order that there be a continuing, flourishing line of descent, husband and wife must be "distinct" from one another in the sense of coming from different surnames. In this narrow sense, "distinction" as a criterion for the relation of husband and wife may indeed be necessary. But both the *Li Ji* and Professor Zhang go on to assign considerably more content to "distinction" than mere incest avoidance. The *Li Ji* treats it as equally natural that women have subordinate, serving roles; Professor Zhang includes a gendered division of labor (with females responsible for caring for children, cooking, and so on) as equally part of the "extremely ancient human phenomenon and principle" that is "distinction between men and women."[11] Professor Zhang is correct that traditional Confucians have typically understood "distinction" in these terms, but it is much more questionable whether such an idea can be justified as natural or necessary. I will return to this issue below.

Turn now to level 5, the specific rituals through which the specific parameters of specifically Confucian relations are taught and expressed. The passage we just examined from the *Li Ji* begins with a reference to the "ritual" of marriage and ends by saying that once distinction has led to affection and thence to righteousness, the resulting ritualized society will exist in a state of "universal repose." The authors of this text see the specific rituals they describe here as both expressing and teaching the underlying relations and their accompanying criteria: it is through acting out the rituals that the relations are made explicit. Do Confucians believe that even these specific rituals (for example, that presents are exchanged before the bride and groom meet one another) are necessary and unchanging? Are they as crucial to the meaning of the relations as are the level 4 criteria themselves?

Some things that Confucians have said seem to answer this question affirmatively. Consider this passage from *Mengzi*:

> In past ages, there were those who did not bury their parents. When their parents died, they took them and abandoned them

in a gulley. The next day they passed them, and foxes were eating them, bugs were sucking on them. Sweat broke out on the survivors' foreheads. They turned away and did not look. It was not for the sake of others that they sweated. What was inside their heart-minds broke through to their countenances. So they went home and, returning with baskets and shovels, covered them. If covering them was really right, then the manner in which filial children and humane people cover their parents must also be part of the way.[12]

And then there is the following passage from *Xunzi*:

Those who cross waters mark out the deep places, but if the markers are not clear, people will fall in. Those who order the people mark out the way, but if the markers are not clear, there will be chaos. The rituals are those markers.[13]

Both of these passages tell us that rituals are to a significant degree necessary and invariant. We must bury our dead, or else we will feel profound discomfort; we must institute and follow the correct rituals, or else we will fall into the deep waters of chaos. It is an objective fact whether water is deep or shallow, so by analogy it must be an objective fact where rituals should mark out human behavior. Admittedly, Mengzi leaves room for different details about burial, and Xunzi says in this passage only that the rituals must be "clear." Much of his "Discourse on Ritual" consists in explaining why rituals must be as they are, though, indicating that for Xunzi at least, even these details have a significant degree of objectivity.[14]

Notwithstanding the degree of objectivity regarding rituals that we find in early texts, we also find clear indications that rituals can change, and this idea is developed further later in the tradition.[15] In the *Analects*, Confucius says that he agrees with the majority of people in his day who now wear silk caps instead of the traditional hemp, and in another passage he makes it explicit that the rituals of the three early dynasties differed from one another.[16] Even more emphatic is the "Evolution of Rituals" chapter of the *Record of Rituals*, which states, "even if they were not among those of the former kings, rituals can be adopted if they spring from righteousness."[17] Given this attitude, it is unsurprising that much later thinkers—aware of many of the changes that have taken place in Chinese society in the intervening millennium—also embrace the idea that rituals can and must change. Zhu Xi explains that he compiles ancient ritual texts simply in order to facilitate his contemporaries' deciding which of the rituals can be employed in his day, not in order to advocate a return to ancient ways, and he also explicitly invokes the "Evolution of Rituals" idea of inventing new rituals so long as they "spring from righteousness."[18] Although this flexible attitude toward rituals has occasional critics within the long Confucian tradition, it is certainly a common and influential view; according to this view, at least, we can expect the specific rituals (level 5) to change with the times, so long as they still succeed in capturing the relations and parameters (levels 3 and 4) that Confucians value.

Taking stock, what are human relations? How seriously do modern Confucians need to take them, and how much can they change? This analysis has shown that relations and their parameters are treated as necessary and objective by most traditional Confucians, though the rituals through which they are taught and expressed are more open to change. We have seen some reasons to think that relations are indeed central to human experience, and later in the chapter I will discuss additional modern arguments that similarly emphasize the importance of relations. For the most part, though, the claim that the specific relations emphasized by Confucianism (level 3) and the specific parameters through which Confucians have historically evaluated relations (level 4) are objective and unchangeable has been taken as an assumption without much explicit philosophical defense. In the next section, I will examine a series of arguments by modern Confucians who seek to defend a traditional conception of relations and thus to argue for quite conservative versions of contemporary social arrangements.

Conservative Arguments

It is now time to look at several ways in which some contemporary Chinese scholars have argued from premises about human relations to conservative social conclusions. I will look at arguments based on nature, texts, metaphysics, instrumental value, and reciprocity, and show that none of them succeed in defending the conservative social relationships that they are meant to champion.

I start with an admittedly extreme example, but I believe that views like this are rather common, even if less commonly expressed in public, so it is worth taking seriously. In a much-discussed book published in 2014, Professor Zeng Yi argues that "the wisdom of the ancients lies in fully understanding the natural aspect of male-female differences, and thus instituting appropriate family norms and behavioral principles that insist on a distinction between inner and outer, with men being in charge of the outer, while women are in charge of the inner."[19] We get a sense of what he means by "natural" differences when he complains that equal division of property in a divorce is "extremely irrational," because "after women go out to the fields, they simply do not have sufficient ability to farm."[20] Let us charitably interpret this not as an insult to women's intelligence, and also ignore all the evidence from around the world of women working in agriculture, and take it as a remark based on the typical differences between men and women in physical strength. The key point to see is that even if we grant this, Professor Zeng has not identified a "natural" difference, because the significance of this difference depends on a specific form of social-economic organization that is increasingly irrelevant in China and around the world. The percentage of Chinese citizens working in agriculture—and especially in agriculture without modern machinery—has declined dramatically, and there is every reason to think that this decline will continue. So even if traditional agricultural society might, to some degree, justify a gendered division of labor, that is no longer the case. The gendered distinction between inner and outer has not been shown to be "natural." To use the language of the previous section, we cannot say that the "natural" level 1 requires the specific Confucian parameter (level 4).

In his recent book, Professor Zhang Xianglong presents an updated version of the argument from "naturalness." Instead of focusing on agricultural society, Zhang discusses gender relations within the hunter-gatherer societies in which humans evolved over many tens of thousands of years. Based on evidence from anthropology and sociobiology, he draws the following conclusions:

1. Male-female parental pair bonds (sometimes with extra females per male) were crucial to human evolutionary success and thus were the standard model throughout this period;

2. Sex-based division of labor, with female "gatherers" taking main responsibility for child-rearing, while male "hunters" ranged widely seeking meat, was also evolutionarily advantageous and the standard model;

3. Because they were evolutionarily adaptive (i.e., they led to evolutionary success), we can conclude that these models for human social relationships are "natural facts" (*ziran shishi* 自然事实).[21]

Zeng's argument depends on an agricultural society, and while it may therefore be able to explain why people in Confucius' day thought about gender relations as they did, it is not able to ground the claim that such ideas of gender are "natural." In contrast, Zhang's argument appeals to the sociobiological principle that human behavior—even today—is shaped by the environment in which our ancient ancestors evolved. Zhang is claiming that because of these early evolutionary adaptations, male-female pair bonds and sex-based division of labor were natural in Confucius' day and are natural today. To return to the language of the previous section, on this view level 1 actually constrains levels 2 through 4 in significant ways, shaping the sorts of relations that males and females can occupy and the parameters we use to evaluate them.

There are two problems with Professor Zhang's argument. First, discussion of sociobiology (also called "evolutionary psychology") has advanced beyond the pioneering works of Edward Wilson from the 1970s, on which Zhang mainly relies. In particular, more emphasis is now put on the crucial fact that the manifestation of biological influences on behavior (i.e., our "phenotype") depends both on underlying genetic material (i.e., our "genotype") and on the environment in which a specific person is born and matures. Even accepting, for sake of argument, that evolutionary pressures shaped hunter-gatherer humans to prefer male-female pair bonds and a sex-based division of labor, there is no good reason to think that the resulting genotype will manifest in the same way in the very different environment of contemporary society. Second, even if there is some influence on contemporary behavior from our ancient evolution—as indeed, there is likely to be, even though we are not yet able to predict what all these effects will be, given the first point—we must distinguish between "natural" psychological promptings and justified ethical principles. We are all familiar with ways in which biological prompts can lead us astray, from overly aggressive responses, to inapt sexual desires, to general selfishness. From early on, Confucian thinkers themselves recognized these phenomena, such as when the *Mengzi* says that the ears and eyes can be "misled by things" (*biyuwu* 蔽於物).[22] I conclude that no matter whether we rely on agricultural practices or on sociobiology, there are not convincing grounds to conclude that traditional Confucian gender relations are "natural" and thus normative for us today.

The two versions of a "nature"-based argument that we just saw both understood "nature" through the lens of modern natural and social science. Now let us look at a form of argument that views what is natural through the lens of the traditional Confucian vocabulary of yin and yang. Yin and yang can be thought of as complementary cosmic forces, or they can be thought of as the receptive and active dimensions of any given situation. Traditional Confucians would in fact see no distinction between these two ways of articulating yin and yang; we moderns might prefer the latter, which lets us use yin and yang as a coherent and revealing "stance" with which to view the world, while still allowing us to adopt other stances (of physics, of intentionality, etc.) at other times.[23] With this in mind, let us consider Zhang Xianglong's appeal to the ideas of yin and yang in the *Book of Changes* in order to argue that while homosexual relations should not be prohibited, Confucians should oppose the institution of gay marriage.[24] Some of Zhang's uses of the *Book of Changes* do not go beyond appealing to textual authority, which I will discuss in a moment,[25] but in other places he relies more on the substantive ideas of the text in order to make his case. In one place he says that homosexuality is not evil, but "is merely a kind of divergence born from incomplete exchanges between yin and yang." He adds that although homosexual couples do have "lesser yin-yang distinctions, following the model of husband and wife, however because they violate the greater yin-yang [process] they have no way of birthing and nurturing descendants."[26] In other words, he imagines that homosexual partners may take on differentiated roles—one more feminine, one more masculine—and yet because human reproduction requires a joining of male and female, they cannot join in this "greater yin-yang" process.

We saw above that in response to arguments from scientific naturalism, two types of responses are available: (1) is the scientific claim correct? (2) even insofar as the scientific claim is correct, does what is "natural" have any normative weight for us? For arguments from yin-yang naturalism, the first type of response is definitely an option. Is Professor Zhang right to distinguish between lesser and greater yin-yang distinctions? Do homosexuals in fact violate the "greater" kind of yin-yang process because of being unable to procreate and nurture? Certainly Zhang is correct that reproduction and growth are central to the general vision of the cosmos of which yin and yang are important parts. The cosmos is constantly undergoing change, and when this dynamism is characterized by harmonious interchanges of yin and yang, we get growth and flourishing. Human procreation is one important part of this, but there is much more to maintaining a vital cosmos than merely human reproduction. Indeed, from a contemporary vantage point, we can see that human overpopulation and human overconsumption can cause significant cosmic disharmonies (as seen, for example, with climate change). In short, it is not so obvious that there is one, and only one, "greater" locus for yin and yang interchanges. In addition, between adoption, surrogacy, and ever-advancing technology, it is by no means the case that homosexual couples cannot reproduce, and certainly they can nurture children (although see below for further discussion of this issue).[27] On this account, homosexuality (including homosexual marriage) is simply another of many kinds of diversity that fill the cosmos, and which we are challenged to harmonize. Finally, what about the second question: is this vision of a life-filled cosmos based on harmony between yin and yang necessarily normative for us? Confucians have long taken the answer to be "yes," and while a thorough discussion will have to wait for another occasion, I find myself sympathetic to this response. Viewing the universe from a scientific stance leads one to recognize certain facts that constrain our possible actions but has no further normative pull on us. Viewing the cosmos from a yin-yang stance, in contrast, is already to take up the role of a caring participant in the whole—one who unavoidably feels connections with other aspects of the cosmos. In short, the strongest grounds for a progressive Confucian to reject Zhang's yin-yang reasoning is to resist his claims about the connection between yin and yang and human procreation, as I have done above.

A third type of argument is based on textual authority: since the Confucian classics tell us how roles should be arranged, we Confucians today must follow their lead. Here is an example. Professor Tang Wenming cites a somewhat obscure text (the "Commentary" to the "Mourning Clothing" chapter of the *Yili*) that he interprets to mean that among the three key roles within the family, that between father and son is essential, while those between husband and wife and between older and younger brothers are less central.[28] Partly on this basis, he later concludes that "in these days of female power, reaffirming the ethic of 'males are superior, females are base' is both necessary and matches with the meaning of the Confucian classics."[29] One problem with this kind of argument is that it may rest on a controversial interpretation of the classics, and in fact the question of priority between husband-wife and father-son (or, more charitably, parent-child) roles is subject to considerable interpretive debate.[30] More basically, though, it is critical to keep in mind what the Classics are. They are the disparate textual records of an internally diverse tradition, some putatively the words of sages, but even these are still only the words of human beings. Even the most revered of the Classics is not taken to be the infallible, revealed word of a god.[31] Given that the historical Confucians largely accepted the patriarchal relations of their society—which may have been reinforced by the dominance of an agricultural mode of production, as we earlier saw Zeng Yi emphasize—it is no surprise that their writings reflect these arrangements. But all inheritors of the complex and internally contested tradition that is Confucianism have been able to pick and choose, emphasizing some texts and themes and downplaying or even rejecting others. I conclude that when we examine a modern claim based on an assertion in an ancient text, we must look at details like which text, how ambiguous the statement is, whether the sentiment is repeated (or contradicted) elsewhere, and so on. Even in a favorable case, though, a bare classical assertion, without further philosophical argument to shore it up, is a very weak basis for modern-day conclusions.

A fourth major set of arguments in favor of a conservative reading of traditional relations is based on instrumental considerations. The basic idea behind these arguments is that changing traditional norms has bad effects. Professor Zhang sees that Confucianism does not recognize "absolute principles that transcend space and time 儒家不承认有超越时空的绝对原则"; for this reason, he spends a good portion of his anti-gay-marriage essay making arguments based not on nature or textual authority, but simply based on the contemporary effects of such a changed official definition of marriage. These arguments are not exclusive to Confucians; indeed, Zhang draws on the reasoning of U.S. Supreme Court Justice Roberts, from Roberts's dissent to the landmark 2015 ruling legalizing gay marriage throughout the United States. I certainly agree that arguments of this kind are relevant to the decision-making process that modern Confucians should employ to determine which sorts of roles and relations, in accord with which sorts of parameters, should be recognized via ritual, and which via law. We should expect that the categories employed in rituals will be much more fine-grained than those recognized by law; here I will use law as my example, but similar considerations should apply when assessing rituals. The basic point of instrumental arguments is that there are costs and benefits, to individuals and to society, from different sorts of legal arrangements. For example, Zhang (following Roberts) says that allowing gay marriage will lead us down a slippery slope to allowing all sorts of other marital arrangements—group marriages, even marriages between humans and nonhuman animals. Zhang also argues that gay marriage will harm the interest that parents and grandparents have in biological continuity, it will harm the ability of other family members to create positive family relations, and it will harm the children raised within gay marriages.[32] Since this is not a chapter specifically on gay marriage, I will not rebut these arguments point by point here. Instead, I will make four more general points. First, these instrumental arguments are not obviously true: they must be assessed with empirical evidence, and in almost all cases it is easy enough to inquire into their veracity.[33] Second, such arguments must be balanced against instrumental arguments based on the potential benefits of revised arrangements.[34] Third, Confucians will insist that when we think about the design of institutions like laws (and rituals), the most important kind of effect to consider is the influence that the institutions will have on the development of virtue by those subject to the institutions. Fourth, I am sure that Confucians will continue to find important value in something that at least partly resembles the traditional relations: family should continue to be of great importance to modern Confucians. As I will discuss in my conclusion, though, families in the twenty-first century may look quite different from premodern families, even as they continue to support us in our growth as virtuous people.

There are two more pro-conservative arguments to consider before moving on. First, very briefly, is the argument that we should continue to treat someone in a certain way because that is what the rituals tell us to do. But as we have already seen, Confucians have long recognized that rituals are appropriately subject to change, so this argument cannot stand on its own. Admittedly, as I have explained elsewhere, rituals are "viscous": that is, by their nature they are somewhat resistant to change.[35] If they did not "stick" with us, they would not be able to perform their various functions. This does not affect the fact that they can—and sometimes must—change, however. Second, a common thing I have heard about traditional Confucian relations is that "they are not (so) bad because they are reciprocal." Men are elevated above women, it is true, but men have responsibilities to women, just as women have to men. These are not simply one-way relations demanding obedience. This is of course true, and is indeed a hallmark of the Confucian conception of human relations. It is not sufficient to discount the possibility that relations and their parameters need to be revised in the modern world, however.

Constitutive Arguments

I now turn to a final perspective that might be able to ground conservative arguments for preserving traditional relations, which is that relations are at least partly constitutive of virtues and agents. That is, we cannot separate virtues or agents from the relations they occupy; there are no virtues or agents in the abstract, independent of relations. I will introduce two versions of this idea, one from Roger Ames and Henry Rosemont, and another from

Tang Wenming. Taken together, their arguments do indeed help us to see why relations are so central to Confucianism, ancient and modern. However, Ames and Rosemont do not believe that strongly conservative implications follow from their interpretation of Confucianism, while Tang Wenming does draw some conservative conclusions. By examining the differences between their two approaches, I will endeavor to trace this difference to its source.

In a series of articles and books dating back to the 1980s, Roger Ames and Henry Rosemont, both singly and together, have advocated the idea that according to Confucianism people and their virtuous qualities are centrally constituted by their relations and roles. If we compare their statements, we will find that there may be at least some differences between them. In an early article, Rosemont writes that "for the early Confucians there can be no *me* in isolation, to be considered abstractly: I am the totality of the roles I live in relation to specific others."[36] In partial contrast, Ames says that to perform ritual is "to contribute oneself to the pattern of relationships which ritual entails, and thereby have a determinative effect on society.... *Li* is not passive deference to external patterns. It is a *making* of society that requires the investment of oneself and one's own sense of importance."[37] I do not want to exaggerate this difference, since Ames is not saying that there is a fully formed self prior to one's involvement with human relations; but still, his formulation does allow for a greater degree of distinction between self and relations. In Ames's case, we can say that the person or agent, and the roles or relations, mutually constitute one another, whereas at least in the statement I have quoted from Rosemont, it is harder to see how the "self" contributes anything distinctive to the nexus of roles and other relations in which one finds oneself.

I will therefore focus more on Ames here. To borrow language that he often uses, we can say that the agent acts as a unique "focus" within a "field" of relationships: by occupying the relevant roles in specific ways, the agent brings into focus or into salience what is of genuine value within all the possibilities made available by the situation. In his more recent *Confucian Role Ethics*, Ames discusses this idea of "value" from several perspectives. For example, he says that value is "nothing more and nothing less than enhanced worth in relations" and that "becoming exemplary as a person . . . is irreducibly collaborative."[38] As the latter quote suggests, Ames believes that "value" and "worth" are both tightly linked to being "exemplary," which he also glosses as demonstrating "virtuosity"—his translation of *de* 德. Ames takes great pains to insist that Confucians understand *de* as an ongoing, holistic process of particularistic activity-in-relations, and not as a set of abstract, reified standards that are independent from the particular actions of particular agents.³⁹ He does think that we can at least partly generalize about the goodness of virtuosity, though, since he regularly appeals to the importance of things like vitality, flourishing, productivity, and growth. For those familiar with the *Book of Changes* or with the Neo-Confucian tradition, this cannot help but resonate with the emphasis we see there on the on-going process of life-giving generativity (*sheng buxi* 生生不息). Summing up, Ames holds that human relations and agents mutually define one another in a process whose success we call "growth" and "flourishing."

In several recent publications, Tang Wenming has argued for a deep connection between human relations and virtue that bears some comparison to Ames's position. Tang's emphasis is on the ways that human relations and virtues are mutually entailing. In the context of an argument against the idea that virtues like humaneness should be understood along Kantian lines as "categorical imperatives," Tang cites a discussion in the *Zhong Yong* of relations and virtues and concludes: "In fact this extremely clearly expresses the connection between virtues and relations (*lunli* 伦理): without virtues, the patterns of human relations (*renlun zhi li* 人伦之理) will have no means of realization, and without the patterns of human relations, virtues will have lost their point."⁴⁰ The similarity to Ames becomes even more explicit when Tang says that "the importance of human relations comes first of all from practical, lived experience, because people do not even for a moment exist apart from human relations."⁴¹ Unlike the Kantian interpreters of Confucianism whom Tang is arguing against, Tang maintains that human relations shape our experience of the world at a fundamental level.⁴²

A specific example of what Tang has in mind will help to flesh out his meaning. In a recent essay Tang (2015) discusses the historian's Chen Yinke's famous assessment of Wang Guowei's 1927 suicide as expressing "independent spirit and freedom of thought."⁴³ As Tang discusses, Wang's background and the part played by loyalty to a lost political system in his decision to commit suicide make it complicated to say exactly wherein lay Wang's freedom and independence. Tang draws on a threefold distinction deriving from Hegel among different senses of freedom in order to draw out what sort of freedom Wang was expressing.⁴⁴ Tang concludes that the most important sense of freedom here is "*lunli ziyou*" (伦理自由), which in the present context we might translate quite literally as "freedom within relationship-patterns" rather than its more typical translation as "ethical freedom," although since (as Tang emphasizes) "ethics" for Hegel is grounded in concrete human relations, perhaps "ethical freedom" is sufficient. In any event, the point is that this kind of freedom is something realized within the framework of the familial, social, and political relationships that unavoidably shape our normative outlooks: it is not a free-floating principle that can be applied in abstraction from our lived contexts. Tang's point is that unlike the unmoored, revolutionary ways that many have interpreted Chen Yinke's statement, the "independence" and "freedom" that Wang Guowei exemplified was actually grounded in quite traditional human relationships.

As Tang's essay makes clear, Wang's decision cannot be simply reduced to the choice to honor the fall of a past dynasty, but there is enough of this meaning to make us wonder what, exactly, Tang means to praise by bringing up the case of Wang Guowei. What if the traditional relation of subject to ruler is somehow problematic; does Tang's picture allow for its critique? Tang explicitly rejects the idea that the ruler-subject relation can be rejected as a "master-slave" relation, because the ruler-subject relation makes reciprocal demands on both ruler and subject: it is not a relation of one-way obedience.[45] In his book, finally, Tang argues that it is one's identification with and embrace of heaven's mandate that leads to our broadening of concern from intimates to others in the larger world.[46] The details of Tang's interpretation here are complex and controversial; for now, suffice it to say that it is not clear how this connection with heaven might lead to the critique of one of Confucianism's traditional roles.

Having now seen two, somewhat similar, arguments that we humans and our virtues are unavoidably constituted by relations, we are left with two questions. First, are these arguments convincing? And second, to the extent that they are convincing, how do such perspectives influence what modern Confucians say about traditional social arrangements? Based on the analysis above, we can begin by saying that Confucians would indeed agree that humans do not exist apart from relations: this is just to reiterate the necessity of level 2. This already covers many of the specific claims that Ames and Tang make, such as Ames's "becoming exemplary as a person . . . is irreducibly collaborative" and Tang's "people do not even for a moment exist apart from relations." The status of virtues requires some further analysis, however. When Tang says that "without virtues, the pattern of human relations will have no means of realization," this might refer to specific criteria for human relations (i.e., level 4), but it might also refer to the seemingly more general—because less obviously tied to specific relations—virtues that the Confucians regularly discuss, like the canonical "humaneness, appropriateness, ritual propriety, and wisdom." It seems that characteristics like humaneness can be manifested within any set of role relations, including relations that Confucians may not have emphasized historically (i.e., level 2 but not level 3). Indeed, some scholars dispute Ames's assertion that value is "nothing more and nothing less than enhanced worth in relations," arguing that virtue can also be expressed nonrelationally.[47] For our purposes, the important point is not whether virtue can be nonrelational, but that some virtues (and virtuosity in general) can be provisionally distinguished from particular relations, so that we can ask, for example, whether a given father, in a given situation, responded with sufficient humaneness, or propriety, or overall virtuosity. This does not mean that humaneness has become the kind of reified, abstract principle that Ames and Tang reject, but rather that just as we understand a given relationship to be characterized by specific criteria that apply across many individual instances of the relation, so too can we understand more general criteria (i.e., virtues) that apply across various types of roles and relations. These virtues are not wholly independent from the particular relationships and contexts in which they are realized—and indeed could not exist without those particularities—but they have sufficient independence for them to be practically useful as well as apt subjects for Confucian theorizing (about how to cultivate them, what their characteristic marks are, and so on). With this clarification in mind, we can conclude that human relations and virtues can indeed be said to constitute one another.

Turn now to the second question: if virtues and relations constitute one another, does this lead to conservativism about human relations and roles? Neither author has addressed this question in detail, but their writings do contain some indications. For Ames, his emphasis on virtuosity as entailing the growth of meaningful relationships has led him to oppose coercive or arbitrary limits on the contours of the relationships we can occupy. For example, Ames argues that hierarchical relationships are not themselves problematic, but whenever such relations are enforced coercively, they should be criticized.[48] Among other things, this means that he believes that Confucians should support gay marriage and oppose a forced, gender-based separation between domestic and public concerns.[49] Tang Wenming, on the other hand, has taken more conservative positions, such as arguing that the father's authority is insufficient today and that in contemporary China, it is necessary—and in keeping with the meaning of the Classics—to re-emphasize the morality of "men are honored; women are lowly" (*nanzun nübei* 男尊女卑).[50] Tang's reference to the Classics helps to remind us that there are multiple arguments from premises concerning relations to conservative conclusions, and it is not at all clear that Tang has the mutuality of relation and virtue in mind when he makes this particular argument. Nonetheless, if we recall his discussion of Wang Guowei, we can see there, too, an implicitly conservative standpoint regarding political relations that is explicitly rooted in the mutual constitution of relations and virtues. Perhaps the key point is this: if relation and virtue constitute one another, is there any further standpoint from which one can criticize existing role-definitions? Ames emphasizes growth, which does seem to lead to progressive possibilities; Tang talks rather abstractly about the commitment to *tian*, but we have not seen any evidence that this can promote change or critique (beyond its original function of moving people beyond caring solely about their close relations). I conclude both that the idea that relations and virtues constitute one another is plausible, and that it need not lead to conservative conclusions. I will elaborate on such a view of human relations in the upcoming section.

Synthesis and Conclusions

For more than one hundred years, traditional Confucian ideas of human relations and the rituals that support them have been under attack in China. According to the analysis of Professor Wu Fei, there have been three main lines of criticism against traditional roles, all of which go back to the late Qing dynasty: first, an effort to replace ritual norms with constitution-based laws, initially spearheaded by Shen Jiaben; second, theories concerning early matriarchal societies that have sources in both Kang Youwei and in Engels's Marxism; and third, an intellectual movement to "replace ritual with humaneness" (*yiren chuli* 以仁黜礼) that gets its clearest early expression from Tan Sitong.[51] Professor Wu offers Lu Xun's argument that children owe no duty to their parents—it is rather parents that owe duties to their children—as an example of the last trend. There may be a distinction worth drawing here, between a modernizing (or progressive) Confucianism based on humaneness (and other virtues), on the one hand, and a liberal-individualist-Kantian perspective, on the other. If so, perhaps we should say that there were four sources of criticism, with the last one emerging a bit later, as part of the New Culture Movement. But in any event, it should be clear that traditional relations have been subject to a longstanding, wide-ranging critique. Professor Wu also suggests that while each of these sources was widely influential, if we probe the reasoning that underlies each one we will find it to be weaker than many have supposed. At least implicitly, then, Wu is suggesting that there may be room for a revival of traditional relations and roles, since the original reasons for their being rejected as "feudal" may have been problematic. And indeed, in the present chapter we have seen considerable evidence of Confucians trying to revive and defend traditional Confucian relationships, and in so doing, endeavoring to restore what they see as the traditional social arrangements that were based on these relations.

The main conclusion that I would like to defend here is that we should neither reject the concept of human relations in favor of pure individualism, nor go back to the full set of traditional Confucian relations and parameters. A contemporary, progressive Confucian perspective argues for a third alternative: accept the insight into the importance of human relations that Confucianism provides, but also accept that these relations and their parameters must change in significant ways. Families and family roles should still be of the utmost importance to contemporary Confucians, but families in the twenty-first century will look quite different from premodern families, even as they continue to support us in our growth as virtuous people. Many of the differences ultimately result from the dramatic changes to our social and economic circumstances that modernization has brought: urbanization, industrialization, and other more recent developments like the internet and robotics revolutions are all having differing but unavoidable impacts in each distinct human society. Of course, modern Confucians should not uncritically accept all the results of modernization in their societies: too often, the narrow pursuit of economic interest has led to problematic social arrangements that put obstacles in the way of the pursuit of moral growth for many. Relying on the Confucian tradition's deep insight into the ways in which selfishness can jeopardize progress in self-cultivation, modern Confucians must be ready to speak out.[52]

The resulting attitude is "critical acceptance of modernity." The vast changes in modern social arrangements challenge Confucians to ask, for each and every type of human relation, how should this relationship be best configured in order to give all participants their best opportunities for growth in virtuosity? How should we interpret or revise age-old teachings in our modern context? (This same question can also be asked in an even more fine-grained way, applying to each specific instance of a given relationship, but my concern here has been with more general social structures.) In answering these questions, we will need to keep in mind the differences among the distinct analytical levels that make up human relations—biology, relation, parameter, and ritual—as well as both ancient insights and modern social scientific research. Two critical touchstones will be the Confucian ideas of "harmony without uniformity (*he er bu tong* 和而不同)," on the one hand, and the "natural equality" of all people (to use Donald Munro's term), on the other. Harmony without uniformity suggests that changing balances of complementary differences are superior to bare uniformity; natural equality means that all people share a nature that gives them the ability to make moral evaluations and develop a virtuous character (in repudiation of earlier ideas of hereditary privilege).[53] Historically, the commitment to natural equality coexisted with many kinds of unequal relations; modern Confucians must now ask which sorts of relationships are justified today.

By way of bringing this chapter to a close, I will consider how one specific type of human relation should be re-thought in the present day. In keeping with my focus throughout the chapter, it makes sense to use the husband-wife relation as our test case. In light of the arguments and analysis of the previous sections, we should ask questions like: Is this relationship necessary? Must this be a relation between one man and one woman? Do the twin roles involved in this relation each have distinct responsibilities? Are the two roles equally important, and do they each maximize the possibilities of each to grow ethically? Is this relation properly governed by the parameter of "distinction," and what rituals properly guide those in these relations?

Let us first think about what the point of such a relationship is. Zhang Xianglong gives us a good start when he says—of the family as a whole, but this surely applies to a spousal relationship as well—that its central function is to "nurture children's maturation so that they can, in turn, raise children of their own."[54] Zhang does not make it explicit, but he would surely agree that this is not a mere biological process: only at least moderately virtuous spouses are likely to do well at raising children who, in turn, will be virtuous enough to do well at raising children in their own right.[55] In this light, we can also say that a critical part of the spousal relationship is mutual support in each partner's growth as an ethical person, both as a partner and in all other relationships: with children, parents, and so on. In this light, it is striking to note what Zhu Xi wrote about the spousal relationship in the twelfth century:

> [The relationship between] husbands and wives is the most intimate and the most private of all human relations. We may not want to tell something to a father or brother, but it can all be told one's wife. These are the most intimate of human affairs and the Way is exercised therein.[56]

Zhu also says that "The Way of the superior person begins its rise in the confidential moments between husband and wife."[57]

On this basis, how should we answer the questions raised in the previous paragraph? It is obvious that I can only sketch some possibilities at this point, since a full investigation of ancient texts and modern social science would require a whole other chapter. Still, how might answers in terms of harmony and natural equality proceed? To begin with, there are many reasons to think that a robust spousal relationship is indeed of great value, both for the moral growth of the partners and their abilities to deal successfully with the various challenges they will inevitably encounter, and for their shared ability to raise children who will mature into admirable adults. What does this tell us about people who do not fit into this favored framework—adults who never marry, divorced or widowed people, orphaned children, and single parents?[58] These are of course complex issues and full answers will again draw on the tradition's discussion of precisely these issues as well as more recent research and insights, but there are two points that will have to be borne in mind. First, even though a robust spousal relationship is of great value, a given, particular relationship may be deeply problematic. Families and society should do their best to nurture positive relationships but must not prohibit the ending of damaging ones, nor demonize individuals who seek to escape them. Second, recognizing the values that come with positive spousal relations means that families and society should do their best to provide these valuable functions to those who are not taking part in such a relationship.

Next, must a spousal relationship be between one man and one woman? Based on everything that has been said up to this point, I see no reason to answer in the affirmative. At the very least, we have seen no compelling reason not to include same-sex partnerships, and there is ample evidence that, in fact, same-sex partners are able to support one another and nurture children just as well as different-sex partners. I am also deliberately leaving open the possibility of spousal relationships with more than two members. This is a complex topic in its own right, and deserves more attention than I can give it here. China's historical experiences provide both reasons for caution and reasons for openness, and I suggest that modern Confucians should be willing to assess the possibility of various kinds of "polyamorous" spousal arrangements.

The remaining questions mainly have to do with how the various responsibilities of living lives together, including raising children and nurturing relationships with other family members—especially parents—are to be apportioned between the spouses. If each partner pays good attention to all the demands on the whole family unit—including professional demands that primarily fall on individuals, as well as more general demands that fall on the family as a whole—and then does what he or she can best do to see the demands are well met, based on caring for his or her spouse, for the other members of the family, and ultimately for the others to whom she or he is connected (professionally; in the neighborhood, city, or country; or simply by virtue of sharing this earth with them); if each spouse responds in this way, then we can expect that responsibilities will be handled differently at different times, based on different capacities.[59] And these capacities themselves can change: for example, one spouse may lose a job and thus have more time at home; or learn a new skill; or become disabled; and so on. Only a few activities are firmly linked to sex differences, such as pregnancy, childbirth, and breastfeeding; and in families that rely on adoption, surrogacy, or other means, even these differences will not be evident. This is not to say that gender differences must disappear. The underlying insight behind Confucian yin-yang cosmology emphasizes the changing, complementary differences in our personalities, situations, and lives. Even in same-sex couples, we should expect role distinctions to emerge, even if they are not permanent through the lives of the spouses.

Finally, does this persistence of distinctions mean that modern Confucians should preserve "distinction" (*bie* 别) as the chief parameter governing spousal relations? I believe not. The kind of distinction that remains appropriate to spousal relations is in fact no different from the sort of distinction implicit in the idea of harmony, and which applies to all roles and relationships. We should not single out spousal roles as marked by an extra level of "distinction," because that will reinforce the old stereotypes that I have argued modern Confucians have no good reason to accept. Instead, drawing on my discussion above, modern Confucians should see a good spousal relationship as marked by deep levels of caring attention.

This brief sketch of what the "husband-wife" human relationship should look like, from the perspective of modern Confucianism, may have raised as many questions as it answers. That is as it should be, because progressive Confucian engagement with modern social challenges is in its infancy. Aside from the early, radical utopianism of Kang Youwei, most modern Confucians have either avoided these questions or taken decidedly conservative—and, I think, insufficiently reflective—stances toward them.

This conservativism, however, misses crucial insights of Confucianism, and undermines the possibility of Confucianism's playing a more active, creative, and positive role in the modern world.

Notes

I owe thanks to many for their feedback on earlier versions of these ideas, including Roger Ames, Youngsun Back, Chen Qiaojian, So-yi Chung, Fang Zhaohui, Max Fong, Gan Chunsong, Peng Guoxiang, Peter Hershock, Elise Springer, and Sor-hoon Tan, as well as other audience members at Zhejiang University, the Confucian Academy, Peking University, Shandong University, Sungkyunkwan University, and East China Normal University.

1. For the way in which an overly rigid idea of "disciplinary role-dependence" has undermined Confucianism in contemporary South Korea, see Kim (2016). As I will discuss further below, conservative or "fundamentalist" Confucians in contemporary China have also led many citizens to be highly skeptical about the possibility of Confucianism playing a constructive part of China's future.
2. *Guanzi*, "*Baguan*."
3. *Mengzi* 3A4; translation from Mengzi (2008, 71), slightly modified.
4. I thank Tang Wenming for emphasizing this point.
5. Chan (2003).
6. Since a given thing or action can be yin from one perspective and yang from another, these are roles, not essences. I discuss yin and yang further below.
7. Zhang (2017), 87–89.
8. *Mengzi* 7A:15; translation from (Mengzi 2008, 175), slightly modified.
9. *Mengzi* 6A4–5.
10. *Li Ji*, "Jiao Te Sheng"; translation from Legge (1885) via The Chinese Text Project (ctext.org/liji/jiao-te-sheng), modified.
11. Zhang (2017,) 107.
12. *Mengzi* 3A:5; translation from Mengzi (2008), 75.
13. *Xunzi* 17; translation from Xunzi (2014), 181.
14. In his "Discourse on Ritual," Xunzi also writes: "Is ritual not perfect indeed! It establishes a lofty standard that is ultimate of its kind, and none under Heaven can add to or subtract from it. *Xunzi* 17; translation from Xunzi (2014), 205. Similarly, in the "Questions on the Three-Year [Mourning Period]" chapter of the *Li Ji*, we read: "What purposes does the three-year mourning ritual serve? The different rules for the mourning rituals were established in harmony with human feelings. By means of them the differences in the social relations are set forth, and close and distant kin relations, as well as ranks of noble and base, are distinguished. They do not admit of being diminished or added to; and are therefore called 'The unchanging rules.' *Liji*, "*San Nian Wen*."

15. Versions of the idea that rituals should not change are also found later in the tradition; for some discussion, see Angle (2012), 93–94.

16. *Analects* 9.3 and 2.23.

17. *Li Ji*, "*Li Yun Pian*," 29.

18. *Zhuzi Yulei* 84 and *Zhuwengong Wenji* 40. I thank Professor Zhang Weihong for extremely helpful discussion of this issue.

19. Zeng and Guo (2014), 178.

20. Zeng and Guo (2014), 175.

21. Zhang (2017), 72 and 85.

22. *Mengzi*, 6A:15.

23. See Dennett (1987) and, for a different but largely compatible view, Kalton (1998).

24. For a helpful discussion of Professor Zhang's arguments, see Fong (2015).

25. For example, he cites a passage that says in part, "There were men and women, and after that there were husbands and wives; there were husbands and wives, and after that there were fathers and sons," and directly concludes that "we can see that Confucianism views men and women, on the one hand, and husbands-wives and parents-children, on the other hand, as intrinsically related to one another. . . . Therefore, in general Confucianism cannot agree to the legitimacy of gay marriage" (Zhang 2017, 226); Zhang is citing the same "Xu Gua" chapter of the *Book of Changes* that we just saw Zeng Yi discussing.

26. Zhang (2017), 226–227.

27. Admittedly, there are complex ethical and scientific issues surrounding some of these options which Confucians should reflect on carefully.

28. Zeng and Guo (2013), 67.

29. Zeng and Guo (2013), 188.

30. Elsewhere in the same book that from which I have been quoting Tang, Zeng Yi attempts to dismiss a well-known passage from the "Xu Gua" chapter of the *Book of Changes* that seems to prioritize husband-wife over father-son (Zeng and Guo 2013, 67–69).

31. Angle (2013).

32. Zhang (2017), 238–243.

33. I cannot help pointing out, though, that Zhang is forced to acknowledge that the only research he can find on the question of whether gay marriages are bad for children actually shows the opposite: that such marriages benefit children. Zhang then calls this research "preliminary" and says we must wait for more mature findings (Zhang 2017, 243).

34. For a series of instrumental arguments in favor of gay marriage, see Bilchitz (2016).

35. Angle (2012), ch. 6.

36. Rosemont (1988), 177.

37. Ames (1988), 200, emphasis in original.

38. Ames (2011), 160 and 188.
39. Ames (2011).
40. See *Zhong Yong*, 20, and Tang (2012), 35.
41. Tang (2012), 35.
42. As Tang reads him, Mou Zongsan's very different interpretation of Confucianism leads Mou to put human relations merely at the level of governance and administrative arrangements (*zhidao* 治道) rather than at the deeper level of moral justification (*zhengdao* 政道) (Tang 2012, 312).
43. A revised version of this essay appears in the present volume as Chapter 6.
44. Tang employs Axel Honneth's interpretation and development of Hegel from Honneth (2014), though he adjusts the final category (which, for Honneth, is "social freedom"). See Tang (2015).
45. Tang (2015).
46. Tang (2012), 36.
47. For example, Joseph Chan argues that "the Confucian ethics of benevolence [*ren*] is ultimately based on a common humanity rather than differentiated social roles—it carries ethical implications beyond these roles. . . . Although the sites for the realization of *ren* are commonly found in personal relationships, such as those between father and son or husband and wife, there are *nonrelational* occasions where moral actions are also required by *ren*" (Chan 2014, 117–118).
48. Rosemont and Ames (2008), 56.
49. Personal communication.
50. Zeng and Guo (2014), 90, 188.
51. Wu Fei, Lecture on "人伦与传统中国: 批判与反思" at Peking University, March 24, 2017.
52. For example, while changes associated with modernity have in some ways undermined the basis for gender inequality, in other ways it has reinforced inequality. While a full discussion is beyond the scope of the present chapter, there are powerful Confucian reasons to critique these modern forms of patriarchy; see Angle (2012), ch. 7, for one such argument. I thank Sor-hoon Tan for discussion of this point.
53. Munro (1969).
54. Zhang (2017), 107.
55. Moderately well-developed virtuosity is quite common in most societies. It should also be clear that virtuous parents are neither necessary nor sufficient for producing virtuous children: even the best will fail sometimes, due to circumstances beyond anyone's control (*ming* 命), and sometimes wonderful children emerge from terrible families, as the story of the ancient sage Shun is meant to remind us.
56. XJSL 6.15/120.
57. XJSL 6.14/120.
58. I thank Youngsun Back for raising this question.
59. The importance of developing good dispositions of "attention" as part of Confucian self-cultivation is one theme of Angle (2009).

References

Ames, Roger T. 1988. Rites as Rights: The Confucian Alternative. In *Human Rights and the World's Religions*, edited by Leroy S. Rouner, 199–216. South Bend, IN: University of Notre Dame Press.
———. 2011. *Confucian Role Ethics: A Vocabulary*. Honolulu: University of Hawai'i Press.
Angle, Stephen C. 2009. *Sagehood: The Contemporary Significance of Neo-Confucian Philosophy*. New York: Oxford University Press.
———. 2012. *Contemporary Confucian Political Philosophy: Toward Progressive Confucianism*. Cambridge, UK: Polity Press.
———. 2013. Contemporary Confucian and Islamic Approaches to Democracy and Human Rights. *Comparative Philosophy* 4(1).
Bilchitz, David. 2016. LBGTI Rights and Legal Reform: A Comparative Approach: Equality, Dignity, and Social Harmony: Exploring the Rationales and Models for Recognizing Same-Sex Relationships in Law." *Frontiers of Law in China* 11(3): 407–432.
Chan, Joseph. 2014. *Confucian Perfectionism: A Political Philosophy for Modern Times*. Princeton, NJ: Princeton University Press.
Chan, Sin Yee. 2013. The Confucian Conception of Gender in the Twenty-First Century. In Daniel A. Bell and Chaibong Hahm (Eds.), *Confucianism for The Modern World* (pp. 312–333). Cambridge: Cambridge University Press.
Dennett, Daniel C. 1987. *The Intentional Stance*. Cambridge, MA: MIT Press.
Fong, Maxwell. 2015. In a World of "Confucius Says" (子曰), What Can Confucius Say About Gay Marriage? *Warp, Weft, and Way*. warpweftandway.com/confucius-%E5%AD%90%E6%9B%B0%EF%BC%89-marriage
Honneth, Axel. 2014. *Freedom's Right: The Social Foundations of Democratic Life*. Translated by Joseph Ganahl. New York: Columbia University Press.
Kalton, Michael C. 1998. Extending the Neo-Confucian Tradition: Questions and Reconceptualization for the Twenty-First Century. In Evelyn Tucker and John Berthrong (Eds.), *Confucianism and Ecology* (pp. 77–101). Cambridge, MA: Harvard University Center for the Study of World Religions.
Kim, Sungmoon. 2016. Beyond a Disciplinary Society: Reimagining Confucian Democracy in South Korea. In P. J. Ivanhoe and Sungmoon Kim (Eds.), *Confucianism, a Habit of the Heart: Bellah, Civil Relgion, and East Asia*. Albany, NY: SUNY Press.
Legge, James. 1885. *Sacred Books of the East, volume 28, part 4: The Li Ki*.
Mengzi. 2008. *Mengzi: With Selections from Traditional Commentaries*. Translated by Bryan Van Norden. Indianapolis: Hackett.
Munro, Donald. 1969. *The Concept of Man in Ancient China*. Stanford, CA: Stanford University Press.

Rosemont Jr., Henry. 1988. Why Take Rights Seriously? A Confucian Critique. In Leroy S. Rouner (Ed.), *Human Rights and the World's Religions* (pp. 167–182). South Bend, IN: University of Notre Dame Press.

Rosemont Jr., Henry, and Roger T. Ames. 2008. *The Chinese Classic of Family Reverence: A Philosophical Translation of the Xiaojing*. Honolulu: University of Hawai'i Press.

Tang, Wenming 唐文明. 2012. 隐秘的颠覆: 牟宗三, 康德与原始儒家. Beijing: Sanlian Shudian.

Tang, Wenming 唐文明. 2015. 从陈寅恪悼念王国维的诗文谈儒教人伦思想中的自由观念. 新浪历史.

Xunzi. 2014. *Xunzi: The Complete Text*. Translated by Eric L. Hutton. Princeton, NJ: Princeton University Press.

Zeng, Yi 曾亦, and Guo, Xiaodong 郭晓东. 2014. 何谓普世? 谁之价值?: 当代儒家论普世价值. Shanghai: Huadong Shifan Daxue Chubanshe.

Zhang, Xianglong. 2017. 张祥龙. 家与孝: 从中西间视野看 [*Family and Filial Piety: As Viewed Between Eastern and Western Perspectives*]. Beijing: Sanlian Shudian.

Chapter 9

From Women's Learning (*Fuxue* 妇学) to Gender Education
Feminist Challenges to Modern Confucianism

SOR-HOON TAN

Introduction

The promotion of Confucianism to offer solutions to contemporary problems, better alternatives to the patently unsatisfactory *status quo* of our world, and the tired ideals that have dominated academic and global discourses should not be mistaken for naïve traditionalism advocating the revival of Confucianism as it was understood and practiced in its historical milieu. This is especially pertinent in the area of gender relations. As Chenyang Li pointed out nearly two decades ago, as "the philosophical-religious tradition that originated in Confucius and was further developed by scholars and supporters of later times . . . there is little doubt that the answer to our first question of whether Confucianism has oppressed women has to be affirmative."[1] Reviewing late twentieth-century studies of Chinese women in traditional society that challenge earlier literature depicting them only as oppressed victims, Li concluded that "While Confucianism's oppression of women was quite severe—indeed undeniably severe—it must have left some room for women's moral cultivation and even social participation."[2]

Li believes that the exploration of common ground between Confucianism and feminism to "find out whether Confucianism is able conceptually to accommodate women's equality" could help to overcome Confucianism's "gender complex."[3] If there is so much affinity between Confucianism and feminism or feminist perspectives, as many interesting explorations of the philosophical common ground between the two have shown, why was Confucianism complicit in the oppression of women in traditional Chinese society? Li suggests two possible answers: (1) aspects of Confucianism that are women-oppressive could be traced to additions by some specific thinkers of later dynasties after Confucius and Mencius, whose core doctrines are free from sexism; (2) restrictive application domain of values or perspectives that have affinity with feminism: "sexist interpretations of *ren* and other core values of Confucianism may have been responsible for excluding women in ancient China. It does not, however, necessarily imply that the concept of *ren* itself is sexist."[4]

Even a scholar who judges that not criticizing the prevailing sexist social arrangements of gender segregation and male dominance rendered Confucius "an accomplice to the continued cultural minimalization of women," sees Confucius as supporting equal opportunity to learn that can be extended to women.[5] While not quite egalitarian in its approach to education for both genders, Confucianism's emphasis on learning provided a way to promote Chinese women's education during historical periods when many societies did not permit women to be educated, let alone see any need to do so. Although Confucius had no female student—even his own daughter and niece are mentioned in the *Analects* only on the occasions of Confucius finding them good husbands (*Analects* 5.1, 5.2) while the text recorded his teaching his own son (*Analects* 16.13)—his views about learning as a central value and "in education, there should be no distinction of kind/class" (*youjiao wulei* 有教无类) (*Analects* 15.38) have been cited as justifying women's equal access to education by contemporary scholars.[6] Given that equal access to education has been granted, at least formally, to women in East Asian societies with Confucian legacies, it seems unproblematic to re-read Confucian texts to discard its sexist accretions in favor of gender equality today.

However, "gender neutral" readings and applications of Confucian ideas despite sexist intentions of their original authors may not be enough to reconcile Confucianism and feminism, let alone construct a Confucian feminism that will offer "a sense of cultural recovery for Chinese feminism."[7] Beyond acknowledging the complicity of Confucianism in past oppressions of women, and resolutely rejecting sexist interpretations, closer scrutiny of how ideas that are not intrinsically sexist have nevertheless supported or even encouraged oppressive practices which diminished women is necessary to prevent Confucianism, if revived today, from repeating its historical errors. Chinese women were not excluded from education by an oversight in limiting the application of Confucian ideas of learning to men. The next section will examine textual historical evidence to show that, throughout China's long history, Confucians paid explicit and serious attention to the education of women; rather than denial of education to women, applying Confucian ideas of learning to women resulted in the gendered education established within Confucian tradition that discriminated against women and entrenched their inferior social position. This exemplifies Lijuan Yuan's observation that, "in a deeply gendered social context, an ostensibly gender-neutral theory may have consequences that are disproportionately damaging for women."[8]

Have the social contexts in today's China, and other Confucian societies, changed sufficiently that Confucian ideas no longer pose a sexist threat? Equal formal access to educational institutions notwithstanding, systematic variations structured along gender as an axis of inequality persist in many aspects of education in many countries, including East Asian countries; gender equality or parity remains an elusive goal even today. Recent empirical studies have shown gender relations worsening insofar as women's well-being and self-realization are concerned despite their impressive gains in education. Whether gender equality or parity is desirable, how to achieve it, and the role of education in that endeavor are issues that a modern (and feminist) Confucian philosophy of education needs to reflect upon so that it could contribute to that conversation, and it needs to do so by going beyond abstract philosophizing to pay serious attention to the multidisciplinary studies of gender, in order to solve real problems confronting women today. Beyond the fact that "*conceptual possibilities* of a traditional idea do little for historically grounded oppressions that are usually tied to conventional interpretations of that very idea," some who are interested in the cultural revival of Confucianism in mainland China advocate revivals of traditional gender roles as well.[9]

> Being a good daughter, a good mother, a good wife, are the necessary demand of women's natural and family attributes, the most basic value basis for measuring the meaning of Chinese women's lives, hence the basis of Chinese women's sense of achievement and belonging. As for participating in the public life of society, being a successful career woman, these are not necessary demands on Chinese women . . .[10]

Jiang's recommendation for modern women's self-cultivation is to revive traditional gendered education based on didactic texts used in the past, such as the *Biographies of Women* (*Lienü Zhuan* 列女传) and *Classic for Daughters* (*Nüer Jing* 女儿经). Given that the social reality in China (and probably all other societies with Confucian influence) still retains significant degree of traditional gender bias associated (even if erroneously so) with Confucianism, there is a real risk of Confucianism repeating and continuing to perpetuate oppression of women. Simply offering contending interpretations of Confucian ideas in the ivory tower is not enough. This chapter will explore what more those who value Confucianism but reject sexism might do to meet feminist challenges.

Education of Women in Confucian Texts and Historical Practice

Education is central to Confucian philosophy. Confucius described himself as one who "stud[ies] without respite and instruct[s] others without growing weary" (*Analects* 7.2).[11] He urged his students to "make an earnest commitment to the love of learning and be steadfast to the death in service to the efficacious way" (*shandao* 善道) (*Analects* 8.13). Whether a Confucian follows Mencius in believing that we are born with four sprouts of humaneness (*ren* 仁), appropriateness (*yi* 义), ritual propriety (*li* 礼), and wisdom (*zhi* 知), constituting natural human goodness, or is more persuaded by Xunzi that the natural qualities of human beings are bad in tending toward greed and conflict in inevitable circumstances of scarcity, she would affirm that personal cultivation, which could be understood as education, is indispensable to becoming human, not the biological human as an animal species, but the normative human as an accomplishment. Mencius's ideal government goes beyond ensuring material prosperity to undertaking the responsibility of educating the people:

> This is the way of the common people: once they have a full belly and warm clothes on their back they degenerate to the level of animals if they are allowed to lead idle lives, without education and discipline. This gave the sage king further cause for concern, and so he appointed Hsieh as the Minister for Education whose duty is to teach the people human relationships: love between father and son, duty between ruler and subject,

distinction between husband and wife, precedence of the old over the young, and faith between friends. (*Mencius*, IIIA4)¹²

Was the learning valued by Confucians and the education to be provided for the people by good governments accessible to women as well as men, or restricted only to the latter, which would render Confucianism a sexist philosophy? While there is no explicit statement in the *Analects* pertinent to this issue, the absence of female students was probably due to Confucius following the tradition ritual norm of segregated education for men and women, a norm that Mencius referred to without criticizing:

> Have you never studied the rites? When a man comes of age his father gives him advice. When a girl marries, her mother gives her advice, and accompanies her to the door with these cautionary words, "When you go to your new home, you must be respectful and circumspect. Do not disobey your husband." It is the way of a wife or concubine to consider obedience and docility the norm. (*Mencius*, IIIB2)

While rejecting obedience and docility as incompatible with being a "great man" (*dazhangfu* 大丈夫), Mencius apparently took for granted that that these are appropriate norms for women. The relation between husband and wife Mencius included in the five basic human relationships is one governed by distinction, this became a more general "distinction between men and women" (*nannü you bie* 男女有别) in the ritual canon and conventional vocabulary of China.¹³ In practice, a gendered approach to education fitted into a larger structure of gender differentiation and segregation defining the ritual order of social relations and cosmic harmony endorsed by the *Record of Rites* (*Liji* 礼记). "If no distinction was observed between men and women, then disorder would arise and grow—such is the nature of heaven and earth."¹⁴ Unlike "measures of weight, length and volume, the fixing of the elegancies of ceremony; the commencement of the year and month; the color of dress; differences of flags and blazonry; vessels and weapons; distinctions in dress," which rulers may change, the "distinction between men and women," together with "what concerned affection for kin, the honor paid to the honorable, the respect due to the aged" among the people, are norms that even sage kings cannot change.¹⁵

Central to the gender distinction is not so much essential nature or biological characteristics but the segregation between the inner (*nei* 内) and outer (*wai* 外) in the division of roles and functions for men and women according to the normative arrangements of family life.

> The observances of ritual propriety commence with a careful attention to the relations between husband and wife. They built the mansion and its apartments, distinguishing between the exterior and interior parts. The men occupied the exterior; the women the interior. The mansion was deep, and the doors were strong, guarded by porter and eunuch. The men did not enter the interior; the women did not come out into the exterior.[16]
>
> The men should not speak of what belongs to the interior, nor the women of what belongs to the exterior. Except at sacrifices and funeral rites, they should not hand vessels to one another. . . . They should not go to the same well nor the same bathing house. They should not share the same mat in lying down; they should not ask or borrow anything from one another; they should not wear similar upper or lower garments. Things spoken inside should not go out; words spoken outside should not come in.[17]

Given the emphasis on division of labor and functional differentiation in the "distinction between men and women," it is not surprising that, insofar as education prepares a child for his or her respective functions as an adult when he or she takes his or her proper place in the family and society, the classical model prescribes different education based on gender.

Differences between the genders are accompanied by commonalities, as evident in the instructions of the *Record of Rites* (*Liji* 礼记) for educating young girls and boys:

> When the child was able to take its own food, it was taught to use the right hand. When it was able to speak, a boy (was taught to) respond boldly and clearly; a girl, submissively and low.
>
> At six years, they were taught the numbers and the names of the cardinal points; at the age of seven, boys and girls did not occupy the same mat nor eat together; at eight, when going out or coming in at a gate or door, and going to their mats to eat and drink, they were required to follow their elders: the teaching of yielding to others was now begun; at nine, they were taught how to number the days.[18]

Gender differentiation is rare in at the earliest stage of education, for which most instructional texts of later dynasties addressed "children" even though boys were in fact their main concern. One exception is the *Words for Little Girls* (*Nü xiaoer yu* 女小儿语) written in the sixteenth century by Lü Desheng 吕得胜, who also authored *Words for Little Children* (*Xiaoer yu* 小儿语). Lü apparently wrote the former due to a perceived inadequacy or unsuitability of the latter for educating girls. The *Words for Little Girls* explicitly steers girls toward domestic life as good wife and mother, whereas teachings for boys to become good husband and father are glaringly absent from the *Words for Little Children*. Nevertheless, despite somewhat different tones, Ping-chen Hsiung finds more similarities than differences between the two, implying that "the lines separating grown-ups from children were immeasurably clearer than those distinguishing gender in early childhood. Furthermore, class or socioeconomic status was unquestionably the second leading factor in formulating these rules and codes, much more so than the separation of the sexes."[19]

Gender differences widened with stricter segregation from ten years old—girls keeping to the inner quarters, and boys no longer allowed in the women's apartments.

> At ten, the boy went to a master outside, and stayed with him even over the night. He learned the different classes of characters and calculation; he did not wear his jacket or trousers of silk; in his manners he followed his early lessons; morning and evening he learned the behavior of a youth; he would ask to be exercised in reading the tablets, and in the forms of polite conversation.[20]

. . .

> A girl at the age of ten ceased to go out from the women's apartments. Her governess taught her the arts of pleasing speech and manners, to be docile and obedient, to handle the hempen fibres, to deal with the cocoons, to weave silks and form fillets, to learn (all) woman's work, how to furnish garments, to watch the sacrifices, to supply the liquors and sauces, to fill the various stands and dishes with pickles and brine, and to assist in setting forth the appurtenances for the ceremonies.[21]

A growing literature for instructing girls and young women written by both men and women over the centuries testifies to the attention given to Chinese women's education. The more famous examples among them include the *Biographies of Exemplary Women* by Liu Xiang 刘向 (ca. 79–78 BCE) and subsequent compilations modeled on it, *The Lessons for Women* (*Nüjie* 女戒) by Ban Zhao (ca. 45–117), *Teachings for Women* (*Nüxun* 女训) by Cai Yong 蔡邕 (133–192), *The Book of Filiality for Women* (*Nü Xiaojing* 女孝经) by Madam Zheng 郑氏 of the Tang dynasty, *The Analects for Women* (*Nü Lunyu* 女论语) by Song Ruoxin 宋若莘 (died 820) and Song Ruozhao 宋若昭 (761–828), *Teachings for the Inner Court* (*Neixun* 内训) by Ming dynasty Empress Xu 徐 (1362–1407), *Short Records of Models for Women* (*Nüfan jielu* 女范捷录) by Madam Liu 刘 (ca. 1480–1570), *Regulations for the Women's Quarters* (*Guifan* 闺范) by Lü Kun 吕坤 (1536–1618), *Women's Learning* (*Nüxue* 女学) by Lan Dingyuan 蓝鼎元 (1680–1733), and *Women's Learning* (*Fuxue* 妇学) by Zhang Xuecheng 章学诚 (1738–1801). Four of these, *The Lessons for Women*, *The Analects for Women*, *Teachings for the Inner Court*, and *Short Records of Models for Women*, all written by women, were compiled and edited with commentaries by Wang Xiang 王相, the son of the Madam Liu, who authored the last of the these works, to form the *Women's Four Books*, published in 1624. Rather than denying women education, gender distinction both in Confucian texts and historical practice had been understood to imply different kinds of education required to cultivate the persons of men and women and prepare them for their different roles in life.

The Chinese didactic literature for women's education all affirm not only the importance of educating women to the flourishing of the family but also its impact on the outside world through the connection between ordering the family and bringing peace to the world in the Confucian ethical project as set out in the "Great Learning" chapter of the *Record of Rites*. According to Liu Xiang's biography in the *Han History*, he composed the *Biographies of Women* to persuade Emperor Cheng to recognize the influence of women on the state at all levels of society, but especially at the level of statecraft.[22] His message was explicitly endorsed by Tang dynasty's Madam Zheng in her *Book of Filiality for Women*.

> It was because of women that the kings of these three dynasties [i.e., Xia, Shang, and Zhou] lost the realm, their lives, and their states. This is even more true at the level of feudal lords, greater officers, and the common people. . . . When viewed in this way,

there are women who deserved credit for founding their families and others who destroyed their families.[23]

Empress Xu of the Ming dynasty saw women "assisting both family and state from the inner quarters," and maintained that, "since ancient times, the foundation of family and state all rely on the virtue of the assistance from the inner quarters."[24] Nor is such impact the sole prerogative of royal ladies, as Madam Liu's *Short Records of Models for Women* intended for a less elevated audience argued that "the way of women's education is even more important than men's. The correct model of the inner realm is prior to the external realm."[25] This was not just a biased gendered perspective of women, as Lü Kun's very popular text of the sixteenth century, *Regulations for the Women's Quarters*, begins by noting that "the ancient kings emphasized the teachings of *yin*, hence women have female teachers . . . Behind the doors of the women's quarters is the source of ten thousand transformations."[26]

Taking the cue from the *Record of Rites*, didactic texts for women from Han dynasty onward seek to impress upon women the "three obediences" (*sancong* 三从) and inculcate in them the "four virtues" (*side* 四德) required of an obedient wife, beginning with what is probably the most famous and influential text of this genre, Ban Zhao's *Lessons for women*.[27]

> A woman (ought to) have four qualifications: (1) womanly virtue; (2) womanly words; (3) womanly bearing; and (4) womanly work. Now what is called womanly virtue need not be brilliant ability, exceptionally different from others. Womanly words need neither be clever in debate nor keen in conversation. Womanly appearance requires neither a pretty nor a perfect face and form. Womanly work need not be work done more skillfully than others.[28]

While advocating the extension of the *Record of Rites* model of boy's education to girls as well, Ban Zhao counselled humility, gentleness, purity, and quietness, being "correct in manner and upright in character" in order to serve her husband with "whole hearted devotion," obedience toward parents-in-law, and harmony with brothers and sisters-in-law.[29] Written nearly seven centuries later, the *Analects for Women*, despite its ambitious title obviously comparing itself to the *Analects*, confines its teachings for women to mundane instructions to conduct themselves with modesty in dress and demeanor, observing ritual propriety in their very limited social sphere, humility and obedience in serving parents, husband and parents in law, industriousness in rising early retiring late, preparing food and sewing clothes for family members, receiving guests with appropriate hospitality, teaching the younger family members, good management of family's resources with frugality and hard work. The *Analects for Women* advises them to value harmony, be filial and respectful above all else, be affectionate toward the younger family members, and should the husband unfortunately die young, a woman "should wear heavy mourning for three years and remain faithful with determination, preserve the family and manage its property, tend to his grave and teach his children diligently to honor him even in death."[30] Given the social limitations placed on women, such gendered education seems to feminists to be little more than survival mechanisms adopted to cope with, and thereby perpetuate, an oppressive patriarchy.

Rather than Chinese society consistently failing to implement Confucian ideals that were relatively more favorable to women, Confucians sometimes resisted social trends that benefitted women, for example, Confucians, Zhu Xi (1130–1200) among them, argued against the expansion of women's property rights during the Song dynasty, citing classical authority of the "descent-line system" (*zongfa* 宗法).[31] The triumph of the Confucian patriarchal view that only males, as "heads of households," should own property from the Yuan dynasty onward has left a legacy of gender bias in property rights and ownership that, even today, has resulted in Chinese women missing out on what is arguably the biggest accumulation of residential property estate wealth in history.[32] Joanna Handlin suggests that the turning point in Confucian attitudes toward women during the Song dynasty could be viewed as "reactions to the aggressive behavior of women, as described in the vernacular fiction, and to the expansion of opportunities for women living in cities."[33] Notwithstanding the increasing sexism endorsed by Confucian ideologies and social practices from late Song dynasty onward, with the increase in women's literacy and contrary evidence, some Confucians in late imperial China did have doubts about the alleged inferiority that apparently excludes one half of humanity from self-cultivation and ethical accomplishment.

Lü Kun, in many ways a conventional Confucian (who was given a place in the Confucian temple after his death), writing for a female audience of different social classes, offered new commentaries on the biographies of exemplary women that praise the heroines "not for their submissiveness, but for independent thinking . . . and for their ingenious use of persuasion."[34]

Rather than exemplars of fidelity, he cited women who supported or saved their menfolk through "expediency in managing matters," maintaining that "the sages value virtue, but more than that, they value virtue accompanied by talent."[35] Lü went so far as to imply that women can be exemplars not only for women but also for "gentlemen aspiring to be exemplary persons" (*shijunzi* 士君子):

> Those who do not have confidence in themselves are unable to trust others. For someone like Mu-lan, how could others gossip about her losing her purity? The multitude of three armies over a period of 12 years did not know that she was a girl. How could they gossip about her? A gentleman in managing the world has a mind of which he alone is aware and which can be tested before the sun in heaven; and his sympathy with others reaches the standard of being able to mix without blighting his splendor with dust. Indeed, Mu-lan is my teacher.[36]

It might seem that, due to the inner-outer gender segregation, only men benefitted from the system of schools that operated outside the family residence, dating back to antiquity.[37] In these institutions, the males were taught various subjects that prepared them for a career outside the family home, while the education of females in the inner quarters was intended to prepare them for lives as wives and mothers taking care of the family and home. Despite girls not attending outside schools before the end of the nineteenth century, we have historical records of Han empresses who were patrons of scholarship and the arts, and Ban Zhao's literary accomplishments. Furthermore, every Chinese dynasty witnessed outstanding women, whose accomplishments which far exceeded domestic care have inspired many, and some of whose writings have been preserved for future generations.[38] Some might think, with good reason, that these are exceptions that proved the rule. However, by the late imperial period, there is ample evidence that literary and even classical education for daughters was a wide-spread practice among gentry families, to the extent that there were millions of literate Chinese women (still, no more than 10 to 20 percent of the female population) during the Qing dynasty, and "places like the Lower Yangtze area were saturated with women who possessed a classical education."[39] Contrary to Xunzi's claim that "a mother can suckle the child but is unable to instruct and correct it," many biographies of Chinese women, often written or commissioned by their sons who were accomplished Confucian scholars testify to their important role as their sons' first teacher who taught them to read the classics.⁴⁰ It has been argued that increased literacy among women—together with disaffection of the scholar official class and the increased economic power of women from the Ming dynasty onward—prompted some Chinese men, such as Lü Kun and later Yuan Mei (1716–1798), to question traditional sexism and argue for the comparability of the two sexes.⁴¹

Ming dynasty gentry were often accommodating, even indulgent toward their daughters, partly in reaction against "the rigid gender prejudice, deplorable social bias, and abhorrent restraints and hardship that daughters had to endure beyond their girlhood."⁴² Among the favors they showered their daughters with was an education that they hoped would guarantee their welfare in the long run. Besides the daughters' personal development, education also enhanced their eligibility in making good marriages as capable spouses and resourceful mothers.⁴³ Daughters often shared lessons with their brothers before the latter started attending school outside; in families with no sons, they were tutored on their own in the home. In many cases, the education of daughters was not limited to domestic skills, even though such skills continue to be emphasized even after the first public school for girls was established in Shanghai in 1898 and arguably even today.⁴⁴ In the Ming dynasty, daughters' education was not confined to the didactic literature of "women's learning," but often included the Confucian classics that sons were introduced to, sometimes by their own mothers or some other educated female relatives, although fathers or male relatives often undertook that role. Some families even hired special tutors or set up "family school for girls" (*nüshu* 女塾) at home. Besides practical skills and moral inculcation, young women were also trained in the classics, history, literature, arts, and philosophy during the Ming dynasty, to the extent this era saw a significant increase in publication, circulation, and marketing of poetry, drama, novels, calligraphy, and paintings by women. Some educated women earned a living selling their literary works or hired themselves out as teachers.⁴⁵

The positive attitudes toward women's education exemplified by Lü Kun in the Ming dynasty continued and broadened during the Qing dynasty, although education for women remained curtailed, and other gender-oppressive beliefs and practices—cults of chastity and virginity, seclusion, footbinding, concubinage, among others—persisted.⁴⁶ The eighteenth-century poet Yuan Mei, accepted female students and encouraged women poets to publish their works.⁴⁷ His views and practices were attacked by Zhang Xuecheng, often viewed as an opponent of women's education in his work, *Women's Learning*. Zhang was defending the traditional Confucian view on gendered education, rather than denying that women are capable of learning and should be educated. Concerned with contemporary moral decline which he associated with poetry, he argued that the popular maxim "Lack of talent is a virtue in women" (女子无才便是德) meant that women should first study to acquire the traditional virtues, Ban Zhao's formula of womanly virtue, words, bearing, and work (德言容功), and poetry should be studied only to improve understanding of propriety, not as a substitute for the latter.[48] Susan Mann points out that Zhang's own treatment of exemplary women portrays them in diverse roles: "He took care that women of talent found a place in the panoply of women's biographies . . . Most notably, Zhang took women seriously as historians in their own rights." Zhang's praise for Ban Zhao in *Women's Learning* makes it clear that he considered "a woman as capable as a man of speaking 'public' language," and rather than supporting the traditional confinement in order to limit their capacity, in Zhang's view, "the inner quarters were the sanctuary where women in the family sustained the pure Dao, free from the corruption that overwhelmed upright men."[49] Notwithstanding Confucian criticisms, by the end of the eighteenth century, women's achievements in poetry, painting, and calligraphy were becoming publicly recognized. Published works by women, which had already appeared in the Ming and early Qing dynasty, increased during the late eighteenth and early nineteenth centuries.[50] However, the gender divide in society, with women assigned to the household and men without, remained largely intact, prompting Mary Rankin's remark, "Education and literary skills, which for men were stepping stones to power and prestige, remained largely an adornment even for the most admired and able women."[51]

Learning from Texts and History

The historical practice of gendered education in China was sexist insofar as it involved a belief that certain differences exist between female and male human beings, which justify unjust social and political arrangements whereby men have power and dominance over women. Confucianism's complicity goes beyond passive acquiescence to pre-existing practices, as Confucian texts from various periods provide important justification for traditional gendered education in its conception of the relation between such education and differentiated gender roles, understood as constituting Confucian social order, sometimes premised on cosmic order. However, dissenting voices have existed from the earliest Confucian discussions of women's roles.[52] While the practice of gendered education as traditional norm did not completely preclude women from receiving education similar to men from the earliest times, what were only exceptions not worthy of philosophical debates became more common in late imperial times and raised questions for traditional norms and generated debates within the Confucian discourse on women's education. From the interaction between textual prescriptions, which may take the form of implicitly or explicitly defending or critiquing existing practices, and historical practices, one may draw a number of lessons for constructing a modern Confucian view on the question of gender in education.

In retrospect, Confucianism might have fared better viz-a-viz gender justice had it been more actively critical of the traditional norms of gendered education, but its insight that education must correspond with the roles that would or must be assumed by the educated so that they could realize themselves within those roles is sound. Its views of gender roles were sexist, and the sexism worsened over time. A rapprochement between Confucianism and feminism requires a reconstruction of Confucian views on gender roles, but this should not and cannot be a matter of replacing them with a borrowed set of given "feminist" gender roles, since there is no consensus on what constitute ideal gender roles among feminists. Reflective inquiry on the problems of gender relations in contemporary contexts and their possibilities in the future is needed for progress in both Confucianism and feminism, and is the most urgent and crucial task in constructing a Confucian feminism or a feminist Confucianism. In contemporary scholarship, reconstructions of Confucian concepts that provide the basis for its gender views, such as *nei-wai* and *yin-yang*, suggest various possibilities of more equitable modern Confucian views of gender roles.[53] Such undertakings do not point in the direction of uncritical acceptance of current gender roles—whether in East Asian societies still influenced by Confucianism or more westernized societies upholding gender equality as idealized by Anglo-European philosophical traditions. As a reflective normative philosophy, Confucianism today cannot simply adapt itself to current gender roles, any more than it should revive traditional roles, which are both far from ideal.

Gender Relations in China Today

Women's liberation was considered central to China's modernization in the nineteenth-century intellectual elite's preoccupation with the "woman question" and the Chinese Communist Party's belief that the achievement of gender equality was necessary for national strength and social progress. Laws and regulations to safeguard the legitimate rights and interests of women in the labor market, to promote gender equality, and to enable women to play more active roles in society have been introduced since the beginning of the twentieth century, with new laws on job promotion, contract labor, and rural land use aimed at promoting gender equality propagated as late as 2008. The Chinese state also adopted a Development Plan for Women for 1995–2000, followed by a second plan for 2001–2010, and a third for 2011–2020.[54] Yet, the modernizers' narrative of Chinese women progressing from a state of subjugation in the premodern period toward liberation and gender equality in modern times is far too simplistic: "Some types of gender inequality have become less common, while others appear to have changed relatively little. Yet other types of gender inequality and some problems for women appear to have been exacerbated or created in the post-Mao period."[55]

Many patriarchal values and practices remained embedded in social, economic, and political policies since 1949, with the aspiration of gender equality subordinated to more urgent agendas. State policies under the Communist Party often built on traditional patriarchal social arrangements and norms to achieve their economic and political goals, and economic reforms have exacerbated some forms and introduced new forms of gender inequality. Chinese women continue to suffer injustice in the revitalized preference for sons in most of China in the post-Mao period and exacerbated by "gender blind-spots" in some policies, in the gendered division of work resulting in women's "double burden" of full time (under)paid work and major responsibilities for child care and housework, under-representation in politics and other domains, especially in positions associated with power and prestige, in the disparity between their shares of economic contributions and benefits both at home and at work, in violence against women in the form of infanticide and wife battering, attitudes about the proper qualities of husbands and wives, and the pressure exerted on young women to get married, often against their economic interests and independence.[56] The era of market reforms and globalization unfortunately has witnessed the commoditization of women through stereotype advertising and other media, leveraging on a return of traditional ideologies of gender bias.

Education is one area where women have benefited significantly from China's modernization, with drastic decreases in gender disparity in school enrollment and average years of education. The population census of 2005 reveals that women who completed senior high school had a significantly higher chance of entering college than men in similar circumstances, and women accounted for 51.1% of students enrolled in college and 49.7% of students enrolled in four-year universities in 2005, although women from economically disadvantaged regions remain a cause for concern.[57] However, China has since reversed this trend: in 2015, 47.1% of college students and 47.6% undergraduates are female. Females accounted for 71.1% of the population with no schooling, which amounts to 8.3% of women aged six and above; in comparison, only 3.2% of men aged six and above have no schooling.[58] While some studies show that industrialization and structural changes, including the growth of gender-specific industries could explain some of the decrease in gender inequality in education, it has also been suggested that the traditional idea that educated women make better wives and mothers plays a part in the expansion of education access for women, as that expansion has not been matched with a corresponding improvement of labor market opportunities and performance, a discrepancy that "can be traced back to the persistent gender norms which, amongst other things, imply the centrality of marriage and non-market unpaid labor for women."[59]

Together with rural-urban residence, provincial residence, and occupation, gender is one of the four major determinants of income inequality (measured as percentage of the Gini coefficient), and its contribution to that inequality more than doubled between 1995 and 2007.[60] While economic development has reduced gender income inequality, market forces have exacerbated it.[61] Several studies have shown that the gender wage gap has widened significantly since the mid-1990s, especially between 2002 and 2007, and according to one study, "this increase was largely due to unexplained components, thereby implying that discrimination against female workers in the urban labor market was rising."[62] Besides discrimination, other studies also attribute the "gender penalty" in income to "a cumulative process of gender-specific 'routing' in the Chinese society: gender-specific childhood process of education, different length of employment in part due to an earlier stipulated retirement age for women, different levels and specializations in educational attainment, different occupations, and different industries."[63] While women's participation in the workforce has increased, they tend to be employed in low-paying industries and positions, and their work performance is often adversely affected by unequal distribution of responsibilities for housework and care for the young and the elderly in the family. Despite self-employment providing more room for work-family balance and the absence of employer discrimination, preliminary findings indicated that the few much-publicized Chinese women entrepreneurs and millionaires are also exceptions that prove the rule of women being relegated to the least rewarding (both in terms of earnings and prestige) self-employment.⁶⁴ Beyond income inequality, the market economy has introduced new forms of gender inequality endangering the futures of Chinese young women: besides "segregating them into work that is low wage, low prestige, and temporary," the new service industry "requires performances of femininity and deference" that perpetuates traditional gender bias in new hierarchical processes.⁶⁵

Despite equal access to gender-neutral education, the traditional "inner-outer" gender division continues to influence students' entries into different disciplines and subsequent entry into different industries, with women concentrated in the social sciences, education, and social work. While the gender difference is small in these fields (55.3 percent men vs. 44.7 percent women in the 2005 graduating cohort), science and engineering graduates are predominantly male (57.5 percent in science/technology and 77.3 percent in engineering).⁶⁶ This is not always due to individual choice, as women face greater difficulty getting jobs in these fields, were given lower starting salaries compared to men despite better academic performance, and some universities require higher University Entrance Examination (UEE) scores for women than for men in recruiting students for majors deemed to relate to "men's work."⁶⁷ The attitudes of the state, educators, potential employers, besides their parents, influence student choice, casting doubt on the extent to which students can choose to study what interest them most and would optimize their self-realization.

Persistence of the "inner-outer" gender norms is also at the root of the disproportionate burden of housework and family care responsibilities shouldered by women even when they hold full-time paid jobs that are no less demanding than their husbands'. A 2008 survey by the National Bureau of Statistics shows that the time spent on unpaid work every week by women is more than twice that of men. Unpaid work takes up 20.2 percent of men's time, but 47.1 percent of women's time.⁶⁸ Another study reported that wives accounted for 64 percent of the total time couples spend on ten major household chores.⁶⁹ In rural China, "domestic work" is considered "women's work" and undertaken almost entirely by women. Tamara Jacka points out,

> This is an important element in women's subordination; not so much because of the work itself but because, firstly, it is, in a number of ways devalued in relation to other work; secondly, women are expected to undertake such work in addition to

other work and hence suffer a double burden; and finally, due to the above two factors, it has certain negative consequences for women's involvement in other types of work.[70]

Some believe that the solution to women's "double burden" is for them to "return home." In 2011, Zhang Xiaomei, a female member of the CPPCC National Committee submitted a law proposal "Encouraging Some Women to Return Home" that triggered a heated debate in the media. According to Shaopeng Song, this is the sixth debate in China over this issue, the first occurring in the 1930s. Earlier advocates of women's return to the home tend to be male, for example in the mid-1990s, a leading sociologist, Zheng Yefu, basically "argued from a market point of view, urging women to accept injustice, or at least to recognize and accept gender injustice, at the current stage of China's development."[71] The 2011 debate saw a woman defending "women returning home" as a voluntary choice that women should be able to make in their own interests, while maintaining that "there are some congenital differences between men and women which cannot be changed," and "women are physiologically more suited to take care of household affairs, housework, caring for the elderly, nursing, educating children, and creating a happy and harmonious family life."[72] Song questions the "voluntariness" of such choices in a gender system still characterized by widespread discrimination against women, and other unjust practices that diminish women's motivation and confidence at work, and make it difficult for women to balance family life and career.[73]

Wither Feminist Encounter with Confucianism?

Rather than adapting to an already modernized ideal gender role of the "liberated woman," Confucian education for women today must answer the question of what "self-cultivation" for women should mean in the current circumstances. Is Zhang Xiaomei's proposal evidence that the ancient wisdom about "distinction between men and women" is correct, and women (or at least some, if not most women) are better off in the "inner quarters"? After all, outstanding Chinese women such as Ban Zhao and the Song sisters believed that the majority of (elite) women should be educated for just such a destiny. The tension between such a belief and their own unusual biographies—all three held official appointments at court, and the Song sisters never married—rather than a sign of inauthenticity that undermines the persuasive force of their advice, perhaps testifies to the practical purpose of their works, aimed at fulfilling what they perceived to be the educational needs of the majority of their female contemporaries, and a realistic acknowledgment that their lives were exceptions to the rule. Nor is the Song sisters' choice of title, *Women's Analects*, necessarily a misguided self-aggrandizing, for Confucius' teachings begin with filial respect toward parents and deference to elders (*Analects* 1.6). It implies that the activities that define the women's role do not preclude Confucian self-cultivation; on the contrary, excellence in their performance requires and sustains self-cultivation. However, the question we must ask is whether the paths that do not lead back to the "inner quarters" are truly open to women today, if they have the abilities and the inclinations to follow such paths, or do such options remain exceptions for external reasons having nothing to do with women's own personal qualities, desires, or values? If so, simply declaring that the Confucian ideal of self-cultivation, in which public life and contributions to society beyond the family are critical, applies to women as much as men will not make much difference without recognizing the need for social changes to remove the structured barriers to women's self-cultivation in diverse forms (and not just confined to the family), explicitly rejecting unexamined traditional gender norms that are unjust even if, perhaps especially if, they are attributed to Confucianism, paying serious attention to women's experience and women's voice, and answering the empirical questions of how to go about doing so in practically efficacious ways. Rather than dogmatically assuming that women's sense of accomplishment and meaning in life lie in being good (traditionally Confucian) daughters, wives, and mothers, feminist Confucians would want to see all opportunities of self-realization in modern societies effectively open to women, and listen seriously to women's own articulation of what kind of accomplishments give them satisfaction and meaning in life.

Lisa Rosenlee argues that, instead of rigid boundaries between static spatial-social domains, the Confucian concept of *nei-wai* implies boundaries that shift with contexts, and permit crossings in practice, so that the relation between inner and outer is one of complementarity, reciprocity, and interdependence.[74] How should such complementary, reciprocal, and interdependent inner-outer roles be distributed among men and women, and what would these demand of them are questions that need answering if Confucians are to educate the next generation appropriately. It may be that no definite prescription is warranted and the answers to these questions will vary from society to society and person to person. It is by no means certain that gender is never a legitimate axis of role differentiations. What is certain is that greater diversity and flexibility in roles that a person, whether male or female, could assume would benefit all; such diversity and flexibility, genuine choice in the roles that one assumes, and authentic evaluation of which roles suit one best in the context of one's network of ethical relationships are not possible without first dismantling the structural inequities posing as tradition.

Notes

1. Chenyang Li, "Confucianism and Feminist Concerns: Overcoming the Confucian 'Gender Complex,'" 188.
2. Chenyang Li, "Confucianism and Feminist Concerns," 191.
3. Chenyang Li, "Confucianism and Feminist Concerns," 192.
4. Chenyang Li, "Confucianism and Feminist Concerns," 193.
5. Terry Woo, "Confucianism and Feminism," 116–117.
6. Ann A. Pang-White, "Introduction: Rereading the Canon," 6; Yu-ning Li, "Historical Roots of Changes in Women's Status in Modern China," 112.
7. Li, "Confucianism and Feminist Concerns," 194.
8. Lijun Yuan, "Ethics of Care and Concept of Ren: A Reply to Chenyang Li," 124.
9. The criticism by Indian feminists identified by Vrinda Dalmiya applies to the appropriation Confucian resources for Chinese feminism as well. Vrinda Dalmiya, "Caring Comparisons: Thoughts on Comparative Care Ethics," 205.
10. Jiang Qing 蒋庆, "Only Confucianism Can Settle Modern Women: The *Biographies of Women* is a Good teaching Resource" (只有儒家能安顿现代女性). For responses to this interview, see Dai Jinhua 戴锦华, "There exists a profound phantom of 'polygamy' in Current Gender Imagination" (当下的性别想象中, 深刻地存在着"多妻制"幽灵), *The Paper* (澎湃), December 15, 2015. www.thepaper.cn/newsDetail_forward_1409159; and several postings on the *Confucianism* website (儒家网), www.rujiazg.com/category/page/1/type/9/small/53
11. Unless otherwise stated, all subsequent in-text citations of *Analects* are from *The Analects of Confucius: A Philosophical Translation*, trans. Roger T. Ames and Henry Jr. Rosemont, 1998.
12. Unless otherwise stated, citations from the *Mencius* are from D. C. Lau, *Mencius*, 1970. See also passages describing "humane government" (*renzheng* 仁政) in *Mencius*, IA3, IA7, and *Analects* 13.9.
13. In the *Record of Rites* (*Liji* 礼记), where this phrase appears in the "Single victim at the border Sacrifice" (*Jiao Te Sheng* 郊特牲, p. 708) chapter, the context is the marriage ceremony, in which the man and woman referred to are (soon to be) husband and wife. Elsewhere in the same text, the distinction is between men

and women, for example in the "Record of small matters in the dress of mourning" (*Sangfu xiaoji* 丧服小记, p. 871), the "Great Treatise" (*Dazhuan* 大传, p. 907), "Record of Music" (*Yueji* 乐记, p. 986), "Different teachings of the different kings" (*Jingjie* 经解, p. 1257), and "The meaning of the marriage ceremony" (昏义, p. 1418). Page numbers are from Sun Xidan 孙希旦, *Record of Rites* (*Liji* 礼记), 3 vols.

14. "Record of Music," 994. Translated in *Li Chi*, trans. James Legge, part II, p. 63.

15. "The Great Treatise" in *Liji*, 907. *Li Chi*, II: 37. For a discussion of other pre-Han and Han texts on the distinction between men and women as definitive of human civilization, see Lisa Raphals, *Sharing the Light*, 207, and Lisa Rosenlee, *Confucianism and Women: A Philosophical Interpretation*, 76–77.

16. "The pattern in the family" (*Neize* 内则), Sun Xidan 孙希旦, *Liji*, 759. *Li Chi*, I: 268.

17. "The pattern in the family" (*Neize* 内则), *Liji*, 735. *Li Chi*, I: 259.

18. "The pattern in the family" (*Neize* 内则), *Liji*, 768–769. *Li Chi*, I: 272–273.

19. Ping-chen Hsiung, *A Tender Voyage: Children and Childhood in Late Imperial China*, 189.

20. Sun Xidan 孙希旦, *Liji*, 769. *Li Chi*, I: 273.

21. *Liji*, 772–773. *Li Chi*, I: 273.

22. Gu 班固 Ban, *Han History* (*Hanshu* 汉书), 36: 1957–1958.

23. Robin R. Wang, ed., *Images of Women in Chinese Thought and Culture*, 390.

24. Yanli 黃嫣梨 Huang, *Women's Four Books with Selected Commentaries* (女四書集注義證), 109, 16, 28, 46. Translation modified from Ann A. Pang-White, "Confucius and the Four Books for Women," 34.

25. Huang, *Women's Four Books*, 168. Pang-White, "Confucius and the Four Books for Women," 34.

26. Lü Kun 吕坤, *Regulations for the Women's Quarters* (*Guifan* 闺范), 236b, author's translation.

27. Sun Xidan 孙希旦, *Liji.*, 709, 1421; cf. justification of translating "*sancong*" as "threefold dependence or following" instead of "three obediences" in Rosenlee, *Confucianism and Women*, 89–90.

28. Nancy Lee Swann, *Pan Chao: Foremost Woman Scholar of China* (New York & London: Century, 1932), 86.

29. Swann, 83–90.

30. Song Ruozhao 宋若昭 and Song Ruoxin 宋若莘, "Analects for Women" (Nü Lunyu 女论语), in *Five Kinds of Transmitted Regulations* (*Wuzhong Yigui* 五种遗规), ed. Hongmou 陈宏谋 Chen, Sibu Beiyao (四部备要), 233b, author's translation. Cf. translation in Wang, *Images of Women in Chinese Thought and Culture*, 340.

31. Bettine Birge, *Women, Property, and Confucian Reaction in Song and Yuan China (960–1368)*, 143–199. Cf a study that confirms the deterioration of women's property rights between Song and Yuan dynasties, but seeks its causes in the different customs and the considerations of political interests rather than the

adoption of Confucian views in You Huiyuan 游惠遠, *Changes in Women's Statuses between Song and Yuan Dynasties* (宋元之際妇女地位的變遷), 203–262.

32. Leta Hong Fincher, *Leftover Women: The Resurgence of Gender Inequality in China*, 113; Lisa Rofel, "Gender as a Categorical Source of Property"; Gail Hershatter, *Women in China's Long Twentieth Century*, 24–25.

33. Joanna F. Handlin, "Lü Kun's New Audience: The Influence of Women's Literacy on Sixteenth Century Thought," 14.

34. Handlin, "Lü Kun's New Audience," 19.

35. Handlin, "Lü Kun's New Audience," 21.

36. Translated in Handlin, "Lü Kun's New Audience," 23. Lü, *Regulations for the Women's Quarters* (*Guifan* 閨範), II:32b.

37. Mencius (IIA3) mentioned these institutions set up by ancient rulers of the *Xia*, *Shang*, and *Zhou* dynasties for the people's education; the "Record on Education" (*Xueji*) of the *Record of Rites* also identifies different educational institutions in antiquity, Sun Xidan 孫希旦, *Liji*, 957. *Li Chi*, Part II, 50.

38. For such writings translated into English, which amount to only a fraction of the total, see Kenneth Rexroth and Ling Chung, eds., *The Orchid Boat: Women Poets of China*; Susan Mann, *Precious Records: Women in China's Long Eighteenth Century*, 76–120; Ellen Widmer and Kang-i Sun Chang, eds., *Writing Women of Late Imperial China*; Kang-i Sun Chang, Haun Saussy, and Charles Yin-tze Kwong, eds., *Women Writers of Traditional China: An Anthology of Poetry and Criticism*; Wilt Idema and Beata Grant, *The Red Brush: Writing Women of Imperial China*.

39. Hsiung, *Tender Voyage*, 205.

40. John Knoblock, *Xunzi: A Translation and Study of the Complete Works*, 71.

41. Handlin, "Lü Kun's New Audience," 27. See also Woo, "Confucianism and Feminism," 134–137. Woo notes that despite his feminist views on women's ability to learn and excel in all areas and the importance of women's economic independence, Lü was a conservative in gender relations who insisted on the differentiation between husband and wife and the gender seggregation of women and men (137). That those who held pro-women attitudes are not without contradictions in their overall outlook is also evident in Yuan Mei's treatment of women, see J. D. Schmidt, "Yuan Mei (1716–98) on Women."

42. Hsiung, *Tender Voyage*, 201.

43. Hsiung, *Tender Voyage*, 215–216.

44. Western missionary schools for Chinese girls were established from the 1840s. While early twentieth-century Chinese schools for girls taught subjects such as ethics, Chinese and foreign languages, arithmetic, history, geography, drawing, and physical education, they nevertheless paid particular attention to "household and family matters" contributing to the cultivation of "virtuous wives and good mothers" (*xianqi liangmu* 贤妻良母). Paul J. Bailey, *Gender and Education in China*, 2, 83–104. For emphasis in the curriculum on domestic education for women in contemporary China, see Sucharita Sinha Mukherjee, "More Educated and More

Equal? A Comparative Analysis of Female Education and Employment in Japan, China, and India," 863.

45. Hsiung, *Tender Voyage*, 205–208.

46. Mary Backus Rankin, "The Emergence of Women at the End of the Ch'ing: The Case of Ch'iu Chin," 40.

47. Schmidt, "Yuan Mei (1716–98) on Women," 140–150.

48. Zhang Xuecheng 章学诚, "Women's Learning" (妇学), 484.

49. Susan Mann, "Women in the Life and Thought of Zhang Xuecheng," 112.

50. Rankin, "Emergence of Women," 41; Dorothy Ko, *Teachers of the Inner Quarter: Women and Culture in Seventeenth Century China*.

51. Rankin, "Emergence of Women," 44. Hsiung's study cited above shows that women's education literary skills had real and important uses in late imperial China, so they were more than "largely an adornment" even though women could not put their education to full use in all domains.

52. An example is Terry's Woo's comparison of Mencius's and Xunzi's views, in Woo, "Confucianism and Feminism," 118–120.

53. Kelly James Clark and Robun R. Wang, 2004, "A Confucian Defense of Gender Equity"; Lisa Rosenlee, "Neiwai, Civility, and Gender Distinctions"; Robin R. Wang, 2005, "Dong Zhongshu's Transformation of Yin-Yang Theory and Contesting Gender Identity."

54. Tania Aneloff and Marylène Lieber, "Equality, Did You Say? Chinese Feminism after 30 Years."

55. "The 'Woman Question' and Gender Inequalities," in Tamara Jacka, Andrew B. Kipnis, and Sally Sargeson, *Contemporary China: Society and Social Change*, 254.

56. She Mingyang, "Changing Trends in Mate Selection among the Young" (青年择偶观的变化趋势), *Marriage and Family* (婚姻与家庭) 3 (1986); Yanjie Bian, "A Preliminary Analysis of the Basic Features of the Life Styles of China's Single-Child Families," *Social Science in China* 8 (1987); Emily Honig and Gail Hershatter, *Personal Voices: Chinese Women in the 1980s*, 273–307; Xiaoling Shu and Yanjie Bian, "Market Transtion and Gender Gap in Earnings in Urban China"; Xiaoling Shu, Yifei Zhu, and Zhanxin Zhang, "Global Economy and Gender Inequalities: The Case of Urban Chinese Market"; Hershatter, *Women in China's Long Twentieth Century*; Gillian Pascall and Sirin Sung, "Gender and East Asian Welfare States: From Confucianism to Gender Equality?"; Hong Fincher, *Leftover Women*; Fenglian Du and Xiaoyuan Dong, "Why Do Women Have Longer Durations of Unemployment Than Men in Post-Restructuring Urban China?"; Huiying Li, "Son Preference and the Tradition of Patriarchy in Rural China."

57. Xiaogang Wu and Zhuoni Zhang, "Educational Inequality in China, 1990–2005: Evidence from the Population Census Data," 143–144; Jun Yang, Xiao Huang, and Xin Liu, "An Analysis of Educaiton Inequality in China"; Junxia Zeng et al., "Gender Inequality in Education in China: A Meta-Regression Analysis."

58. "Population aged 6 and Over by Sex, Educational Attainment and Region (2015)," table 2.14. www.stats.gov.cn/tjsj/ndsj/2016/indexeh.htm

59. Ming-Hsuan Lee, "Schooling and Industrialization in China: Gender Differences in School Enrollment." Cf. Mukherjee, "More Educated and More Equal?," 846.

60. Shi Li, Guanghua Wan, and Juzhong Zhuang, "Income Inequality and Redistributive Policy in the People's Republic of China," 336–337. This is not to say that China is worse than other countries. Indeed, the picture for gender equality is gloomy and worsening worldwide, and according to one study China's urban gender wage gap is still one of the smallest among developing countries. Jane Nolan, "Gender and Equality of Opportunity in China's Labor Market," 160; Martin King Whyte, "Sexual Inequality under Socialism: The Chinese Case in Perspective." Despite widespread global injustices, feminists and other philosophers remain positive in offering possible solutions in a special issue of *Philosophical Topics* (37.2, 2009) on global gender justice.

61. Gloria Guangye He and Xiaogang Wu, "Gender Earnings Inequality in Reform-Era Urban China"; Philip N. Cohen and Wang Feng, "Market and Gender Pay Equity: Have Chinese Reforms Narrowed the Gap?"

62. Shi Li and Jin Song, "Changes in the Gender-Wage Gap in Urban China, 1995–2007," 402. See also Liqin Zhang and Xiao-Yuan Dong, "Male-Female Wage Discrimination in Chinese Industry: Investigation Using Firm-Level Data"; Min Qin et al., "Gender Inequalities in Employment and Wage-Earning among Internal Labor Migrants in Chinese Cities."

63. Feng Wang, *Boundaries and Categories: Rising Inequality in Post-Socialist China*, 119. See also Eileen Otis, *Markets and Bodies: Women, Service Work, and the Making of Inequality in China*, 6; Bohong Lui, Ling Li, and Chunyu Yang, "Gender (in)Equality and China's Economic Transition," 26–42.

64. Qian Forrest Zhang, "Gender Disparities in Self-Employment in Urban China's Market Transition: Income Inequality, Occupational Segregation and Mobility Processes." Cf. more complicated picture in Jing Song, "Women and Self-Employment in Post-Socialist Rural China: Side Job, Individual Career or Family Venture."

65. Otis, *Markets and Bodies*, 6. See also Xin Tong, "Gender, Division of Labor, and Social Mobility in Small-Scale Restaurants in China."

66. Congbin Guo, Mun C. Tsang, and Xiaohao Ding, "Gender Disparities in Science and Engineering in Chinese Universities." See also Xiaoling Shu, "Market Transition and Gender Seggregation in Urban China."

67. Guo, Tsang, and Ding, "Gender Disparities in Science and Engineering in Chinese Universities"; Didi Kirsten Tatlow, "Women in China Face Rising University Entrance Barriers."

68. Lui, Li, and Yang, "Gender (in)Equality and China's Economic Transition," 40.

69. Joyce Lai Ting Leong, Sylvia Xiaohua Chen, and Michael Harris Bond, "Housework Allocation and Gender (In)Equality," 85. The publication does not specify the date when the research was carried out.

70. Tamara Jacka, *Women's Work in Rural China*, 119. Women in advanced Western societies also continue to have difficulties combining work and family as a result of inequitable distribution of housework and care responsibilities and persistence of traditional gender ideology. Arlie Russell Hochschild, *The Second Shift*; Ann Crittenden, *The Price of Motherhood: Why the Most Important Job in the World Is Still the Least Valued*; Emily Monosson, ed. *Motherhood, the Elephant in the Laboratory: Women Scientists Speak Out*; Man Yee Kan and Jonathan Gershuny, "Gender Segregation and Bargaining in Domestic Labour: Evidence from the Longitudinal Time-Use Data"; Sheryl Sandberg and Arlie Russell, *Lean In: Women, Work, and the Will to Lead*.

71. Shaopeng Song, "'Returning Home' or 'Being Returned Home'?": The Debate over Women Returning to the Home and Changing Values," 72; Yefu Zheng, "Sociological Reflections on Gender Equality" (男女平等的社会学思考).

72. Song, "'Returning Home' or 'Being Returned Home'?," 61.

73. Song, "'Returning Home' or 'Being Returned Home'?," 62. For more evidence that, rather than a voluntary choice of family over work, Chinese women since the 1990s have been pushed into leaving work by market forces and inadequate state policies to protect their rights, see Jieyu Liu, *Gender and Work in Urban China: Women Workers of the Unlucky Genderation*, ch. 6; Tamara Jacka, "Back to the Wok: Women and Employment in Chinese Industry in the 1980s"; *Women's Work in Rural China*, 106–108; Shirin M. Rai, "Gender in China," in *China in the 1990s*, 190. For a general philosophical discussion of when and why feminists worry about gendered preferences, not just because they are adaptive, even to the extent of arguing for overriding voluntary preferences of many actual women and men, see Ann Levey, "Liberalism, Adaptive Preferences, and Gender Equality."

74. Rosenlee, *Confucianism and Women*, 70.

References

The Analects of Confucius: A Philosophical Translation. 1998. Translated by Roger T. Ames and Henry Jr. Rosemont. New York: Ballantine.
Aneloff, Tania, and Marylène Lieber. 2012. Equality, Did You Say? Chinese Feminism after 30 Years. *China Perspectives* 4: 17–24.
Bailey, Paul J. 2007. *Gender and Education in China*. Routledge Contemporary China. New York: Taylor & Francis.
Ban Gu 班固. 1975. *Han History (Hanshu* 汉书) [Chinese]. Beijing: Zhonghua Shuju.
Bian, Yanjie. 1987. A Preliminary Analysis of the Basic Features of the Life Styles of China's Single-Child Families. *Social Science in China* 8: 189–209.

Chang, Kang-i Sun, Haun Saussy, and Charles Yin-tze Kwong (Eds.). 1999. *Women Writers of Traditional China: An Anthology of Poetry and Criticism*. Stanford, CA: Stanford University Press.
Clark, Kelly James, and Robun R. Wang. 2004. A Confucian Defense of Gender Equity. *Journal of American Academy of Religion* 72(2) : 395–422.
Cohen, Philip N., and Wang Feng. 2009. Market and Gender Pay Equity: Have Chinese Reforms Narrowed the Gap? In Deborah S. Davis and Wang Feng (Eds.), *Creating Wealth and Poverty in Postsocialist China* (pp. 37–53). Stanford, CA: Stanford University Press.
Crittenden, Ann. 2001. *The Price of Motherhood: Why the Most Important Job in the World Is Still the Least Valued*. New York: Picador.
Dalmiya, Vrinda. 2009. Caring Comparisons: Thoughts on Comparative Care Ethics. *Journal of Chinese Philosophy* 36(2): 192–209.
Du, Fenglian, and Xiaoyuan Dong. 2009. Why Do Women Have Longer Durations of Unemployment Than Men in Post-Restructuring Urban China? *Cambridge Journal of Economics* 33(2): 233–252.
Guo, Congbin, Mun C. Tsang, and Xiaohao Ding. 2010. Gender Disparities in Science and Engineering in Chinese Universities. *Economics of Education Review* 29: 225–235.
Handlin, Joanna F1975. Lü Kun's New Audience: The Influence of Women's Literacy on Sixteenth Century Thought. In Margery Wolf and Roxane Witke (Eds.), *Women in Chinese Society*, 13–38. Stanford, CA: Stanford University Press.
He, Gloria Guangye, and Xiaogang Wu. 2014. Gender Earnings Inequality in Reform-Era Urban China. Michigan Population Studies Center, University of Michigan Institute for Social Research.
Hershatter, Gail. 2007. *Women in China's Long Twentieth Century*. Berkeley: University of California Press.
Hochschild, Arlie Russell. 1989. *The Second Shift*. New York: Quill.
Hong Fincher, Leta. 2014. *Leftover Women: The Resurgence of Gender Inequality in China*. London and New York: Zed Books.
Honig, Emily, and Gail Hershatter. 1988. *Personal Voices: Chinese Women in the 1980s*. Stanford, CA: Stanford University Press.
Hsiung, Ping-chen. 2005. *A Tender Voyage: Children and Childhood in Late Imperial China*. Stanford, CA: Stanford University Press.
Huang, Yanli 黃嫣梨. 2008. *Women's Four Books with Selected Commentaries* (女四書集注義證). Hong Kong: Commercial Press.
Idema, Wilt, and Beata Grant. 2004. *The Red Brush: Writing Women of Imperial China*. Cambridge, MA: Harvard University Asia Center.
Jacka, Tamara. 1990. Back to the Wok: Women and Employment in Chinese Industry in the 1980s. *Australian Journal of Chinese Affairs* 24: 1–24.
———. 1997. *Women's Work in Rural China*. Cambridge: Cambridge University Press.

Jacka, Tamara, Andrew B. Kipnis, and Sally Sargeson. 2013. *Contemporary China: Society and Social Change*. New York: Cambridge University Press.

K'ung Fu-tzu. *Li Chi*. 2008. Translated by James Legge. London: Forgotten Books.

Kan, Man Yee, and Jonathan Gershuny. 2010. Gender Segregation and Bargaining in Domestic Labour: Evidence from the Longitudinal Time-Use Data. In *Gender Inequalities in the 21st Century: New Barriers and Continuing Constraints*. Cheltenham: Edward Elgar.

Knoblock, John. 1994. *Xunzi: A Translation and Study of the Complete Works*. 3 vols. Vol. III. Stanford, CA: Stanford University Press.

Ko, Dorothy. 1994. *Teachers of the Inner Quarter: Women and Culture in Seventeenth Century China*. Stanford, CA: Stanford University Press.

Lau, D. C. 1970. *Mencius*. Harmondsworth: Penguin.

Lee, Ming-Hsuan. 2014. Schooling and Industrialization in China: Gender Differences in School Enrollment. *Comparative Education Review* 58(2): 241–277.

Leong, Joyce Lai Ting, Sylvia Xiaohua Chen, and Michael Harris Bond. 2015. Housework Allocation and Gender (in)Equality. In Saba Safdar and Natasza Kosakowska-Berezecka (Eds.), *Psychology of Gender through the Lens of Culture* (pp. 77–91). Cham, Switzerland: Springer International.

Levey, Ann. 2005. Liberalism, Adaptive Preferences, and Gender Equality. *Hypatia* 204: 127–143.

Li, Chenyang. 2000. Confucianism and Feminist Concerns: Overcoming the Confucian "Gender Complex." *Journal of Chinese Philosophy* 27(2): 187–199.

Li, Huiying. 2016. Son Preference and the Tradition of Patriarchy in Rural China. In Qi Wang, Min Dongchao, and Bo Aerenlund Sorensen (Eds.), *Revisiting Gender Inequality: Perspectives from the People's Republic of China* (pp. 137–156). Basingstoke: Palgrave Macmillan.

Li, Shi, and Jin Song. 2013. Changes in the Gender-Wage Gap in Urban China, 1995–2007. In Li Shi, Hiroshi Sato, and Terry Sicular (Eds.), *Rising Inequality in China: Challenges to a Harmonious Society* (pp. 384–413). New York: Cambridge University Press.

Li, Shi, Guanghua Wan, and Juzhong Zhuang. 2014. Income Inequality and Redistributive Policy in the People's Republic of China. In Ravi Kanbur, Changyong Rhee, and Juzhong Zhuang (Eds.), *Inequality in Asia and the Pacific* (pp. 329–350). Abingdon: Routledge.

Li, Yu-ning. 1992. Historical Roots of Changes in Women's Status in Modern China. In Yu-ning Li (Ed.), *Chinese Women through Chinese Eyes*, 102–122. Armonk: M. E. Sharpe.

Liu, Jieyu. 2007. *Gender and Work in Urban China: Women Workers of the Unlucky Genderation*. New York: Routledge.

Lü Kun 吕坤. 1927. *Regulations for the Women's Quarters (Guifan* 闺范*)*. [Publisher unknown.]

Lui, Bohong, Ling Li, and Chunyu Yang. 2016. Gender (In)Equality and China's Economic Transition. In Qi Wang, Min Dongchao, and Bo Aerenlund Sorensen (Eds.), *Revisiting Gender Inequality: Perspectives from the People's Republic of China* (pp. 21–57). Basingstoke: Palgrave Macmillan.

Mann, Susan. 1997. *Precious Records: Women in China's Long Eighteenth Century.* Stanford, CA: Stanford University Press.

———. 1997. Women in the Life and Thought of Zhang Xuecheng. In Philip J. Ivanhoe (Ed.), *Chinese Language, Thought, and Culture: Nivison and His Critics* (pp. 94–120). La Salle, IL: Open Court.

Monosson, Emily (Ed.). 2008. *Motherhood, the Elephant in the Laboratory: Women Scientists Speak Out.* Ithaca, NY: Cornell University Press.

Mukherjee, Sucharita Sinha. 2015. More Educated and More Equal? A Comparative Analysis of Female Education and Employment in Japan, China, and India. *Gender and Education* 27(7): 846–870.

Nolan, Jane. 2010. Gender and Equality of Opportunity in China's Labor Market. In Mustafa F. Özbilgin and Jawad Syed (Eds.), *Managing Gender Diversity in Asia: A Research Companion* (pp. 160–182). Cheltenham, UK: Edward Elgar Publishing.

Otis, Eileen. 2012. *Markets and Bodies: Women, Service Work, and the Making of Inequality in China.* Stanford, CA: Stanford University Press.

Pang-White, Ann A. 2016. Confucius and the Four Books for Women. In Mathew Foust and Sor-hoon Tan (Eds.), *Feminist Encounters with Confucius*: London: Brill.

———. 2016. Introduction: Rereading the Canon. In Ann A. Pang-White (Ed.), *Bloomsbury Research Handbook of Chinese Philosophy and Gender* (pp. 1–21). New York & London: Bloomsbury.

Pascall, Gillian, and Sirin Sung. 2007. Gender and East Asian Welfare States: From Confucianism to Gender Equality? East Asia, Fourth Anneal East Asian Social Policy Research Network (EASP) International Conference. Tokyo.

Qin, Min, James J. Brown, Sabu S. Padmadas, Bohua Li, JIanan Qi, and Jane Falkingham. 2016. Gender Inequalities in Employment and Wage-Earning among Internal Labor Migrants in Chinese Cities. *Demographic Research* 34: 175–202.

Rai, Shirin M. 1995. Gender in China. In Robert Benewick and Paul Wingrove (Eds.), *China in the 1990s* (pp. 181–192). Basingstoke: Macmillan.

Rankin, Mary Backus. 1975. The Emergence of Women at the End of the Ch'ing: The Case of Ch'iu Chin. In Margery Wolf and Roxane Witke (Eds.), *Women in Chinese Society* (pp. 39–66). Stanford, CA: Stanford University Press.

Raphals, Lisa. 1998. *Sharing the Light.* Albany, NY: SUNY Press.

Rexroth, Kenneth, and Ling Chung (Eds.). 1972. *The Orchid Boat: Women Poets of China.* New York: McGraw-Hill.

Rofel, Lisa. 2013. Gender as a Categorical Source of Property. In Wanning Sun and Yingjie Guo (Eds.), *Unequal China: The Political Economy and Cultural Politics of Inequality* (pp. 168–183). New York: Routledge.

Rosenlee, Lisa. 2006. *Confucianism and Women: A Philosophical Interpretation*. Albany, NY: SUNY Press.

———. 2004. Neiwai, Civility, and Gender Distinctions. *Asian Philosophy* 14(1): 41–58.

Sandberg, Sheryl, and Arlie Russell. 2013. *Lean In: Women, Work, and the Will to Lead*. New York: Alfred A. Knopf.

Schmidt, J. D. 2008. Yuan Mei (1716–98) on Women. *Late Imperial China* 29(2): 129–185.

She Mingyang. 1986. Changing Trends in Mate Selection among the Young (青年择偶观的变化趋势). *Marriage and Family* (婚姻与家庭) 3: 147–165.

Shu, Xiaoling. 2005. Market Transition and Gender Segregation in Urban China. *Social Science Quarterly* 86(5): 1299–1323.

Shu, Xiaoling, and Yanjie Bian. 2003. Market Transition and Gender Gap in Earnings in Urban China. *Social Forces* 81(4): 1107–1145.

Shu, Xiaoling, Yifei Zhu, and Zhanxin Zhang. 2007. Global Economy and Gender Inequalities: The Case of Urban Chinese Market. *Social Science Quarterly* 88(5): 1307–1332.

Song, Jing. 2015. Women and Self-Employment in Post-Socialist Rural China: Side Job, Individual Career or Family Venture. *The China Quarterly* 221: 229–242.

Song, Shaopeng. 2016. "Returning Home" or "Being Returned Home"? The Debate over Women Returning to the Home and Changing Values. In Qi Wang, Min Dongchao, and Bo Aerenlund Sorensen (Eds.), *Revisiting Gender Inequality: Perspectives from the People's Republic of China* (pp. 59–84). Basingstoke: Palgrave Macmillan.

Song Ruoxin 宋若莘, and Song Ruozhao 宋若昭. 1935. Analects for Women (Nü Lunyu 女论语). In Chen Hongmou 陈宏谋 and Sibu Beiyao (四部备要) (Eds.), *Five Kinds of Transmitted Regulations* (五种遗规). Shanghai: Commercial Press.

Sun Xidan 孙希旦. 1989. *Record of Rites* (礼记). 3 vols. Beijing: Zhonghua Shuju.

Swann, Nancy Lee. 1932. *Pan Chao: Foremost Woman Scholar of China*. New York & London: Century.

Tatlow, Didi Kirsten. 2012 (October 7). Women in China Face Rising University Entrance Barriers. *New York Times*.

Tong, Xin. 2011. Gender, Division of Labor, and Social Mobility in Small-Scale Restaurants in China. In Esther Ngan-Ling Chow, Marcia Texler Segal, and Lin Tan (Eds.), *Analyzing Gender, Intersectionality, and Multiple Inequalities* (pp. 121–137). Bingley, UK: Emerald.

Wang, Feng. 2008. *Boundaries and Categories: Rising Inequality in Post-Socialist China*. Stanford, CA: Stanford University Press.

Wang, Robin R. 2005. Dong Zhongshu's Transformation of Yin-Yang Theory and Contesting Gender Identity. *Philosohy East and West* 55(2): 209–231.

Wang, Robin R. (Ed.). 2003. *Images of Women in Chinese Thought and Culture*. Indianapolis: Hackett.

Whyte, Martin King. 2010. Sexual Inequality under Socialism: The Chinese Case in Perspective. In James L. Watson (Ed.), *Class and Social Stratification in Post-Revolutionary China*. Cambridge: Cambridge University Press.

Widmer, Ellen, and Kang-i Sun Chang (Eds.). 1997. *Writing Women of Late Imperial China*. Stanford, CA: Stanford University Press.

Woo, Terry. 1999. Confucianism and Feminism. In Arvind Sharma and Katherine K. Young (Eds.), *Feminism and World Religions* (pp. 110–147). Albany, NY: SUNY Press.

Wu, Xiaogang, and Zhuoni Zhang. 2010. Educational Inequality in China, 1990–2005: Evidence from the Population Census Data. In Emily Hannum, Hyunjoon Park, and Yuko Goto Butler (Eds.), *Globalization, Changing Demographics, and Educational Challenges in East Asia*. Bingley, UK: Emerald.

Yang, Jun, Xiao Huang, and Xin Liu. 2014. An Analysis of Education Inequality in China. *International Journal of Educational Development* 37: 2–10.

You Huiyuan 游惠遠. 2003. *Changes in Women's Statuses between Song and Yuan Dynasties* (宋元之際婦女地位的變遷). Taipei: Xin Wen Feng.

Yuan, Lijun. 2002. Ethics of Care and Concept of Ren: A Reply to Chenyang Li. *Hypatia* 17(1): 107–129.

Zeng, Junxia, Xiaopeng Pang, Linxiu Zhang, Alexis Medina, and Scott Rozelle. 2014. Gender Inequality in Education in China: A Meta-Regression Analysis. *Contemporary Economic Policy* 32(2): 474–491.

Zhang, Liqin, and Xiao-Yuan Dong. 2008. Male-Female Wage Discrimination in Chinese Industry: Investigation Using Firm-Level Data. *Economics of Transition* 16(1): 85–112.

Zhang, Qian Forrest. 2013. Gender Disparities in Self-Employment in Urban China's Market Transition: Income Inequality, Occupational Segregation and Mobility Processes. *The China Quarterly* 215: 744–763.

Zhang Xuecheng 章学诚. 1984. Women's Learning (妇学). In *Conshu Jicheng Xianbian* (pp. 482–484). Taipei: Xin Wen Feng Publishing.

Zheng Yefu. 1994. Sociological Reflections on Gender Equality (男女平等的社会学思考). *Sociological Studies* (社会学研究) 2: 108–113.

Chapter 10

Perspectives on Human Personhood and the Self from the *Zhuangzi*

David B. Wong

Introduction

I address the guiding questions of this volume through my interpretation of the *Zhuangzi*, a text that has its origins in the fourth century BCE and that later came to be regarded as one of the great canonical texts of Daoism. It is useful to contrast the *Zhuangzi*'s view of what it is to be a human being and a person with the view to be found in Confucianism: human beings are social creatures who find their fulfillment in right and harmonious social relationship with each other and in doing so they are acting in accord with *tiandao* 天道 (Heaven's Way). This is a view with which I have a great deal of sympathy, but I also have a great deal of sympathy with the Zhuangzi's view, which I shall put somewhat pugnaciously: that human beings are just another part of Nature (also *tian* 天 and usually translated as "Heaven" but perhaps less misleading conceived for this text as Nature), who foolishly regard themselves as above Nature; we are presumptuous "know-it-alls." However, our redeeming quality is our latent ability to shed our arrogant dispositions and place ourselves in more productive relationships to other things in Nature, both human and nonhuman.

A Playful Skepticism about Human Pretension

The text does not give us an argument against human pretension, because it is suspicious of argument. Argument is a tool for those who want to win the day for their point of view, but it is not good for much of anything else. Instead of argument, the text seeks to playfully and humorously evoke something that we (or at least many of us) have suspected all along but conveniently ignore. It disarms us through its humor, prods us through parables to stop taking ourselves so seriously, and in doing so prompts us to come around to accepting our limitations. But as it turns out, this very acceptance is empowering and allows us to transcend the very limitations we place on ourselves by presuming that we know. Let me explain this curious dialectic.

In the *Xiao yao you* 逍遙遊 chapter ("Going Rambling without a Destination"), we are invited to inhabit the perspective of a huge fish that transforms into a huge bird, *Peng* 鵬 "Breeze," whose wings are like "clouds all over the sky," and who sets off a six-month gale when she takes flight. The *Zhuangzi* then poses the question of how things look up there to Peng compared to how we normally see the sky standing on the ground and looking up into the distance:

> Horse-shaped clouds, motes of dust, living things blowing breath at each other—is the blue-green of Heaven its proper color or just its being so endlessly far away? It looks just the same to her gazing down from above. (translation by Kjellberg 2011, 209[1])

The *Zhuangzi* is bringing home the relativity of perceptual perspective to the scale of the creature and how it is able to move about in its environment. When humans look up into the sky and Peng looks down to earth, everyone sees blue-green. Yet we see other things from our earth-bound location that Peng does not see from up high, and so we are made to realize that our view of what's up there may be as limited as Peng's view of what's down here.

A Constructive Skepticism

The skeptical stance taken in the text is not dogmatic or doctrinal. The intention is not to establish that we know nothing. Rather, the therapeutic point is to open us to new possibilities of what might become new knowledge and insight, though new discoveries are never immune to questioning in turn, especially when they calcify into received wisdom.

This, I believe, is the point of the story about Huizi and the gourds.[2] Huizi, Zhuangzi's friend and philosophical sparring partner, grew some seeds that turned into huge gourds. When he tried to put them to some use, he found they were not sturdy enough to be water containers, and too big to be ladles. Huizi gives up, smashing them to pieces. Zhuangzi chastises his friend:

> "Now you had these gigantic gourds. Why not lash them together like big buoys and go floating on the rivers and lakes instead of worrying that they were too big to dip into anything? Your mind is full of underbrush, my friend." (Kjellberg 2011, 213)

Huizi is so wedded to his ideas of how to use the gourds that he could not think of another way they could be useful: not to *hold* water but rather to float *upon* it.

Now human beings wouldn't be what they are without concepts and language. They enable us selectively abstract from the potentially overwhelming flow of experience, and to focus on resources in the world that we use to satisfy our needs. But precisely because they enable us to *selectively* abstract from experience, they also limit us. We tend to rely on what has worked for us in the past, even if the present has significantly changed. We tend to focus on what we already want, instead of what we might want if we only encounter it. Our concepts and language, which reflect our past experience and what we already want, bring certain things into the foreground of perception and push other potentially valuable things into the blurry background. The *Zhuangzi* seeks to remind us that the world is too rich and diverse and dynamic to fit inside our limited perspectives.

This skeptical stance is constructive in two ways. First, the prospect of overturning received ideas is greeted not with anxiety but with delight. The nearest contemporary analogue to the sort of healthy and constructive skepticism I see in this text is to be found in science. For example, some scientists expressed disappointment at the news that experimental studies in the Large Hadron Collider had confirmed the existence of the Higgs Boson particle, which in turn provided further confirmation of the Standard Model of particle physics. It had been thirty-five years since the appearance of a new particle had surprised the field, Stephen Wolfram remarked in a tone of sadness (2012). He expressed desire for a discovery that needed to be reckoned with and required further exploration.

Recall that Zhuangzi chastises his friend for not clearing his mind of the underbrush of fixed conceptions of how the gourds are to be used, implying that the underbrush can be cleared, at least some of it. More generally, the implication is that we can become aware of how our entrenched concepts and names for things can become limiting and as a result strive to broaden our current perspectives. We can do this by learning something from the perspectives of others (in this case of Zhuangzi himself). We can learn from nonhuman others as well, as we observe how their perceptual fields differ from our own and from each other's. This is the point of the subsequent commentary from the cicada and the student-dove on Peng's soaring flight. These little creatures laugh at Peng, saying, "When we start up and fly up, we struggle for the elm or the sandalwood [tree]. Sometimes we don't make it and just plunk down to the ground. What is she doing rising ninety thousand li and heading south?" (209). In comparing the perspectives of different animals, we can recognize that each has a distinctive perceptual world. And we realize this applies to ourselves.

Human beings are like the cicada and student-dove in measuring what is possible or sensible on the basis of their own limited experience: "People who know how to do one job, handle a small town, or impress a ruler to get put in charge of a state see themselves like this" (2003, 210). The skepticism of the *Zhuangzi* is continually put to positive use: to pry loose the grip of our preconceptions of what is of use and value, to dent our confidence that we already know what is important, so that we are open to new possibilities. If we realize that our presumptions might be like those of the cicada and student-dove, we may attend more closely to clues as to what others might know and have done that we have not even dreamt of.

Pluralism of Value and Identity

Among those who presume to know the difference between the right way and the wrong way to act are Confucians, who hold that the degree and nature of one's concern for others should vary with one's relationship to them (e.g., more is owed to family members), and the Mohists, who hold that impartial and equal concern is owed to all. Each calls right what the other calls wrong, and each calls wrong what the other calls right. The *Zhuangzi* is skeptical of the power of argument to resolve the differences between those who like the Mohists and Confucians insist on their rights and wrongs.

I am sympathetic with this skepticism for a Zhuangist sort of reason: the world of *value* is too rich to be contained within a single coherent conceptual framework. The Confucians have got something right in holding that the nature of one's relationships is a source of duty: being raised and nurtured by one's parents can give rise to duties to honor and serve *them*; and this basis of duty is different from what we owe to any person in virtue of his or her humanity. Similarly, the fact that one has brought a child into the world, has given birth to life with tremendous vulnerability and possibility, gives rise to a special duty toward *that* child. The moral perspective that focuses on what in particular happens between people as a primary basis of duty to them is fundamental to Confucian ethics. On the other side, Mohists begin with a perspective that abstracts from the particularity of relationships and brings to our attention the vulnerability and possibility of each person, and lays a claim to our equal concern for everyone on that basis. Each perspective has powerful appeal. The duties each gives rise to can conflict with one another, especially in a world where many strangers can be in desperate need of the resources that we are accustomed to channel to those close to us in hopes of helping them to thrive, not merely survive.

It is in accord with a Zhuangist perspective that even if one starts out with a view of the rights and wrongs, one should be able to see why others can hold very different views. One can come to recognize that each moral code, even one's own, succeeds in honoring certain basic values at the cost of sacrificing others. Every coherent moral code cuts out something of genuine value. Every coherent code, in defining what is right, also requires what is wrong according to some other coherent and viable code. This sort of recognition is certainly not peculiar to the *Zhuangzi*. In Western ethical thought, it has a history represented by thinkers such as Montaigne, Isaiah Berlin, Bernard Williams, and Joseph Raz. Value pluralism as I've just characterized it can put us in a dilemma that Joseph Raz vividly characterizes. He holds that it is impossible to recognize a plurality of equally justified ways of life and to remain engaged with one's own way. Imagine, he asks us, that the

> Skills and character traits cherished by my way of life are a handicap for those pursuing one or another of its alternatives. I value long contemplation and patient examination: these are the

> qualities I require in my chosen course. Their life, by contrast, requires impetuosity, swift responses, and decisive action, and they despise the slow contemplative types as indecisive. They almost have to. To succeed in their chosen way, they have to be committed to it and to believe that the virtues it requires should be cultivated. They therefore cannot regard those others as virtues for them. By the same token it is only natural that they will value in others what they choose to emulate themselves. . . . Of course, pluralists can step back from their personal commitments and appreciate in the abstract the value of other ways of life. But this acknowledgment coexists with, and cannot replace, the feelings of rejection and dismissiveness. Tension is an inevitable concomitant of value pluralism. And it is a tension without stability, without the prospect of reconciliation of the two perspectives, the one recognizing the validity of competing values and the one hostile to them. One is forever moving from one to the other. (Raz 1994, 73)

Pluralists, as Raz describes them, are continually alternating between a detached perspective from which they step back from their personal commitments and appreciate in the abstract the value of other ways of life on the one hand and the engaged perspective from which they cannot help but be dismissive of other ways on the other hand. Raz, I think, has identified a genuine dilemma that morally serious people of broad and open minds can fall into. The *Zhuangzi*, I believe, offers a way out of that dilemma.

Recall that in the story of Huizi and the gourds, Zhuangzi does not deny that the more ordinary uses are *genuine* uses for the gourds, and clearly, they are. Rather, Zhuangzi's idea of clearing the underbrush from our heads is to encourage an *enlarged* view of what is of value. More generally, the *Zhuangzi* seeks to undermine the assumption that our own perspectives on value are uniquely correct not by discrediting them but by undermining their claim to have exhausted what there is to see and value, and this involves opening our minds to perspectives other than our own. Thus we are not disabused of the notion that our moral codes embody real values. Rather, we are encouraged to recognize that others embody real values just as ours do. The *Zhuangzi*'s appreciation for diversity is consistent with its being a moral stance at the same time that it constitutes a distancing from one's own original moral commitments: not the kind of distancing that debunks the values one believes in, but the kind that recognizes they are not the only values worth defending. Falling into Raz's dilemma, I believe, presupposes that commitment to one's values as genuine requires denying that the competing values of others are not genuine. The *Zhuangzi* suggests that this presupposition is not necessary.

Raz's path to his dilemma is the assumption that the detached perspective from which we recognize the worth of other commitments undermines the engaged perspective defined by our own commitments. The swift responders and decisive actors "almost have" to despise the long contemplators and patient examiners. To regard the qualities they prize as virtues, they cannot regard qualities of patience as virtues for them. By the same token, says Raz, it is only natural that they will value in others what they choose to emulate themselves. Detachment and engagement cannot co-exist at the same time in the same mind, but must alternate in ascendancy.

The *Zhuangzi*'s challenge to our narrow perspectives offers a way to make the detached and engaged perspectives sit more easily with each other. The detached perspective from which we recognize a broader array of genuine values is also an engaged perspective from which we come to appreciate the values that others hold. The *Zhuangzi*'s constructive skepticism holds that typical normative perspectives go astray in claiming an exclusive and comprehensive insight into value, and while it does not undermine the status of our own commitments as based on genuine values, it also encourages us to expand our view of what other commitments have a similar status.

Consider again Raz's example. The swift responders and decisive actors may not strive to realize the patient qualities in themselves, but recognition of such qualities as virtues may take other forms. It may involve seeing that the long contemplators and patient examiners have their place as well, perhaps even in one's own society. Perhaps the two sets of qualities are complementary to each other within a larger social context, where some are needed to be swift and decisive, but others needed to give a view from a larger and longer perspective. One may value swiftness and decisiveness in oneself, because, say, one views it as an admirable trait and one has the temperament to do that sort of thing well, but that does not mean that one needs to denigrate those qualities that enable others to give the longer view. Perhaps many do tend to value in others what they value in themselves, but it is not inevitable.

Now of course there will be cases in which what it takes to realize one way of life will exclude what it takes to realize another way of life. Even if one recognizes the worth of both those ways of life, one cannot make equal effort to realize both of them. That is why it is perfectly acceptable to dedicate oneself to the realization of one way of life among the many ways one might find equally valuable. We can certainly remain committed to our own way of life because we could not possibly strive equally to realize all valuable ways. But to choose our own way for this reason need not result in despising or dismissing the other ways.

We can go beyond compatibility. The Zhuangist perspective should encourage more than mere acceptance of other ways of life while one remains set on one's originally narrow course. Recognizing the worth of other ways of life can and often should have a deeper and wider effect on one's original moral commitments. If one genuinely appreciates the use of gourds as tubs to float around in, one is unlikely to remain the sort of person who smashes them when one fails to use them as water dippers. If one opens up one's mind to new sources of value, one should sometimes go beyond acceptance of the new toward incorporating it into one's commitments. One need not try to incorporate an entirely different way of life into one's commitments. Alternatively, one can seek to affirm certain values underlying that other way of life by balancing one's efforts to realize them in relation to values one already affirms. If we take this sort of project seriously, and are open to the possibility of incorporating new values into our original commitments, then we must be ready to make our commitments open-ended and flexible, to leave them to a certain degree indeterminate with respect to what values are affirmed and what the relationship of priority is among those values in case of conflict. The Zhuangist perspective would have us leave behind the comfort of moral certitude, but I would suggest that such certitude is unavailable for the thoughtful among us in any case. For those who affirm their strong duties to particular others in virtue of their relationships to them, and I number myself among such people, it is always a disturbing question of whether one has properly balanced one's duties to strangers in great need and suffering oppression.

Implications for the Good, the Bad, and the Ugly

For this volume we are asked to draw implications from the perspective discussed for the good life in contrast with the bad life, the best life in contrast with the worst, and responsibilities to others (and also to the self).[3] The previous section shows a way to think about these kinds of lives in a culture where we receive much encouragement to think positively about cultural diversity but in which the practical upshot is not often taken beyond a liberal sampling of a variety of ethnic restaurants. How can we enrich our thinking about what goes into a good life by learning about and attempting to appreciate what others have found profoundly satisfying about their ways of life?

We would do well in addressing such questions by starting with the *Zhuangzi*'s constructive skepticism. And perhaps an answer to a bad life, and perhaps the worst life, comes from the *Zhuangzi*'s stories of creatures whose pride is premised on not seeing beyond the small worlds of their experience. Besides the cicada and student-dove, there is the frog in the caved-in-well of the *Qiushui* 秋水 ("Autumn Floods") chapter. He surveys his domain and says, "Look around at the larvae and shrimp and polliwogs. None of them can match me! To control the water of an entire gully and straddle the happiness of a whole collapsed well—this is really getting somewhere!" When the frog invites the turtle of the Eastern Sea to step in and enjoy the well, the turtle can't even get two feet in before one becomes stuck in the mud. He tells the frog of the vastness and changelessness of the Eastern Sea: "In Yu's time there were floods nine years in ten, but its waters never rose. In Tang's time there were droughts seven years in eight, but its shores never receded" (Kjellberg 2011, 246). This made the frog splutter in surprise, and he forgot who he was.

Here again is the *Zhuangzi*'s concern with presumptuous know-it-alls who insist on their superiority. The frog's sense of who he is depends on his sense of superiority, perhaps in analogy to those human beings who think that the worth of their ways of life depends on their superiority to others. If they are shocked out of that sense of superiority, they lose that sense of who they are. The *Zhuangzi* suggests that such a forgetting of one's superior self is not a bad thing at all, and to be imprisoned within that sense is perhaps the worst kind of life. The human capacity to forget the self is part of our power to transcend the limitations of our presumptions to know.

Let me briefly introduce what I think is one of the most fertile possibilities for combining two values that are often in tension with one another and that each form the core of a way of life. On the one hand there is the value of a life of common project with others in which one's interdependence with others is prized and one's responsibilities and duties to others help to secure those goods. On the other hand, there is the value of a life of individual freedom in which independence and self-sufficiency is prized and rights conceived as protections against the encroachment and interference of others.

Obviously the tensions between these values are real, but so are the possible connections between them. Even in the closest of relationships, there can be conflicts of interest between the parties and the need to give the other some space and protection of legitimate interests. On the other hand, a successful society built around individual rights sometimes needs its members to act in common project, such as securing the rights of the vulnerable and oppressed, and it is not clear that the degree of commitment such projects would require can be forthcoming without genuine mutual concern and civic friendship. That American society is lacking in such values of relationship, I believe, is connected to our shamefully inadequate education for its most vulnerable children and by our rate of imprisonment, which is by far the highest of any country in the world. There is fertile territory in which the two values that are usually opposed can also be placed in mutual support (which is not to deny that there is tension and outright conflict between them also, but to a value pluralist this is the normal state of affairs). But we will never get there if advocates of each way of life "insist on their rights and wrongs" as the Confucians and Mohists do.

More Good

There is a lot more the *Zhuangzi* has to say about the good life. Let me tap just one more vein. Once we read this text as calling into question our assumptions about what we think we know and what there is to value, it makes a great deal of sense that the activities that come in for praise are not those of the Confucian literati but those of artisans such as Cook Ding, wheelwright Bian, the cicada catcher, and the ferryman. In the most famous of the skill stories, Cook Ding says that when he first began cutting up oxen, he did not see anything but oxen, but after three years, he couldn't see the whole ox.[4] Now he has so mastered the art that he performs his task in dance-like fashion and does not need to look with his eyes when moving the knife through an ox's joints and spaces. He encounters them with "spirit" (shen 神). He relies "on the Heavenly patterns" (*tianli* 天理), "strikes in the big gaps," and is "guided by the large fissures."

The stories of marvelously skilled artisans have led some to interpret the *Zhuangzi* as advocating a kind of inexplicable, mystical access to the natural patterns of the world that enables superlatively effective action. I do not deny that there are textual passages that could easily be taken to support such an interpretation, but these stories have multiple levels of meaning, one of which conveys, often in metaphorical terms, what it feels like to have attained and to perform real-life intuitive skills. Such skills are not in principle inexplicable or accessible only to the mystic.

The cook's saying that at the beginning he saw nothing but oxen can be taken to suggest the experience of beginners in a craft as needing to pay attention to seemingly all aspects of the skill activity, having to keep everything in mind all at once, and hence having to self-consciously direct oneself in performing the many aspects of the activity that one is exceedingly clumsy. "Seeing with one's eyes" in the apprentice stage is a metaphorical expression of having to self-consciously watch oneself performing all the prescribed moves. Later stages at which one acquires some skill involve mastery through repetition of the basic moves so that one can focus one's attention on doing the things that confer excellence on what one is doing.

"Encountering with spirit" conveys the sense of having acquired a "feel" for what one has to be doing in the moment that does not typically involve thinking about what one is doing but does involve paying very close attention, even intense concentration. In certain kinds of skilled activity, one has the feeling of being totally absorbed in what one is doing: there is no Cartesian pilot in the head directing the body and not even a unified person distinct from the activity she is performing but simply the doing. Some psychologists and neuroscientists have identified human capabilities for something like intuitive attunement. These are capabilities for processing of information at the nonconscious level, which can be very fast compared to conscious thought that involves the manipulation of symbolic representations according to articulable rules.

A related feature of skill stories such as Cook Ding's is the embodied nature of the activity. A current trend in cognitive psychology and philosophy of mind has turned on the insight that much of our perception and action in the world is not well understood by conceiving of our brains as information processors that construct representations of the world based on sensory information and then formulate plans of action based on these representations. Rather, much perception and action flow from the whole of a person's body interacting with the environment. The philosopher of mind Sean Gallagher (2006) has written about the way in which embodiment shapes our minds through our "body schemas," the sensory-motor capacities that give us a sense of our bodies in space.

When we close our eyes and raise an arm, our body schemas enable us to know exactly where our arm is located. When we perceive and act, our body schemas become engaged with the environment and with whatever in the environment we can use to help us accomplish our task. When we get good at using these available things, they in effect become part of our body schemas, at least in that context. The psychologist Louise Barrett gives the basic example of picking up a pencil and using it to poke something (2011, 200). When we do that, we feel the object we are poking at, not our fingers clutching the pencil and the pencil encountering resistance. The pencil becomes part of our bodily schema. Or to take another example, when one first learns to ride a bicycle, one does not follow an instruction manual one has memorized and represented in one's mind. Just as we learned as young children to stand upright and walk, coordinating our movements with the proprioceptive feel of moving forward and maintaining balance, we learn to coordinate our movements with the proprioceptive feel of our bodies on the bicycle as we move forward and maintain balance. Our subjective experience in such cases of using things in the environment is not of using our minds to direct our bodies in the manipulation of tools, but closer to our unselfconscious actions as embodied creatures such as poking something with our fingers or walking or running on our feet. The feeling is one of having enhanced embodied selves through our engagement with parts of our environment, making these parts extensions of our bodies.

Go back to Cook Ding's feats of cutting. In terms of what we have come to understand about embodied action in the world, he has made his knife part of his body schema in such a way that he cuts in the unselfconscious way one can write with a pencil or a pen or ride a bicycle. Keeping in mind that on the early Chinese conception, *qi* is the animating energy-stuff of the body, there is a genuine sense in which, as Cook Ding intimates, that we perform skillful activity with our *qi* and not just with the part that composes the brain.

The embodied nature of skill activity is also exemplified in the story of the cicada catcher of the nineteenth *Dasheng* 達生 chapter ("Grasping Life"). His skill in using a pole to catch cicadas is such that he is using the pole as if it were his hand. Moreover, he describes his path to his skill, which lay in learning to balance an increasing number of balls on the top of his pole. One might say that he is learning to incorporate the pole into his body schemas. He does not have to pay attention to how he is holding and manipulating the pole. He can pay full attention to the cicadas. And indeed, when he describes his experience of catching cicadas, he says he is aware of nothing but cicadas.

There is a feature of the Cook Ding story indicating that his skill activity is not totally an automated process that is unmediated by conscious conceptualization about goals, methods, and self-consciousness. When Cook Ding comes to a difficult spot in the ox, he says he must pause and gather himself to make careful effort. This moment in the cook's description of his own activity implies that experiential immersion in one's activity is never absolute and total, nor the feeling of flowing effortless. The capability for taking self-conscious control of one's activity gets triggered, perhaps when there is an interruption in the feel of flowing effortlessness. A more complex picture of intuitive activity emerges, one that allows conscious thought, goal-directness, and being guided by thoughts of method to interact and/or alternate with automatic nonconscious doing. Conscious awareness and method seem most crucial at the beginning when one launches oneself into the learning of skilled activity; and it may play a crucial role later when one's automatic skill has reached a plateau that cannot be transcended without thought about how to go on.

This point should not be taken to diminish the role of nonconscious activity, however. There seem to be crucial aspects of the activity that are very difficult if not possible for conscious awareness and thoughts of methods to access. One may never be able to fully articulate how one does something skillfully. The wheelwright of the *Tian dao* 天道 ("Heaven's Way") chapter says he cannot pass onto his son the right way to chisel a wheel, and likens his situation to the ancients who left their words in texts but not what they accomplished and how, knowledge that died with them.

The *Renjianshi* 人間世 ("In the Human World") chapter presents a rather unusual intuitive skill activity (unusual for the *Zhuangzi*) in that it involves people. Confucius and his favorite student Yan Hui are set up as characters to convey through their dialogue a presumably Zhuangist way of dealing with people in an intuitively skillful way. Yan Hui wants to go to a state and reform its young ruler, who is careless of the lives of his people. Confucius is pessimistic about the prospects for success, but if Yan Hui is determined to go, he should not bring into the situation any preconceived plans for accomplishing his goal. Just as the cook must develop his ability to intuitively find with his knife the great hollows and cavities of the ox, so Yan Hui, if he puts aside his ambitions and his preconceived plans for changing the young ruler (what Confucius in this chapter calls 心齋 fasting the mind), has a chance of navigating skillfully his way inside the psyche of this ruler and turning him toward a better course. Yan Hui must listen not with his mind but with his *qi* (无聽之以心而聽之以氣). The implication is that the mind imposes its preconceived names and conceptions of how things and people are, while the body's energies are responsive to how things on the outside are.

This echoes the previously discussed theme that human interaction with the world is necessarily embodied. There is further resonance with

Damasio's seminal theory of somatic markers (1994). On this theory subjective feeling is constituted by the mental states arising from the neural representation of various changes occurring within the chemical landscape of the body. These somatic changes are responses to a precipitating event or stimulus, and may serve the role of making one ready for action. Our interactions with others are among these precipitating events or stimuli, and can produce positive and negative effects that get embodied in somatic markers. It is not uncommon that we get positive or negative "vibes" from our interactions with particular people without being able put our mental fingers on what exactly it is about those people that accounts for the vibes. It may not be the particular content of what is said, but how they say it or their expressions or the way they gesture. In the ancient Chinese conception of the person, our interactions with others leave their marks on our *qi*. Our bodily energies record the positive and negative impressions others make on us. Knowledge of who they are is embedded in us, waiting to be taken advantage of if we are open to their input.

In fact, we humans do have impressive abilities to read one another's nonverbal language of physical postures, gestures, and facial expressions, and this kind of knowledge often sits below the level of conscious awareness and is not recorded in propositions. Participants in one study were able to identify facial expressions they glimpsed for only five milliseconds (Rosenthal et al. 1979). In another study (Edwards 1998), participants were able to order fourteen photographs of the temporal sequence of an emotion unfolding over the course of less than one second. A third study (Lewicki 1986) reported that participants were able to detect minute violations of the basic proportions of the human face. They felt something was wrong with the faces, but none of them were able to identify what was wrong. Such skill in "nonverbal decoding" improves from early childhood through early adulthood (Cohen, Prather, Town, and Hynd 1990; Dimitrovsky 1964; Hamilton 1973; Rosenthal et al. 1979). As Matthew Lieberman observes, "the dance of nonverbal communication between people occurs intuitively, and when we get a sense of the other's state of mind as a result of the nonverbal cues the other has presented, we often have nothing other than our intuition to justify our inferences" (Lieberman 2000, 123).

Interestingly, some evidence suggests that deliberate, conscious learning can interfere with the kind of "implicit" or nonconscious learning under discussion (Lieberman 2000, 121[5]). Thus the relation between conscious activity guided by thoughts of method and intuitive nonconscious activity is complex. Thought focused on method can lead to practice aimed at acquiring skill so that much of what is initially guided consciously can subsequently become automatic. Conscious thought can also take over when unconscious activity hits a problematic spot. But at other times, it can be better to suspend conscious thought in favor of nonconscious processing because the two can interfere with one another. This point returns us to the Zhuangist point that our names, concepts, and existing likes and dislikes can filter from our experience much of what could be potentially valuable to us. Our penchant for naming things and pinning them down with our concepts can cut off a more informative receptivity to who they are.

To appreciate the value of automatic processing, we must distinguish between different kinds of processing. Not so relevant to the Zhuangist point is the kind of automatic processing that involves the application of "heuristic biases" that allow us to respond in quick and messy ways to events and things in the world that are critical to our survival and reproduction. I hardly need to mention Kahneman and Tversky's work as enormously influential in this regard (see Tversky and Kahneman 1973; Kahneman 2011). Much of the psychological work on intuition in their wake draws attention to the extensive influence of such heuristically guided processes and to the way they can lead us astray.

For example, the "availability" heuristic functions to estimate the probabilities or frequencies of events that fall into a certain class of events E. We are disposed to judge the occurrence rate of events in E on the basis of the ease with which examples of E can be retrieved from memory. Ease of retrieval serves as a proxy for frequency of occurrence because what is frequently encountered can also be easily retrieved. The availability heuristic should provide accurate estimates most of the time, or enough of the time to make the disposition to use the heuristic adaptive and selected for during the course of human evolution. Problems arise, however, when ease of retrieval is influenced by other factors such as the salience of an event that attracts one's attention (bad behavior by celebrities) or its dramatic nature (a plane crash, for example) that would cause one to overestimate frequency of occurrence.

The *Zhuangzi* draws our attention to the possibilities of getting what our words and customary conceptual frameworks don't get. Picking up the patterns that reflect the emotions of human facial expressions is a process extended over time, and what it is that is picked up cannot be fully articulated. This kind of automatic processing involves capabilities of picking up on very complex patterns that get revealed after repeated experiences of the relevant sequence of events.

Connectionist models of the brain are based on the basic architecture of neural tissues, "in which each neuron interacts simultaneously with many others" and "automatically registers complex co-occurrences and interacting regularities" (Isenman 2013, 153; Churchland 1992; French and Cleeremans 2002; Glöckner and Betsch 2008). As Isenman suggests, some of our most useful intuitions are produced not through a simplifying heuristic applied to a thin slice of experience, but nonconscious processing that integrates multiple clues into a meaningful complex pattern that may be "too multi-dimensional and interwoven for the conscious mind, with its ability to hold a very limited amount of information at the same time, to comprehend, never mind articulate" (Isenman 2013, 160). This nonconscious processing is holistic and relational in nature. Thus if there is sometimes competition between the automatic processing of experience and explicit, deliberate analysis, and if relevant experiential patterns are too complex for conscious analysis, it may make sense, as the *Zhuangzi* does, to encourage suspension of the latter in favor of the former. This is one way we can place ourselves in a more constructive relationship to our surroundings. Instead of always trying to analyze and regiment the meaning of our experience with names and concepts, we can promote a receptive attitude toward things and other people, waiting for them to teach us, and being receptive to what our bodies and nonconscious levels of mind have to say about what we have been taught.

Taking Advantage of Zhuangist Insights

One of the most direct applications of the Zhuangist insights discussed here is education and the ideals of intelligence, judgment, and wisdom that implicitly guide education, or should guide it. Most recent efforts at improving the quality of the U.S. educational system are depressingly simple-minded and focused on success in test taking. This is not only to focus exclusively on the results of conscious, deliberate processing of experience but only on the parts that are most easily measured, not necessarily the most useful or important parts. We need to develop more respect for those processes of mind that take in wider swaths of experience and are able to integrate multiple aspects of experience that can be integrated into complex patterns that are not necessarily articulable. We need to appreciate patience and the ability to wait on things, and on the quieter parts of oneself, as virtues.

This of course is not to dismiss the value of conscious deliberative thought. In fact, one of its most valuable uses may be to help us identify which deliverances of intuition are likely trustworthy. While conscious thought might not produce the content of intuitions that track complex patterns too challenging for our conceptual and linguistic frameworks, it might help us to better understand the circumstances under which intuition is on track rather than misleading. For example, psychological and neuroscientific study has already helped us to distinguish intuitions based on heuristics that have proven adaptive for the human species but also produce serious error when based on on-off cases or thin slices of evidence. This is different from automatic holistic processing of information that over time integrates multiple experiential clues and that might provide useful insight that conscious analysis cannot.

We might also think about the implications for choice of leaders. We usually focus on the types, to invoke Raz's example, who are decisive and definite in their policies and programs. Perhaps we would do better to make room for leaders who are not so quick to say that they know what to do, who admit that they were wrong, or who admit to changing their minds. As Isenman remarks in her analysis of Jerome Groopman's book on the difficulties of diagnosis and judgment in the medical profession, sometimes the path to a better answer is confessing that one doesn't know, or that there are conflicting indications that form a puzzle yet to be solved (Isenman 2013, 161–163). Such a confession might lead to a Zhuangist constructive skepticism that makes one more receptive to something one has not named or conceptualized but that has been tracked through one's bodily *qi*. The solution to the puzzle might not come from pressing further and more intensely with conscious analytic thought, but waiting on those quieter parts of the self to process what is too much for the conscious mind to handle.

We have therefore traveled from a critical perspective of human persons in the *Zhuangzi* as presumptuous know-it-alls to its encouragement to treat all the different parts of ourselves as our potential teachers: our embodied parts that interact with and explore the rest of nature, the nonconscious parts that take in what our conscious minds cannot name and regiment into simple patterns. The *Qiwulun* 齊物論 chapter ("Equalizing All Things") observes that "it seems as though there is a true master, but you can't get a glimpse of it. In our actions we take the self on faith, but we can't see its form. There is essence but no form" (Kjellberg 2011, 216). The conscious parts nominate themselves as the boss of that often disorganized congregation of voices we call the self. The *Zhuangzi* tells the conscious parts to pipe down. They might learn something from their supposed servants.

Notes

1. Paul Kjellberg's partial translation of the text in *Readings in Classical Chinese Philosophy*, 2nd ed., edited by Philip J. Ivanhoe and Bryan W. Van Norden is a very nice balance between readability to contemporary English readers and scholarly accuracy.

2. Also in the *Xiao yao you* 逍遙遊 chapter ("Going Rambling without a Destination").

3. I will trim my ambitions and stop short of discussing the relative merits of this life versus the afterlife.

4. In the *Yang sheng zhu* 養生主 chapter ("Nurturing Life").

5. Also, in an fMRI study of the probabilistic-classification task, Poldrack et al. (1999) found caudate activation coupled with medial temporal lobe deactivations. The findings of Rauch et al. (1995) and of Poldrack et al. (1999) are consistent with animal lesion studies showing that tasks for which learning is impaired by basal ganglia lesions are actually learned more quickly after hippocampal lesions (McDonald and White 1993; Packard, Hirsh, and White 1989).

References

Barrett, Louise. 2011. *Beyond the Brain: How Body and Environment Shape Animal and Human Minds*. Princeton, NJ: Princeton University Press. Kindle Edition.

Churchland, Paul. 1992. *A Neurocomputational Perspective*. Cambridge, MA: MIT Press.

Cohen, Morris, Anne Prather, Patricia Town, and George Hynd. 1990. Neurodevelopmental Differences in Emotional Prosody in Normal Children and Children with Left and Right Temporal Lobe Epilepsy. *Brain & Language* 38: 122–134.

Damasio, Antonio R. 1994. *Descartes' Error: Emotion, Reason, and the Human Brain*. New York: Putnam.

Dimitrovsky, Lily. 1964. The Ability to Identify the Emotional Meaning of Vocal Expressions at Successive Age Levels. In Joel R. Davitz (Ed.), *The Communication of Emotional Meaning*, 69–86. New York: McGraw-Hill.

Edwards, Kari. 1998. The Face of Time: Temporal Cues in Facial Expressions of Emotion. *Psychological Science* 9: 270–276.

French, Robert, and Axel Cleeremans. 2002. *Implicit Learning and Consciousness: An Empirical, Philosophical and Computational Consensus in the Making*. Hove, UK: Psychology Press.

Gallagher, Sean. 2006. *How the Body Shapes the Mind*. Oxford: Oxford University Press.

Glöckner, Andreas. 2007. Does Intuition Beat Fast and Frugal Heuristics? A Systematic Empirical Analysis. In Henning Plessner, Cornelia Betsch, and Tilmann

Betsch (Eds.), *Intuition in Judgment and Decision Making* (pp. 309–325). New York: Lawrence Erlbaum.
Hamilton, Marshall L. 1973. Imitative Behavior and Expressive Ability in Facial Expressions of Emotions. *Developmental Psychology* 8: 138.
Isenman, Lois. 2013. Understanding Unconscious Intelligence and Intuition: *"Blink"* and Beyond. *Perspectives in Biology and Medicine* 56(1): 148–166.
Kahneman, Daniel. 2011. *Thinking, Fast and Slow.* New York: Farrar, Straus and Giroux.
Kjellberg, Paul. 2011. Translation of selections from the *Zhuangzi*, in *Readings in Classical Chinese Philosophy*, 2nd ed. Edited by Philip J. Ivanhoe and Bryan W. Van Norden. Indianapolis: Hackett Publishing Company.
Lewicki, Pawel. 1986. *Nonconscious Social Information Processing.* New York: Academic Press.
Lieberman, Matthew D. 2000. Intuition: A Social Cognitive Neuroscience Approach. *Psychological Bulletin* 126: 100–137.
McDonald, Robert J., and Norman M. White. 1993. A Triple Dissociation of Memory Systems: Hippocampus, Amygdala, and Dorsal Striatum. *Behavioral Neuroscience* 107: 3–22.
Packard, Mark G., Richard Hirsh, and Norman M. White. 1989. Differential Effects of Fornix and Caudate Nucleus Lesions on Two Radial Maze Tasks: Evidence for Multiple Memory Systems. *Journal of Neuroscience* 9: 1465–1472.
Poldrack, Russell A., Vivek Prahakharan, Carol Seger, and John D. E. Gabrieli. 1999. Striatal Activation during Acquisition of a Cognitive Skill. *Neuropsychology* 13(4): 564–574.
Rauch, Scott L., Cary R. Savage, Halle D. Brown, Tim Curran, Nathaniel M. Alpert, Adair Kendrick, Alan J. Fischman, and Stephen M. Kosslyn. 1995. A PET Investigation of Implicit and Explicit Sequence Learning. *Human Brain Mapping* 3: 271–286.
Raz, Joseph. 1994. Multiculturalism: A Liberal Perspective. *Dissent* 41: 67–79.
Rosenthal, Robert, Judith A. Hall, M. Robin DiMatteo, Peter L. Rogers, and Dane Archer. 1979. *Sensitivity to Nonverbal Communication: The PONS Test.* Baltimore: John Hopkins University Press.
Tversky, Amos, and Daniel Kahneman. 1974. Judgment under Uncertainty: Heuristics and Biases. *Science* 185: 1124–1130.
Wolfram, Stephen. 2012 (July 5). A Moment for Particle Physics: The End of a 40-Year Story? Online blog.stephenwolfram.com/2012/07/a-moment-for-particle-physics-the-end-of-a-40-year-story

Contributors

Roger T. Ames is Humanities Chair Professor at Peking University, co-chair of the Academic Advisory Committee of the Peking University Berggruen Research Center, and Professor Emeritus of philosophy at the University of Hawai`i. He is former editor of *Philosophy East & West* and founding editor of *China Review International*. Ames has authored several interpretative studies of Chinese philosophy and culture: *Thinking through Confucius* (1987), *Anticipating China* (1995), *Thinking from the Han* (1998), and *Democracy of the Dead* (1999) (all with D. L. Hall), *Confucian Role Ethics: A Vocabulary* (2011), and most recently *Human Becomings: Theorizing "Persons" for Confucian Role Ethics* (2020). His publications also include translations of Chinese classics: *Sun-tzu: The Art of Warfare* (1993); *Sun Pin: The Art of Warfare* (1996) (with D. C. Lau); the *Confucian Analects* (1998); and the *Classic of Family Reverence: The Xiaojing* (2009) (both with H. Rosemont); *Focusing the Familiar: The Zhongyong* (2001); and *The Daodejing* (with D.L. Hall) (2003). Almost all of his publications are now available in Chinese translation, including his philosophical translations of Chinese canonical texts. He has most recently been engaged in compiling the new *Sourcebook of Classical Confucian Philosophy*, and in writing articles promoting a conversation between American pragmatism and Confucianism.

Stephen C. Angle is director of the Fries Center for Global Studies, Mansfield Freeman Professor of East Asian Studies, and professor of philosophy at Wesleyan University. Angle specializes in Chinese philosophy, Confucianism, Neo-Confucianism, and comparative philosophy. He is the author of *Human Rights and Chinese Thought: A Cross-Cultural Inquiry* (2002; Chinese edition, 2012), *Sagehood: The Contemporary Significance of Neo-Confucian Philosophy* (2009; Chinese edition, 2017), *Contemporary Confucian Political*

Philosophy: Toward Progressive Confucianism (2012; Chinese edition, 2015), and co-author (with Justin Tiwald) of *Neo-Confucianism: A Philosophical Introduction* (2017). His blog on Chinese and comparative philosophy is warpweftandway.com.

Gan Chunsong is a professor of philosophy and vice director of the Confucius Research Institute at Peking University. His major social affiliations include serving as the executive vice president of Chinese Confucian Academy, as the director of International Confucian Association, and as a member of the Academic Committee of China Confucius Foundation. His work now focuses on Confucianism and Chinese modern philosophy. He also works as a specialist in Taishan Scholar Scheme, and is a research fellow of Berggruen Institute. Dr. Gan earned his bachelor and master degrees in philosophy from Renmin University of China and a PhD in philosophy from the Chinese Academy of Social Sciences. His books include *A Concise Reader if Chinese Culture* (2019) and *Back to Wangdao: Confucianism and the World Order* (2012).

Peter D. Hershock is director of the Asian Studies Development Program at the East-West Center in Honolulu, and holds a PhD in Asian and Comparative Philosophy from the University of Hawai`i. His philosophical work makes use of Buddhist conceptual resources to address contemporary issues of global concern. He has authored or edited more than a dozen books on Buddhism, Asian philosophy, and contemporary issues, including *Liberating Intimacy: Enlightenment and Social Virtuosity in Ch'an Buddhism* (1996); *Reinventing the Wheel: A Buddhist Response to the Information Age* (1999); *Chan Buddhism* (2005); *Buddhism in the Public Sphere: Reorienting Global Interdependence* (2006); *Valuing Diversity: Buddhist Reflection on Realizing a More Equitable Global Future* (2012); and *Public Zen, Personal Zen: A Buddhist Introduction* (2014). His current project, initiated as a 2017–2018 Fellow of the Berggruen Institute in China, is a monograph on *Buddhism and Intelligent Technology: Toward a More Humane Future* (forthcoming, 2021)—a reflection on the personal and societal impacts of the attention economy and artificial intelligence.

Hwang Kwang-Kuo obtained his PhD in social psychology from the University of Hawai`i, Honolulu. He is the founder of the Research Center for Cultural China, professor emeritus of National Taiwan University, and national chair professor, awarded by the Ministry of Education, Republic of China. Professor Hwang has endeavored to promote the indigenization movement in psychology and the social sciences in Chinese society since the early 1980s. He has published more than 150 articles on related issues in both Chinese and English in addition to more than ten books, including *Foundations of Chinese Psychology: Confucian Social Relations* (2012); *Inner Sageliness and Outer Kingliness: The accomplishment and Unfolding of Confucianism* (in Chinese; 2018); and *Culture-Inclusive Theories: An Epistemological Strategy* (2019). He is past president of the Asian Association of Indigenous and Cultural Psychology (2010–2014) and of the Asian Association of Social Psychology (2003–2005).

Jin Li is professor of education and human development at Brown University. Her research focuses on East Asian virtue-oriented and Western mind-oriented learning models and how these models shape children's learning beliefs, parental socialization, and development. She is the author of *Cultural Foundations of Learning: East and West*. She was one of the inaugural Berggruen Fellows, 2015–17 at the Center for Advanced Study in Behavioral Sciences, Stanford University and at Schwarzman College, Tsinghua University, China. Supported by the Berggruen Instituted, Dr. Li is writing her current book, *Self in the West and East Asia*, where she synthesizes philosophy with psychological research to examine how the self is conceptualized and functions in these two cultural systems.

Peimin Ni is a professor in the department of philosophy at Grand Valley State University. He holds a PhD from the University of Connecticut and an MA and BA from Fudan University, Shanghai. Ni is the author of *Understanding the Analects of Confucius—A New Translation of Lunyu with Annotations*; *Confucius—the Man and the Way of Gongfu*; *Wandering-Brush and Pen in Philosophical Reflection* (with Stephen Rowe); *On Reid*; and *On Confucius*. He is co-editor, with Chenyang Li, of *Moral Cultivation and Confucian Character: Engaging Joel J. Kupperman*. He is a founder and former president of the Association of Chinese Philosophers in America (ACPA) and former president of the Society of Asian and Comparative Philosophy. He is the editor-in-chief of the ACPA book series "Chinese and Comparative Philosophy." He also served as an executive vice-director of the Institute for Advanced Humanistic Studies at Peking University.

Sor-hoon Tan is professor of philosophy at Singapore Management University. Her research focuses on comparative studies of Confucianism and

John Dewey's pragmatism. She has published *Confucian Democracy: A Deweyan Reconstruction*, articles in *Philosophy East and West*, *Dao*, *Journal of Chinese Philosophy*, *Transactions of the C.S. Peirce Society*, *Contemporary Pragmatism*, *History and Theory*, *Journal of Value inquiry*, *Australasian Journal of Philosophy*, among others, and chapters in various anthologies, including the *Oxford Handbook of Dewey* and the *Oxford Handbook of Secularism*. She edited the *Bloomsbury Research handbook on Chinese Philosophy Methodologies*, and *Challenging Citizenship: Group Membership and Cultural Identity in a Global Age*. She is co-editor of *Filial Piety in Chinese History and Thought*; *The Moral Circle and the Self: Chinese and Western Perspectives*; *Democracy as Culture: Deweyan Pragmatism in a Globalizing World*; and *Feminist Encounters with Confucius*.

Tang Wenming graduated from Peking University and received his PhD in philosophy in 2001. He is currently a professor and doctoral student supervisor at Tsinghua University. He is also vice-dean of the Institute for Ethics and Religions, director of the Center for Confucian Studies at Tsinghua University, and secretary general of the Chinese Confucius Society. His main interests are Chinese philosophy, ethics, and religious studies. He has been visiting professor at Graduate Theological Union at Berkeley, Harvard-Yenching Institute, Chinese University of Hong Kong, Taiwan University, and Institute of Sino-Christian Studies at Hong Kong. He has published six books and more than one hundred academic papers. Some of his books and papers have been translated into English and Korean. He is currently the chief editor of *Public Confucianism*.

David B. Wong is the Susan Fox Beischer and George D. Beischer Professor of Philosophy at Duke University. Before coming to Duke, he was the Harry Austryn Wolfson Professor of Philosophy at Brandeis University and the John M. Findlay Visiting Professor of Philosophy at Boston University. He has written widely on issues in contemporary ethical theory, moral psychology, and classical Chinese philosophy. His books are *Moral Relativity* (1984) and *Natural Moralities* (2006), and with Kwong-loi Shun he is the co-editor of *Confucian Ethics: A Comparative Study of Self, Autonomy and Community* (2004). *Moral Relativism and Chinese Philosophy: David Wong and his Critics*, edited by Yang Xiao and Yong Huang (2014), is a book of critical commentaries on *Natural Moralities* and contains responses to each of the commentaries.

Index

Ames, Roger, 121, 176, 182, 200–202, 204–205
Analects, the, 39–41, 91, 95–96, 171–172, 178, 181–183, 216 218
analytic dualism, 122, 137
Archer, Margaret S., 137
Arendt, Hannah, 157–161
Aristotle, 39, 123, 160
art, 174–175, 177
attention, 19, 32; and economy, 18–19, 22

Baidu, 28
Ban Zhao, 222, 223, 227, 232
Barrett, Louise, 255–256
Berlin, Isaiah, 155, 249
Bhaskar, Roy, 132
bodhisattva, 25–27, 35
Book of Documents, The (shangshu 尚书), 70–71
Book of Odes, the, 54, 142
Book of Songs, 52–53, 182
Buddhism, 22–26
Buddhaghosa, 25

Castells, Manual, 18
Chen Duansheng, 161
Chen Yinke, 149, 152, 154, 161–162
Cheng Hao, 172

Cheng Yaotian, 78
Chenyang Li, 215
Chinese, and aesthetic spirit, 169, 176–177, 180, 184; agriculture, 195; Communist Party, 228–229; cosmology, 41–42, 44, 64; family system, 99–100; feminism, 216; international relations, 86–87; natural cosmology, 40–42, 44–45, 55; society, 86–87; Western cultures, 122–123; women, 229–230; women's education, 215–217, 224–225, 228; women's education literature, 222–223
climate change, 12–14, 197
commonality, 80, 182
compassion, 21–25
Confucianism, and aesthetic ideal, 177; aesthetic spirit, 169, 180; aesthetics, 184; appreciation of beauty, 181–182; art, 170, 177–179, 184; benevolence, 138–140, 144–145; Chinese culture, 121; conceptions of destiny, 138; cosmology of naturalism, the 130; cultivation, 172; Daoism, 130, 169; economic policies, 81; education, 218; ethical system, 131; ethics, 69, 86; ethics and morality, 132, 145; feminism,

269

Confucianism *(continued)*
216–217, 228; freedom, 154; gender relations, 196; heritage cultures, 93; human relations, 200–206; human self, 94–95, 115; human virtues, 96, 100; interpersonal relations, 152–153; learning, 170–171, 184, 216–217; learning tradition, 93; moral lessons, 179; morphogenesis, 122; morphostasis, 122; music, 178; naturalism, 142–143; new Confucianism (Hong Kong and Taiwan), 132; oppression of women, 215; pre-Qin Confucianism, 138; progressive Confucianism, 188, 205; relationalism, 132; responsiveness, 121; righteousness, 138–140, 144–145; self-cultivation, 91–116, 142; six arts, 175, 177–178; subjectivity, 170; virtues, 96, 101, 111; women's education, 217

consciousness, 61–63
constructive realism, 127–128, 136
constructive skepticism, 246–253, 261
contending (*zheng* 争), 78–80, 85
Cook Ding, 254–256
creative transformation, 121–122, 126, 142, 144
culture (*wenhua* 文化), 42–44, 150; as system, 122–123, 137; as traditions, 106, 127

Damasio, Antonio, 257–258
dao 道 (way), 39, 43, 129–130, 172, 227
Daodejing, 130
Daoism, 76–77, 128, 130, 140, 169–170, 172, 179–180, 184, 245
dasein (human being), 123–124
Daxue, 39, 41, 49, 76, 82–83, 142
de 德 (virtue), 182, 201–202
Descartes, 123

Dewey, John, 60–63
diversity, 86, 234, 250, 252
Dong Zhongshu (董仲舒), 53, 72
Durkheim, Emile, 103

Eckensberger, Lutz H., 125
Ellul, Jacques, 17
emotional engagement, 103, 105–106, 116
equality, 134, 136; as natural, 207–208
ethics (*lunli* 伦理), 158–159, 161; and freedom, 162–163

face and favor model, 127, 133–134, 136–138
Facebook, 27
family, 41, 56, 93, 198–200, 207, 209; and parent-child bonds, 99–100, 198; and reverence, 41, 52–53
Farquhar, Judith, 57
Fei Xiaotong, 84
Feng Youlan, 170
filial piety, 96, 98–99, 103, 106, 115–116, 143
Fiske, Alan P., 134, 136
five cardinal relationships (*wu lun*), 140–141, 187
Floridi, Luciano, 14
François Jullien, 128
freedom, 149–150, 160–161; individual, 156, 158, 159, 161, 163; negative freedom, 155–159, 163; reflexive, 156–158, 160–161, 163

Gallagher, Sean, 255
Gaozi, 143–144
gender: bias, 218, 224, 229, 231; and complex, 216; and differentiation, 219, 221; and education, 217–218, 224, 227–228; and equality, 216–217, 228–229; and inequality,

229–231; and relations, 20, 162, 195–196, 215, 217, 228–232; and segregation, 216, 225
Giddens, Anthony, 125
Goldberg, Stephen, 170
Gongdu Zi, 143
Google, 28
Guanzi, 190

Hall, David, 176
Handlin, Joanna, 224
he 和 (harmony), 56, 79, 85–86, 96, 172, 182
Harris, Grace G., 125
He Lin, 153, 162
heart-mind, 77–78, 173, 177–178, 180–181, 193
Hegel, Georg Wilhelm Friedrich, 157–158, 160, 162–163
Heidegger, Martin, 123–124, 128–129
Herder, Johann Gottfried, 157
Higgs Boson particle, 247
Hobbes, Thomas, 155
homosexuality, 197–199
Honneth, Axel, 155–157
human, and development, 87, 92, 99, 102; humaneness, 191, 202–205; and nature (*renxing* 人性), 47–49, 64; and relations (*renlun* 人伦), 159, 187–194
humility, 23, 96, 223–224

independence, 202–203, 253
Instagram, 27
Isenman, Lois, 260

James, William, 50, 60–61, 63

Kant, Immanuel, 34, 156–157, 202; moral autonomy, 157; moral goodness, 175; morality, 174
karma, 13, 15, 19, 24, 32–35

Kong Rong, 80
Kong Yingda, 71

Laozi, 77, 130
Legalism, 81–83
Li Shenzhi, 149
li 禮/礼 (ritual propriety), 54–56, 64, 74, 78, 81, 96, 175, 178, 182, 218, 220, 224
Liang Qichao, 84, 154
Liang Shuming, 84–85
Lieberman, Matthew, 258
lifeworld, 19, 125–128, 132, 144, 155
Liji, the (礼记), 46, 53, 74, 141, 178–179, 183, 191–192, 219–220, 222–223
Lijuan Yuan, 217
Lin Yusheng, 121
Liu Gongquan, 180
Liu Rushi, 161–162
Liu Xiang, 43
Liu Xie, 43
love, 98–99, 191, 218; familial, 41, 94, 116, 191, 218; humane (*renai* 仁爱), 76
Lü Kun, 224–226
Lu Xun, 205
Lunyu (the Analects), 69, 74, 78
Luo Zhenyu, 154

Mahayana Buddhism, 15, 25–26, 33
Mann, Susan, 227
Marcuse, Herbert, 34
Marx, Karl, 177
Master Zeng, 52
May 4th era, 122, 188
Mencius/Mengzi, 56–59, 69, 72–73, 83, 143, 187, 189–193, 196, 218–219
Mill, John Stuart, 157
Mohism (*mojia* 墨家), 71, 76, 248–249, 254

morality, and duty, 100, 116; and education, 80, 170; as exemplarity, 94, 104; and goodness, 175, 180–181; and subjectivity, 170, 177; topography of, 124, 141
Morozov, Evgeny, 31
Morris, Meaghan, 20
Mozi (墨子), 76–77

Nancy, Jean-Luc, 20
natural law, 82, 156
natural tendencies (*xing*), 45–46, 58, 64, 96
Neuhouser, Frederick, 157
Nussbaum, Martha, 21–22

participatory sharing, 71–74, 79–82, 86–88
personal identity, 50–51, 94, 125, 160
personhood, 11, 13, 21, 138, 141; *ren* (person), 170, 172, 216
Ping-chen Hsiung, 221
Plato, 39, 123, 152
pleasure, 23, 73–74, 80–81, 98, 126, 173, 181
privacy, 30–32
propriety, 70, 73–75, 138–140, 144–145, 227

qi 氣/气 (vital energy), 40, 57, 183, 256–258, 261
Qu Yuan, 183

Ran You, 171
Raz, Joseph, 249–251, 261
Record of Rituals, 52, 193
reflexivity, 125–126, 144–145
ren 仁, as benevolence, 70, 73, 76, 96; as consummate conduct, 64; as human becoming, 39, 40; as human hearted, 179; as humaneness, 218; as relational virtuosity, 44, 49–50

reverence, 52, 142–143, 191
righteousness, 73, 191–193
Rosemont, Henry, 182, 200–201
Rousseau, Jean-Jacques, 156

Sakai, Naoki, 20
Sang Hongyang, 83
self, and cultivation, 92–115, 170, 176, 206, 232–233; and identity, 126, 141; and improvement, 102–103, 106, 116; and realization, 157, 217, 231, 233; and reflection, 95, 102–103, 106, 116, 125–126
sexism, 216–219, 224, 226–228
Sima Guang, 83
Sima Qian, 175
Sivin, Nathan, 53
Socrates, 39
Sommer, Deborah, 54–55
soul, 39, 49–51, 55, 60, 62, 64, 94
structuralism, 128, 134–139
Su Shi, 180
Sundararajan, Louise, 136

Tang Junyi, 44–49
Tang Wenming, 198, 201–202, 204
Taylor, Charles, 124–126, 129–130, 136
Three Character Classic (*sanzi jing* 三字经), 80
ti 體 (body), 51–55
tiyong 體用, 57
tian (heaven), 46; and *tiandao* 天道 (Heaven's Way), 245, 257; and *tianli* 天理 (heavenly order/patterns), 82, 254; and *tianxia* 天下 (all under heaven), 71, 74
trustworthiness (信), 96
Tsinghua University, 149, 154
Turkle, Sherry, 29
Twitter, 27

United Nations, 88

virtue, 223, 227 (see also, *de* 德)

Wang Anshi, 83
Wang Baoxin, 150
Wang Guowei, 149–163, 202–203
Weibo, 27
Wenming, Tang, 200–202, 204
Whitebrook, Maureen, 21
Williams, Bernard, 249
Williams, Raymond, 42
Wilson, Edward, 196
wisdom (*zhi* 知), 218
Wolfram, Stephen, 247–248
women, and equality, 216; and learning, 226; and liberation, 228–229; oppression of, 215–216, 218
Wu Fei, 205
Wu Mi, 154, 162

Xi Jinping, 86
xing 性 (human nature), 42–49
Xu Fuguan, 169, 176, 180
Xunzi, 81, 179, 193, 218, 225

Yan Hui, 175, 257
Yang Zhu, 84
Ye Dehui, 150

Ye Lang, 182
Yeh Chizheng, 122
Yi Jing, 190
yi 義/义 (appropriateness), 49, 51, 64, 70, 96, 218
Yijing, 130–132, 142
yin-yang, 54, 130, 190, 196–198, 209, 228
Yingshi Yu, 122
YouTube, 27
Yuan Mei, 226

Zen, 171–172, 180
Zeng Dian, 171–172
Zeng Shen, 142
Zeng Yi, 194, 198
Zhang Huaiguan, 180
Zhang Xianglong, 190, 192, 195, 207
Zhang Xiaomei, 232
Zhang Xuecheng, 226–227
Zheng Yefu, 232
Zhongyong (中庸), 46, 50–51 131, 141, 172, 182, 202
Zhu Xi, 193, 207, 224
Zhuangzi, 169, 176–177, 245–248
Zi Gong, 69, 142
Zihua, 171
Zilu, 78, 153, 171, 173

www.ingramcontent.com/pod-product-compliance
Lightning Source LLC
Chambersburg PA
CBHW020642230426
43665CB00008B/283